Space, Time and Structure
in the Modern Novel

Space, Time and Structure in the Modern Novel

Sharon Spencer

THE SWALLOW PRESS INC.
CHICAGO

To my mother and to Srdjan

Published by
The Swallow Press Incorporated
1139 South Wabash Avenue
Chicago, Illinois 60605

Acknowledgments

Quotation from Guillaume Apollinaire, "L'Esprit nouveau et les poetes," copyright © 1918 by Jacques Haumont. Reprinted here by permission of Jacques Haumont.

Quotations from Monique Nathan, Jean Duvignaud, Georges-Albert Astre, and Michel Mourlet, from "Cinema et roman—elements d'appreciation," edited by G.-A. Astre, *La Revue des lettres modernes,* vol. V, Nos. 36-38, 1958, are reprinted here by permission of *La Revue des lettres modernes.*

Quotation from Djuna Barnes, *Nightwood,* copyright © 1937 by Djuna Barnes. Reprinted here by permission of New Directions Publishing Corp.

Quotation from Roland Barthes, "Litterature et discontinu," and "L'Activite structuraliste," in *Essais Critiques,* copyright © 1964 by Editions du Seuil. Reprinted here by permission of Editions du Seuil.

Quotation from Bernard Bergonzi, *The Listener,* copyright © 1967 by Bernard Bergonzi. Reprinted here with the permission of the author.

Quotation from George Bluestone, *Novels into Film,* copyright © 1961 by The Johns Hopkins Press. Reprinted here by permission of The Johns Hopkins Press.

Quotation from Wayne C. Booth, *The Rhetoric of Fiction,* copyright © 1961 by The University of Chicago Press. Reprinted here by permission of The University of Chicago Press.

Quotation from Sergei Eisenstein, *Film Form,* translated by Jay Leyda, copyright © 1957 by Harcourt Brace Jovanovich, Inc. Reprinted here by permission of Harcourt Brace Jovanovich, Inc.

Quotation from Maurice Fourre, *Tete-de-Negre,* copyright © 1960 by Editions Gallimard. Reprinted here by permission of Editions Gallimard.

Quotation from Joseph Frank, "Spatial Form in Modern Literature," in *The Sewanee Review,* copyright © 1945 by The University of the South. Reprinted here by permission of *The Sewanee Review.*

Quotation from Waldo Frank, "The Major Issue," *The Novel of Tomorrow and the Scope of Fiction: By Twelve American Novelists,* copyright © 1922 by The Bobbs-Merrill Company, Inc. Reprinted here by permission of The Bobbs-Merrill Company, Inc.

Quotation from Carlos Fuentes, *Cambio de Piel,* reprinted here by permission of Editorial Joaquin Mortiz, S.A. *Change of Skin* copyright © 1967 by Farrar, Straus and Giroux, Inc. for the United States, and by Carlos Fuentes and Jonathan Cape, Ltd. for the British Commonwealth. Reprinted here with the permission of Carlos Fuentes, Jonathan Cape, Ltd. and Farrar, Straus and Giroux, Inc.

Quotation from Andre Gide, *Les Faux-Monnayeurs,* and *Journal des "Faux-Monnayeurs,"* copyright © 1925 by Editions Gallimard. Reprinted here by permission of Editions Gallimard.

Quotation from Christian Zervos, "Interview with Picasso," from *The Creative Process,* edited by Brewster Ghiselin, copyright by University of California Press. Reprinted here with permission of The Regents of the University of California.

Quotation from Sigfried Giedion, *Space, Time and Architecture: The Growth of a New Tradition,* copyright © 1967 by the Harvard University Press. Reprinted here by permission of the Harvard University Press.

Quotation from Arnold Hauser, *The Social History of Art,* copyright © by Random House, Inc. Reprinted by permission of Random House.

Quotation from John Hawkes, *The Cannibal,* copyright © 1949 by New Directions Publishing Corporation. Quotation from Hawkes, *Second Skin,* copyright © 1964 by John Hawkes. Quotation from

© 1968 by Princeton University Press. Reprinted here with the permission of Princeton University Press.

Quotation from Jose Ortega y Gasset, "The Doctrine of the Point of View," reprinted by permission of Curtis Brown, Ltd.

Quotation from Jose Ortega y Gasset, *Obras Completas, III*, reprinted here with the permission of Revista de Occidente, S.A.

Quotation from Sir Herbert Read, *A Concise History of Modern Sculpture,* copyright © 1966 by Praeger Publishers, Inc. Reprinted here by permission of Praeger Publishers, Inc. for the United States and by permission of Thames and Hudson, Limited, for the British Commonwealth.

Quotation from Sir Herbert Read, *The Philosophy of Modern Art,* copyright © 1952 by Horizon Press. Reprinted here by permission of Horizon Press, New York for the United States and Faber and Faber Ltd., for the British Commonwealth.

Quotation from Alain Robbe-Grillet, *Pour un Nouveau Roman,* reprinted here by permission of Les Editions de Minuit. *For A New Novel,* copyright © 1965 by Grove Press. Published by Grove Press, Inc. and reprinted here with their permission.

Quotation from Alain Robbe-Grillet, *Dans le Labyrinthe,* reprinted by permission of Les Editions de Minuit. *In the Labyrinth,* copyright © 1960 by Grove Press. Published by Grove Press, Inc. and reprinted here with their permission.

Quotation from G. di San Lazzaro, *Klee: A Study of His Life and Work,* reprinted here by permission of the Praeger Publishers, Inc. for the United States and Thames and Hudson, Ltd. for the British Commonwealth.

Quotation from Marc Saporta, *Composition No. 1,* reprinted here with the permission of Editions du Seuil.

Quotation from Jean-Paul Sartre, *Situations I,* copyright © 1947 by Editions Gallimard. Reprinted here with the permission of Editions Gallimard.

Quotation from Robert Scholes, "For Nonrealistic Fiction," in *The New York Times Book Review,* copyright © 1967 by the New York Times Company. Reprinted by permission.

Contents

Introduction

Space, Time and Structure is a study of the genre from 1910 to the present, but only of those types of novels whose authors have designed them to be of this age, of the twentieth century, and who have sought to express those relationships in time and space and among characters that are distinctly "modern." "It is a curious anomaly," wrote Anaïs Nin in 1968 "that we listen to jazz, we look at modern paintings, we live in modern houses of modern design, we travel in jet planes, yet we continue to read novels written in a tempo and style which is not of our time and not related to any of these influences." She says that the new novel "could be born of Freud, Einstein, jazz, and science." [1] It *"could be,"* yes, and it has been and is still arising from those immensely fertile sources enumerated by Miss Nin: "Freud, Einstein, jazz, and science."

The difficulty is not that the "new" novel does not exist. It has been and is still being created by such writers as: Djuna Barnes, Hermann Broch, Michel Butor, Julio Cortázar, Robert Desnos, Alfred Döblin, John Dos Passos, Maurice Fourré, Carlos Fuentes, André Gide, John Hawkes, Michel Leiris, Robert Musil, Vladimir Nabokov, Alain Robbe-Grillet, Raymond Roussel, Edoardo Sanguineti, Marc Saporta, Nathalie Sarraute, Gertrude Stein, Virginia Woolf, Anaïs Nin herself, and many others. The real difficulty is that readers are too often intimidated by the books written by these authors, and, oddly enough, these readers are usually the very same persons who spend their Sunday afternoons in museums of modern art, who have written off Stravinsky as passé, who make it a point to see all the major films directed by Bergman, Buñuel, Fellini, and Antonioni, and who are least aware of the general nature of Professor McLuhan's theories about media. For a variety of social and cultural reasons, one of which is the continued domination of the American literary imagination by English literary values, the same people who accept and enjoy modernist works in other media seem instinctively to recoil from the modernist novel.

Space, Time and Structure is an attempt to rectify this situation by describing the expressive aspirations that lie at the source of so many "difficult" novels and by calling attention to vital relationships between experimental books and modern music and painting. The French novelist and critic Michel Butor has asserted that "Far from being in opposition to realism, as is too often supposed in critiques written from a nearsighted view; in the novel, formal invention is the essential condition of a more vital realism." [2] The author of the present study shares this belief and has based her ideas upon it, along with a serene confidence that the novel, far from being "dead," is a lively and flexible literary form, ever-capable of the evolutionary changes in style and structure that are indispensable to its continuing "realism."

If one visits a large city bookstore or reads *The New York Times Book Review,* he could receive the impression that the novel is the only contemporary art form that has not yet become "modern," that has not been deeply influenced by such crucial twentieth-century developments as the theory of relativity, by the exploration of dreams and their significance, by the concept of the closed field in mathematics, by serial production in the cinema, and by the invention of various types of cameras. This would be a false impression, for although the popular novel of the twentieth century is scarcely different from that of the nineteenth, newer, more ambitious, more daring, and often more "realistic" types of novels are consigned to obscurity, or are never published, simply because the public has never been taught how to read them. For a wide range of reasons that do not come within the scope of this study, the evolution of the modern novel has received slight critical attention in the United States and, consequently, scarcely any consideration from all but a very small number of readers.

Novel readers continue, by and large, to seek in fiction the classic ideals of a joyous realism along with a "story," a "plot," and "characters" depicted in the nineteenth-century manner. But this spirit and its formalistic manifestations are usually not found in the works of the most serious novelists of the modern age, no more than in those of painters, sculptors, composers, playwrights, and poets. Thus, readers continue to expect characters rendered according to principles of external and psychological verisimilitude; dialogue that approximates actual speech; plots, actions, and themes that reproduce the sociological and psychological preoccupations of the majority of normal, middle-class men; and a story, or a sequence of events, that moves forward from point to point from a definite beginning toward a definite conclusion. When these same readers are confronted with characters that seem perverse or fantastic, with streams of highly intellectual or highly poetic language, with confusing patterns of narration, and with inexplicable temporal arrangements, they become frustrated, hostile, and defensively contemptuous. No wonder that some fifty years after the advent of cubism, an earnest literary critic found it necessary virtually to beg readers and critics alike to give experimental novels a chance: "In order to deal with life in a more vital and meaningful way, fiction must abandon the worn-out type of realism and focus on the world in different ways." [3] So wrote Robert Scholes in 1967. Modern novelists who think of themselves as artists are rarely realists in the traditional sense. But most readers fail to understand this because they have not applied what they *know* about the ways in which the twentieth century is different from the nineteenth to their apprehension of all those novels that they find so intimidating.

At the center of the misunderstanding is the issue of the fictional character. Character is to the novel what the melody is to music and what the identifiable representational subject is to painting and sculpture. It provides the element of the familiar and the recognizable. Its presence is a signal, a code, a sign that reassures the reader that he knows what the work is "about." The diminished and diminishing role of character for its own sake, along with changing methods of depicting character, arouses in the unprepared reader insecurity and anxiety and, eventually, anger. He revenges himself upon the book and its author by becoming scornful of the "modern." This transformation in the function of the character in the novel is perhaps the major source of bewilderment for unsophisticated readers and of attack for unsympathetic critics.

At the same time, the novelist's loss of interest in character created and analyzed for its own sake is perfectly natural. For one thing, in our time, psychology and sociology have taken over many of the novel's functions with regard to the presentation and analysis of human behavior. For another, psychology and especially the discoveries of Freud, has shown us how very little of the truth about a human being lies on the surface that novelists learned how to depict so brilliantly during the nineteenth century, and how very misleading that surface can really be. To portray character with depth and truth, the novelist must abandon the surface and find some way of penetrating the inner reality of his subject. Finally, the increasingly abstract treatment of character in the modernist novel is but one manifestation of a broad trend in the arts: the "dehumanization" which José Ortega y Gasset described in 1925: "Wherever we look we see the same thing: flight from the human person." [4] In contrast to virtually all Western art since the Renaissance, in contemporary times man himself occupies a relatively small place in most serious compositions, regardless of their stylistic mode of expression.[5] "It will not be easy," wrote Ortega, "to interest a person under thirty in a book that under the pretext of art reports on the doings of some men and women. To him, such a thing smacks of sociology or psychology. He would accept it gladly if issues were not confused and those facts were told him in sociological and psychological terms. But art means something else to him." [6]

Whether the dehumanization of the novel is a sign of spiritual deterioration as is claimed by critics with traditional orientations, or is instead a long overdue rejection of complacent, egotistic anthropomorphism, a movement toward a more universal cosmic conception of existence, as is claimed by such experimenters as Alain Robbe-Grillet,[7] is a question, however fascinating, that cannot be considered in these pages. What does seem certain is that this marked tendency toward dehumanization in fiction is related to the drive toward abstraction that has characterized all the arts of the modern age and whose psychological sources were perhaps definitively explained in Wilhelm Worringer's book of 1908, *Abstraction and Empathy (Abstraktion und Einfühlung)*. Briefly, during historical periods when man feels uneasy, oppressed, overwhelmed, and terrified by both his natural and his human environment, artists tend to abandon realism for a style that seeks exaggeration, distortion, and, ultimately, abstraction; images of the world that are simplified, stripped of details, purified, reduced to essences, provide a comforting sense of the basic stability of life. A broad impulse toward expressionism underlies all the modern arts. Furthermore, the modern artist has received immensely fertile suggestions for new styles and structures from the revelation of the significance of dreams (in which the dreamer is released from all limitations of time, space, and personal identity) and from newly evolving concepts of time and space as they have been formulated since 1905 when the "new" physics of relativity was announced by Albert Einstein. The novels that are examined in the following pages are—not necessarily with the conscious intentions of their authors—responses, adjustments to the new theories of the nature of reality that arise from the speculations of modern science.

Especially vital for the ideas underlying this study of the novel are changes in the manner of regarding time and space that have taken place since Einstein published his famous theory. The ultimate scientific truth of Einstein's ideas does not matter. What counts in terms of their impact on literature is their power and prevalence in the emotional and intellectual atmosphere of the age, which cannot but be inadvertently absorbed by the more sensitive and the more aesthetically ambitious of modern novelists. In our time, space is conceived not as one-sided or linear—as in the Renaissance idea of perspective—but as many-sided and virtually space

inexhaustible in its potentiality for relationships, none of which are mutually exclusive. Consequently, absolute description of any object or area is impossible from a single point of reference. Each position which provides a perspective will reveal a different aspect of the subject of observation or contemplation, for in modern physics, space is conceived as relative to a moving point of reference.

The historical and aesthetic implications of this revision of spatial perspective have been explored by José Ortega y Gasset in two essays printed in *The Modern Theme* (*El Tema de Nuestro Tiempo*) of 1923: "The Doctrine of the Point of View" and "The Historical Significance of the Theory of Einstein" ("La Doctrina del Punto de Vista" and "Del Sentido Histórico de la Teoría de Einstein"). Together, these essays constitute the major aspects of a theory of "perspectivity." The Spanish thinker concludes that ultimate, or absolute, perception can be achieved only by linking up endlessly individual points of view until a complete panorama is attained. The only "false" perspective is the one that claims to be total; such a view renders obsolete the convention of the exclusive perspective of the omniscient author, whose authority was unquestioned until the twentieth century:

> The persistent error that has hitherto been made is the supposition that reality possesses in itself, independently of the point of view from which it is observed, a physiognomy of its own. Such a theory clearly implies that no view of reality relative to any one particular standpoint would coincide with its absolute aspect, and consequently all such views would be false. But reality happens to be, like a landscape, possessed of an infinite number of perspectives, all equally veracious and authentic. The sole false perspective is that which claims to be the only one there is.[8]

time   Our idea of time, no less than that of space, has undergone alteration. Time is now regarded by physicists and mathematicians as the fourth dimension, that is, as an interdependent and inseparable aspect of space dynamically conceived. Sigfried Giedion in his book, *Space, Time and Architecture*, explains:

Previously, time had been regarded in one of two ways: either realistically, as something going on and existing without an observer, independent of the existence of other objects and without any necessary relation to other phenomena; or subjectively, as something having no existence apart from an observer and present only in sense experience. Now [in 1908] came another and new way of regarding time, one involving implications of the greatest significance, the consequences of which cannot today be minimized or ignored.

He attributes the first statement of the interdependence of time and space to Hermann Minkowski, a mathematician who in 1908 proclaimed: " 'Henceforth . . . space alone or time alone is doomed to fade into a mere shadow; only a kind of union of both will preserve their existence.' " [9]

The discovery and existence of these concepts, along with the (scientific validity given to dreams,) impose an obligation upon the serious novelist. If he is to create works that reflect the reality of his age, he must search for ways of attaining a fusion of time and space. The challenge is a grave one, for fiction is perhaps the most closely bound of all the arts to the concept of sequential time—to the idea of time regarded "realistically, as something going on and existing without an observer, independent of the existence of other objects and without any necessary relation to other phenomena." This is the "time" of most so-called "realistic" fiction. In the first decades of the century, however, a very great transformation in the orientation of the novel to the concept of time was achieved by the ("stream of consciousness") and its relation to ideas articulated by Henri Bergson. These were reflected in Dorothy Richardson's *Pilgrimage,* in James Joyce's *Ulysses,* in Marcel Proust's *A la recherche du temps perdu,* in Virginia Woolf's novels, and in hordes of lesser works that embody "subjective" time schemes: the notion that time is "something having no existence apart from an observer and present only in sense experience."

The "new" view of time makes time an aspect of space. For example, on earth today there exists virtually every historical period in the "progressive" history of man, ranging from the

primitive culture of New Guinea to those societies whose tech-
nologies enable them to send men to walk on the moon. All these
historical periods are *simultaneous.* What has changed is not their
existence in time, but our *awareness* of their existence, an awareness that is made possible by the multiplication of perspectives
achieved by cameras, radios, television, and tape recorders. Every
location in space, every *lieu*, is infused with its own time, or
simultaneity of times. In an important sense, time has lost its
meaning apart from its aspect as a function of space as perceived
by some individual from a changing point of view. The revision
of the concept of time as linear and sequential has been carried
still further by the great liberties offered us by the dream. In
dreams—waking, sleeping, or drug-induced—each of us can be
wherever he (or his unconscious) wishes, backward or forward in
time; in all sorts of "times" at once; in every country or realm
he has ever experienced directly, read about, viewed in a movie,
or is capable of imagining; he can be as many persons as he
wishes—and all at the same time. Finally, by offering us the swift
language of visual images in film and television, technology has
shown us new ways of organizing what our senses receive: we take
in sensations and words all at once instead of sequentially. It is
no wonder that sequential, linear time—the time of the novel
as a narration—has increasingly lost its relevance for the arts. In
the novel, which is especially closely bound to the linear because
of the physical nature of the book, there exists an observable
struggle to subdue the patterns suggested by time in its accustomed
sense to those existing in its new spatial sense.

   Space, Time and Structure in the Modern Novel studies books
that embody approximations of time-space fusions achieved by
various ingenious structural procedures. For the sake of convenience, the doubtless imperfect term "architectonic" has been used
throughout to distinguish these novels from more nearly traditional ones.[10] Although, like many modern novels, the architectonic novel manifests an avoidance of character developed for its
intrinsic interest, its essential feature is neither thematic nor
stylistic, but structural. Its goal is the evocation of the illusion of
a spatial entity, either representational or abstract, constructed

from prose fragments of diverse types and lengths and arranged by means of the principle of juxtaposition so as to include a comprehensive view of the book's subject. The "truth" of the total vision of such a novel is a composite truth obtained from the reader's apprehension of a great many relationships among the fragments that make up the book's totality. Treating perspective as "the aspect of an object of thought from a particular standpoint," [11] the author of an architectonic novel chooses to represent his subject either from a single exclusively maintained and often unusual perspective, or from a great variety of perspectives simultaneously focused upon the subject. These alternate modes of "seeing" the materials of the novel result in two opposed types of structures: "closed" and "open." And both of these types of structures may be either stable or mobile, depending upon the ways in which they have been constructed.

The architectonic novelist's desire to simulate in the reader's imagination a plastic structure necessitates the abandonment of the principle of narration (that is, the concept of the novel as a series of logically connected incidents related by an omniscient and concealed, or by a revealed, author or narrator) and the adoption, in place of narration, of the procedure of construction by means of juxtaposition (that is, the setting beside one another without connectives of types of prose).[12] Narration necessarily assumes a linear shape, for it proceeds from point to point from a definite beginning toward a definite end. However, the whole idea of beginning and ending is annihilated by the procedure of juxtaposition, which abolishes all overt transitions as well as the suggestion of causality, and which renders possible the free creation of all sort of relationships among the items juxtaposed. Nevertheless, as Roger Shattuck carefully points out in "The Art of Stillness" in *The Banquet Years*, juxtaposition does imply the notion of succession, even if it is random or haphazard succession. Juxtaposition embodies the idea of dynamic movement. "Ultimately," Shattuck has written, "it becomes apparent that the mutually conflicting elements . . . are to be conceived not successively but *simultaneously*, to converge in our minds as contemporaneous events." He concludes: "The aspiration of simulantism is to grasp the moment in its total significance or, more ambitiously, to manufacture a moment which surpasses our usual perception of time and space." [13]

Among the vast number of architectonic books that have been written during the past half century, the following are not only the best known but also provide the clearest illustrative relationships for purposes of study. A few have not yet been translated into English; in many cases, one has not felt it necessary to supply an English title, since most readers will know enough French to translate the names of the books in question for themselves. Throughout the text, occasional French phrases, chapter headings, and titles of essays have been left untranslated. On the other hand, all titles of German books, whether translated into English or not, have been rendered into English for the convenience of the reader. The works on which the present study is based are these: Djuna Barnes's *Nightwood;* the *Ficciones* of Jorge Luis Borges; Hermann Broch's *The Sleepwalkers (Die Schlafwandler)*, *The Death of Virgil (Der Tod des Vergil)*, and *The Innocent (Die Schuldlosen)*; Michel Butor's *Degrees (Degrés)*, *Passing Time (L'Emploi du temps)* and *Mobile: Study for a Representation of the United States (Mobile: étude pour une représentation des États-Unis)*; Julio Cortázar's *Hopscotch (Rayuela)*; Robert Desnos' *La Liberté ou l'amour!;* Alfred Döblin's *Alexanderplatz Berlin (Berlin Alexanderplatz)*; John Dos Passos' *U.S.A.;* Maurice Fourré's *Tête-de-Nègre;* Carlos Fuentes' *Change of Skin (Cambio de piel)*; André Gide's *The Counterfeiters (Les Faux-Monnayeurs)*; John Hawkes's *The Cannibal, The Lime Twig* and *Second Skin;* Michel Leiris' *Aurora;* Robert Musil's *The Man Without Qualities (Der Mann Ohne Eigenschaften)*; Vladimir Nabokov's *Pale Fire;* Anaïs Nin's *Cities of the Interior, Collages,* and *House of Incest;* Alain Robbe-Grillet's *In the Labyrinth (Dans le labyrinthe)*, *Jealousy (La Jalousie)*, and *La Maison de Rendez-vous;* Raymond Roussel's *Impressions d'Afrique;* Edoardo Sanguineti's *Capriccio italiano;* Marc Saporta's *Composition No. 1;* Gertrude Stein's *The Making of Americans, Tender Buttons,* and *Three Lives;* Virginia Woolf's *To the Lighthouse, Mrs. Dalloway,* and *The Waves.*

Another observer of the changing structural procedures of the novel might have made very different selections. The novels cited here are intended to be representative; they provide examples of general ideas to be advanced and developed in the following pages. It seems necessary, however, to explain certain omissions and selections. *Ulysses* and other works by James Joyce have been excluded because the author, although fully aware of their germinal importance for modern fiction, believes that they have been more than adequately discussed and analyzed. Excluded for a different reason are those many novels which, because of their subject, tone, attitude, or mode of humor, seem strikingly "modern," but are, in fact, structurally traditional. Examples of this type of novel are Günther Grass's *The Tin Drum* (*Die Blechtrommel*), Nathanael West's *Miss Lonelyhearts* and *The Day of the Locust*, and Norman Mailer's *An American Dream*. Although Virginia Woolf's work is generally thought of as belonging to the Symbolist-influenced "stream-of-consciousness" novel, *To the Lighthouse* and *The Waves* contain examples of architectonic structure that are felt to be of value in illustrating the general argument of this study. The *U.S.A.* of John Dos Passos has been included because of the author's belief that its narrative originality has generally been overlooked, especially by American critics who have shown far more interest in Dos Passos' politics than in his novels.[14]

With unlimited space, one would certainly have examined some of the many other courageous works that might be characterized as "architectonic." Among such books are stories by the Austrian poet Ingeborg Bachmann, the novels of Uwe Johnson and Jürgen Becker; of Italy's Carlo Emilio Gadda and the various writings of the members of "Gruppo 63." From current French literature, one might have included Michel Butor's *Niagara* (a "stereophonic" novel), books by Jean Cayrol, Maurice Blanchot, Marguerite Duras, Robert Pinget, Joyce Mansour, and Claude Simon. A more complete treatment of works by American writers might have included Charles G. Finney's *The Circus of Dr. Lao*, William Gaddis' *The Recognitions*, Harry Matthews' *Tlooth*, books by William Burroughs and Thomas Pynchon, and certainly Marguerite Young's *Miss MacIntosh, My Darling*. Finally, there is Julio Cortázar's experiment, *Ultimo Round*. This list might well go on and on, and doubtless every reader will wish to make

his own additions. Whatever they may be, one hopes to have
provided, in the pages that follow, at least a few fresh ways of
thinking about novels that may help to bridge the present chasm
between the intentions of serious novelists and the overly simple
expectations, even of those readers who are most amply prepared
with intelligence, imagination, and good will.

Notes

Following each reference to a work written in a language other than English
will be a reference to the publication in the original language, followed by
the citation in that language. If no English version of a book is cited, then
the reader may assume that it has not been translated into English and that
the text citation has been translated by the author of this study.

1. Anaïs Nin, *The Novel of the Future* (New York, 1968), p. 29.
2. Michel Butor, "Le roman comme recherche," *Répertoire*, II (Paris, 1963), p. 9: "L'invention formelle dans le roman, bien loin de s'opposer au réalisme comme l'imagine trop souvent une critique à courte vue, est la condition *sine qua non* d'un réalisme plus poussé."
3. "For Nonrealistic Fiction," *The New York Times Book Review* (October 22, 1967), p. 2.
4. José Ortega y Gasset, *The Dehumanization of Art and Other Writings on Art and Culture* (New York, 1956), p. 30. The publisher, Doubleday and Company, does not give the name of the translator. "La Deshumanización del Arte," *Obras completas*, III (Madrid, 1947), p. 372: "Por todas partes salimos a lo mismo: huída de la persona humana."
5. See, for example, the contrasting arguments of Miss Mary McCarthy in "Characters in Fiction," *The Humanist in the Bathtub* (New York, 1964) and of the French critic Jean Bloch-Michel in "Nouveau roman et culture des masses," *Preuves* (March, 1961).
6. José Ortega y Gasset, p. 30. "La Deshumanización del Arte," p. 372: "Es muy difícil que a un contemporáneo menor de treinta años le interese un libro donde, so pretexto de arte, se le refieran las idas y venidas de unos hombres y unas mujeres. Todo eso le sabe a sociología, a psicología, y lo aceptaría con gusto si, no confundiendo las cosas, se le hablase sociológicamente o psicológicamente de ello. Pero el arte para él es otra cosa."
7. See Robbe-Grillet's essays on the novel, collected under the title *Pour un nouveau roman* (Paris, 1963), but especially "Nature, humanisme, tragédie." Translated by Richard Howard as "Nature, Humanism, Tragedy," *For a New Novel* (New York, 1965).
8. José Ortega y Gasset, "The Doctrine of the Point of View," *The Modern Theme* (New York, 1961), pp. 91–92. "La Doctrina del Punto

de Vista," "El Tema de Nuestro Tiempo," *Obras completas,* III (Madrid, 1947), 200: "El error inveterado consistía en suponer que la realidad tenía por sí misma, e independentemente del punto de vista que sobre ella se tomara, una fisonomía propia. Pensando así, claro está, toda visión de ella desde un punto determinando no coincidería con ese su aspecto absoluto y, por tanto, sería falsa. Pero es el caso que la realidad, como un paisaje, tiene infinitas perspectivas, todas ellas igualmente verídicas y auténticas. La sola perspectiva falsa es esa que pretende ser la única."

9. Sigfried Giedion, *Space, Time and Architecture* (Cambridge, Massachusetts, 1941), pp. 368–69.

10. The author believes that the use of the term "architectonic" to describe a clearly definable type of novel is original in this study. However, the germinal idea, the suggestion that space might provide the key to many a book commonly thought to be obscure, came from an essay written by Joseph Frank and published in 1945, "Spatial Form in the Modern Novel." He was concerned primarily with novelists' apparent need to "break up temporal sequence" in order to compose and "fix" for a moment, necessarily in space, the instant of perception in which time and space are fused. Frank's argument depends upon his belief that "since language proceeds in time, it is impossible to approach this simultaneity of perception without recourse to the creation of a spatial dimension": "Spatial Form in the Modern Novel," *Critiques and Essays in Modern Fiction: 1920–1951,* edited by John W. Aldridge (New York, 1952), p. 43. Apart from Frank's study of spatial form, there exist scarcely any explorations of the topic in English and American criticism, although much has been done with the subject in France.

11. *Webster's New Collegiate Dictionary* (Springfield, Massachusetts, 1949).

12. For an interesting examination of the ways in which typography has altered the concept of the book as a recorded narrative, see Hugh Kenner's *Flaubert, Joyce and Beckett: The Stoic Comedians* (Boston, 1962).

13. Roger Shattuck, *The Banquet Years* (New York, 1961), p. 345.

14. In fact, Dos Passos' work is virtually ignored by American critics. And yet his unusual narrative techniques have influenced many foreign writers, including Hermann Broch and Carlos Fuentes. See Theodore Ziolkowski, *Hermann Broch* (New York, 1964), and Luis Harss and Barbara Dohmann, "Carlos Fuentes, or the New Heresy," in *Into the Mainstream: Conversations with Latin American Writers* (New York, 1967). In 1938, Jean-Paul Sartre wrote: "Je tiens Dos Passos pour le plus grand écrivain de notre temps." ("I regard Dos Passos as the greatest writer of our time."): "A Propos de John Dos Passos," *Situations I* (Paris, 1947), p. 25.

The poet of space, if he is writing a novel, will want to arrange the elements of his book so as to create a world, or a realm, either of his own design or as an imaginative replica of some pre-existent form. At once there comes to mind the idea of a novel as an approximation of a city. Or, it might be of a world: Raymond Roussel's Africa or Lewis Carroll's "wonderland." The literary spatialist need not have in mind a representational model, such as, for example, a circle, a triangle, a maze, or a straight line. He may, instead, invent from combinations of such forms a nonrepresentational structure on which to base the spatial illusion embodied in the fiction he is creating. And once one has passed into the realm of the nonrepresentational, the available variety of models becomes, for all practical purposes, infinite. Such nonrepresentational concepts, whether regarded as spatial bases for novels or as works of sculpture, are well demonstrated by the

1

"constructs" invented by the Russian-born sculptors, Naum Gabo and Antoine Pevsner.

Regardless of whether the plastic model on which the novel's structure is based—be it a familiar city or a unique abstract form—is representational or nonrepresentational, the finished structure will often reflect a great diminution or alteration of the role that is usually taken by character. This is natural. The creator of a world will want to put in people, but much more besides: streets; buildings; parks; stores; cars; animals; systems of thought; replicas of art works; religious attitudes; theories of economics, government, psychology; and so on. The character becomes, then, but one of many elements of the total world.

But more important than this general reduction of the role of the character is a definite change in the way in which the author uses the character. The literary spatialist wishes to exploit the character's point of view of the reality of the world the novelist is creating. Thus, characters are chosen or invented less because they are interesting or important in their own right than because they are capable of providing various masks for the author. Generally, characters are used by the literary spatialist as perspectives, as points of reference from which the subject of the book is perceived. If the novelist wishes to evoke a bizarre world, he may select an insane man as a point of reference. If he wishes to evoke a complex world filled with intellectual and ethical alternatives, he will select a great many characters as points of reference: a businessman, a priest, a very old person, a child, a young woman, a middleaged man, a foreigner, an artist, and so on. And he will bring together the perspectives of each of these persons upon the subject of the novel. The variety of architectonic structures and the ways in which characters are employed as the foundations of these structures provide the material for discussion in Chapter 1.

Chapters 2 and 3 are devoted to "closed" and to "open" structures, respectively. Each type of novel is constructed upon a different utilization of perspective. The closed structure is a world in itself: a self-enclosed, private, usually intense, and often extremely haunting world in which the accustomed types of literary characters and the usual relationships in time and space are inappropriate. The closed structure depends for its enclosure upon the restriction of the perspective to one exclusively maintained emotional and intellectual attitude toward the subject. The closed structure may embody a first-person narrative technique, but not necessarily, for narrative point of view is but one type of literary perspective. The open structure, by contrast, reflects a vast, diffuse, confusing, complex world which is just as independent of conventional ideas of characterization and of time and space as is that of the closed structure. However, its structural nature is very different. It gives an impression of asymmetry. It seems jagged, full of points and thrusts, poorly balanced, and it perhaps even conveys the notion that it is either in motion or is capable of motion. Since it demonstrates the deliberate violation of classical ideals of proportion among parts, of harmony of tone and diction, of balance, of unity, and of a sense of being finished or rounded off, the open-structured novel may be said to be an "antinovel."

The concept of closed and open forms is not usually applied to literature, but it is a relatively old idea, having been formulated by Heinrich Wölfflin as a means of distinguishing classical from baroque forms in Renaissance art. The essential characteristic of open form is that the work of art seems to project itself into space. Of the open form in modern sculpture, Sir Herbert Read has written: "Far from seeking a point of rest and stability on a horizontal plane, it takes off the ground and seeks an ideal movement in space. Far from conforming to the ideal of *containment*, it is essentially articulated, and accosts the spectator with aggressive spikes. It may sometimes present a polished surface, but only to emphasize a predominant roughness." [1] These sentences very aptly describe the ultimate effect on the reader of a novel with an open structure. By contrast, the novel with a closed structure suggests containment, a single strong emotion, an insistence upon its own mood and point of view, and a sense of calm and of inward-directed energy. However, both modes of structure express the author's clearly realistic attempt to approximate a comprehensive view of reality by means of perspective: in the case of the closed structure, by insisting upon the crucial nature of some generally

I began to write fiction on the assumption that the true enemies of the novel were plot, character, setting, and theme . . . totality of vision or structure was really all that remained.

—John Hawkes [1]

1.

Character: A Medium of Expression for the Novelist

John Hawkes was most certainly not joking when he told an interviewer that he "began to write fiction on the assumption that the true enemies of the novel were plot, character, setting, and theme." This is as explicit a statement as one could want of José Ortega y Gasset's assertion, when writing of the dehumanization of art in 1925, that "the art of which we speak is inhuman not only because it contains no things human, but also because it is an explicit act of dehumanization." [2] (This deliberate reduction of the role that character has traditionally played in the novel is but one of the most striking results of the novelist's desire to evoke a world, a realm, a "totality" which will include either a special perspective on reality or as many diverse perspectives as he is capable of expressing.) Such an aspiration implies that the individual character, instead of being the focal point, the purpose for which the fiction was created, becomes, instead, a medium for the expression of some particularized view of the reality constructed in the book in which he appears. What captures the excitement of the novelist is the possibility of a character as a "persona," a

5

voice through which the author may express a special attitude toward reality.

Any character, with his individual temperament, intelligence, sensibility, language, culture, prejudices, and convictions, is a natural mouthpiece. Sometimes this exploitation of the character as a medium results in an intentional blurring of his individuality and a consequent heightening of his typicality. This occurs, for example, in such novels as Robert Musil's *The Man Without Qualities (Der Mann Ohne Eigenschaften)*, André Gide's *The Counterfeiters (Les Faux-Monnayeurs)*, and Virginia Woolf's *The Waves,* all of whose themes propose coexisting concepts of reality. Sometimes, too, deliberately bizarre characters are chosen as media for the expression of unusual or distorted perspectives on life; this occurs in many Surrealist novels, for example in *Aurora,* and in works by such typical "nonrealists" as Djuna Barnes, Nathanael West, and John Hawkes. In still other cases, particularly in novels like Raymond Roussel's *Impressions d'Afrique* and Alain Robbe-Grillet's *In the Labyrinth (Dans le labyrinthe)* in which the processes of dream and of art provide both the substance and the technique by means of which it is portrayed, character is likely altogether to disappear in a composition that is preoccupied with itself *as a composition.*

Character has become but one of many components that, conceived and handled by the novelist as though they were building materials, contribute to the erection of a spatial structure. And this spatial structure, be it as abstract as that of Alain Robbe-Grillet's *La Maison de Rendez-vous* or as concrete as the hopscotch of Julio Cortázar's *Hopscotch (Rayuela)*, has been designed deliberately as an embodiment of one or more complementary perspectives on the novel's subject matter. "Literary spatialism" is merely one way of describing the novelist's attempt to discover, already existing in reality, or to invent, from the resources of his imagination, the most appropriate structure for the book he wishes to create. And character is the most obvious, the most readily available, and perhaps the most flexible vehicle for the containment of whatever perspective, or combination of perspectives, is to be employed as a foundation for any architectonic novel's particular structure.

Perhaps the best way to illustrate the subordination of character to a vision of "totality" conceived and wrought structurally is to compare the different treatments of character in a traditional and in an architectonic novel. For this purpose, Robert Musil's *The Man Without Qualities* and Malcolm Lowry's *Under the Volcano* will serve very well. Their respective protagonists are very similar, and yet the uses to which they are put are extremely different. Both novels portray highly intellectual central figures, and both embody meticulously and powerfully wrought evocations of place: the former, Vienna just before World War I; the latter, Mexico just before World War II. Lowry's interest in the Consul always dominates other elements of the novel. Whatever his intention, he succeeds in alluding to imminent worldwide destruction *through* the willful self-destruction of his protagonist. By contrast, Musil contrives to make certain that Vienna always dominates his secondary elements, among which must be included the character of Ulrich. In the traditional sense, Ulrich is not a character at all. He is a collection of splendid possibilities detached from action, a mind abstracted from human feelings, a mind set free to ponder endlessly himself, the city of Vienna, and the predominant intellectual problems of the early part of the century.

Ulrich and the Consul have much in common. Both are handsome, strong, athletically powerful, charming, extraordinarily intelligent, meticulous and obsessive by temperament, and profoundly rebellious. And yet, despite these parallels, the Consul exists for the reader with a force and a palpability that are deliberately denied to the perverse Ulrich. Musil's refusal to define Ulrich is intentional, and in this refusal lies the ultimate point of the book. By employing Ulrich as a perceptor, as a mental container for a spectrum of ideas whose opposites are represented by the other "characters," Musil is erecting upon the foundations of Vienna an intellectual edifice. Vienna provides the finite boundaries required by Musil's spatialization of reality. Malcolm Lowry, in strong contrast to Robert Musil, displays a conventional interest in place or *lieu*. He is interested in Mexico partly because he desires a vivid and alien setting that will lend itself to symbolic treatment and partly because he wishes to extend the implications of the Consul's spiritual collapse by means of an elaborate super-imposed metaphor.

One of the finest achievements of *Under the Volcano* is the brilliance of Lowry's evocation of Mexico. The country itself is constantly sensed as a presence, a savage and dangerous bird brooding over the action with wings spread and claws open. Throughout Lowry's novel, place references embody allusions to the action and to the relationships among the characters. The two volcanos, Popocatepetl and Xctaccihuatl, suggest the former strength of Yvonne and Geoffrey in marriage; a huge split rock called "La Despidida" represents their sundered condition at the time of the Consul's death; the Calle Nicaragua, the street on which he lives in a run-down unkempt house, suggests his course downward toward destruction. The barranca, a deep ravine that runs all the way through the village and its surroundings and cuts across the Calle Nicaragua, is a clear embodiment of damnation, or simply of a terrifying emptiness (the Consul is thrown into the barranca after he is murdered). Mexico herself, with her rank ebullient growth of flowers and bushes, her powerful odors and general steamy air, is a paradoxical symbol both of heaven (an earthly Eden, sexual love and fruition) and of hell (as suggested by the fires within the volcanoes and the many violent storms).

The fearful and beautiful presence of Mexico does not, however, delude anyone into thinking that *Under the Volcano* is not first and foremost a book about a man. There is never any doubt about its emphasis nor about what it is that Lowry wishes to depict. Mexico is for him a vast objective correlative for the condition of the Consul, a condition that is clearly meant to convey larger suggestions about the spiritual disintegration of modern man.

The Man Without Qualities opens, not with a presentation of Ulrich, but with a presentation of Vienna. Chapter I consists of a dry, stoically rendered, measured, prose approximation of the streets of Vienna on an August day in 1913:

> Motor-cars came shooting out of deep, narrow streets into the shallows of bright squares. Dark patches of pedestrian bustle formed into cloudy streams. Where stronger lines of

speed transected their loose-woven hurrying, they clotted up—only to trickle on all the faster then and after a few ripples regain their regular pulse-beat. Hundreds of sounds were intertwined into a coil of wiry noise, with single barbs projecting, sharp edges running along it and submerging again, and clear notes splintering off—flying and scattering.[3]

As a futher indication of the subordination of character to place, Musil reserves his introduction of Ulrich for the second chapter. And it is not even the man, but his house that is presented first. From this point onward, Musil composes his enormous work in very short chapters of some five to eight pages, each of which carries a comic old-fashioned title that parodies those of Victorian novels. There is no "story," only a great number of relationships of relatively increasing or decreasing tension, most of which are centered around the "Collateral Campaign," an effort to restore Austria's prestige in the face of growing Prussian power by publicizing her ostensible cultural and spiritual glories.

The Man Without Qualities receives both its structural principle and its substance from dialectical confrontation, from a thorough and consistent opposition of sets of twos. In this respect, the novel is a good example of the idea elaborated by Hugh Kenner in "Art in a Closed Field," in which he demonstrates how certain novelists, taking their cue from mathematics, are creating novels by defining an arbitrary and fixed number of elements and by subsequently arranging these elements into patterns dictated by an arbitrary and invariable plan. "The closed field," Kenner explains, "contains a finite number of elements to be combined according to fixed rules." [4] The key to the selection of bipolarity in Musil's novel is found in Ulrich's conviction that all ideas come in twos: in their positive and negative propositions. In accordance with this "law," the characters are played off against each other in sets, each member of which is the opposite of the other. Ulrich's opposite is Paul Arnheim, Diotima's is Bonadea, Tuzzi's is General Stumm von Bohdwehr, Clarisse's is Agathe. Moosbrugger's violence is the opposite of Prince Leinsdorf's control.

But the alternation of twos exists on a more complicated level of organization as well: the novel is a structure erected upon alternations and contrasts among two types of basic relationships: those of love or lust (as between Bonadea and Ulrich, Walter and Clarisse, Clarisse and Ulrich, Ulrich and Diotima, Diotima and Arnheim, Rachael and Soliman, Rachael and Ulrich, and, finally, Ulrich and Agathe) and those of competitive antagonism between men (as between Ulrich and Arnheim, Ulrich and Walter, Ulrich and Tuzzi, General Stumm von Bohdwehr and Arnheim, Leinsdorf and Arnheim, Tuzzi and Ulrich, Meingast and Ulrich, Ulrich and Leinsdorf, Ulrich and Lindner, Ulrich and Moosbrugger, and so on). In this composition of oppositions, the polar extremities are represented by Moosbrugger (the insane sex maniac and murderer who suggests what society is to become) and Count Leinsdorf (the cultured, dignified man of honor and self-control who represents the values that are lost to the twentieth century). Each of the other characters adheres largely to one or the other of these extremes.

In *The Man Without Qualities* Musil has given three-dimensional being to mere patterns of thought by embodying these patterns in contrasting perspectives that, in their multiplicity and diversity, suggest the spatial busyness, the complexity, and the perpetual conflict of a city. José Ortega y Gasset has remarked in his discussion of the dehumanization of art, with special reference to Luigi Pirandello's *Six Characters in Search of an Author*, that there is a marked tendency in modern literature to attempt the objectification of the subjective:

> if, turning our back on alleged reality, we take the ideas for what they are—mere subjective patterns—and make them live as such, lean and angular, but pure and transparent; in short, if we deliberately propose to "realize" our ideas—then we have dehumanized and, as it were, derealized them. For ideas are really unreal. To regard them as reality is an idealization, a candid falsification. On the other hand, making them live in their very unreality is—let us express it this way—realizing the unreal as such. In this way we do not move from the mind to the world. On the contrary, we give three-dimensional being to mere patterns, we objectify the subjective, we "worldify" the immanent.[5]

The Man Without Qualities is an extreme example of this "world-ification" of ideas and of how, in an attempt to achieve it, characters in fiction may be employed as elements in the construction of a spatially conceived entity that contains, as does reality, alternative perceptions and metaphysical approaches to the comprehension of that same reality.

In the novel, the spatialization of concepts has a very long history. One has only to think of one of the novel's ancestors, the Odyssey, to realize how ancient is the use of the quest or journey to portray human search and to provide a natural structure for a literary work that traces such a search. From the quest, which may assume either a linear or a circular pattern, are derived the spatial edifices of such architectonic works as *Aurora, Tête-de-Nègre, Second Skin, Hopscotch, Seduction of the Minotaur, Mobile,* and *Change of Skin.* The maze is another ancient form that is useful as a structural model; in fact, Julio Cortázar originally intended to use it, instead of the hopscotch, as the basic design for *Rayuela.* [6] In twentieth-century literature, the city is perhaps the most commonly adopted model for an architectonic novel.

The model need not, however, be representative. Ingenious novelists have invented all sorts of abstract structures, some of which, like *Cities of the Interior, Mobile,* and *Composition No. 1,* are literally mobile. A few others, although they appear to be motionless, do, in fact, contain—compressed and nearly concealed—the illusion of circular movement. The gyroscope provides a model of the sort of motion that is embodied in such "circular" works. Still other literary structures are based upon simple mathematical relationships. We have already seen how negative and positive statements of the same proposition gave Robert Musil the organizing principle of *The Man Without Qualities.* Sets of twos—doubles and opposites—provide the spatial coordinates of several fine novels.

Mrs. Dalloway, for example, consists of a fine network of sensations and perceptions, a network that suggests a cobweb in which there are two complementary and mutually sustaining patterns: those woven by Septimus Warren Smith and by Clarissa Dalloway. Together they constitute the "total vision" glimpsed by Clarissa during the middle of her party when she watches an old woman in a window opposite her own preparing for bed. *To the Lighthouse* also manifests an underlying plan of dual spatial organization. It proposes a representation of two bodies of land some distance from each other; these two points are designated as the window of the house on the shore and as the lighthouse standing on an island that is visible from this window. They are related or joined only when the boy James makes his long-desired trip to the lighthouse—that is, by the motion of the boat between the two points. Each of the three components of this design, which fuses time and space, is represented by one of the novel's three divisions: "The Window" (the land); "Time Passes" (death and inactivity); "To the Lighthouse" (the resumption of action and the fulfillment of the journey that unites the two points in space). Still another example of organization by twos is Vladimir Nabokov's *Pale Fire.* This novel, which consists of a long poem and a critical comment on the poem, is a duologue; the two opposed visions of the same reality must be read concurrently if a comprehensive point of view is to be attained.

A most interesting example of a total vision rendered in twos is Samuel Beckett's novel, *Molloy.* Like Musil, Beckett uses the novel as a means of "objectifying" his ideas. His characters, who are designated either by an initial or by a cryptic name, are abstract in the extreme. They consist of various modalities of irritated confusion animated by a sleight of the authorial hand that concentrates all their life energy in some trick of wearing their clothing, of walking, or of riding a bicycle. Beckett swiftly sketches a comic figure in a humiliating situation—crawling or falling off his bicycle—and then sets him off on an improbable pedantic monologue that slyly parodies the process of thought in general and, frequently, of philosophical (systematic) thought in particular.

Molloy depicts man—generalized man—in two cultural and metaphysical situations. There is no attempt at literary counterpoint, as there is in *Pale Fire;* and the doubles are employed with a structural simplicity that is in strong contrast to the complex engineering of Robert Musil's vast novel. Very simply, the first half of *Molloy* presents the journey of an old man who thinks (he cannot quite remember) that he wants to visit his mother; the second part presents the search of one Jacques Moran (another "M") for Molloy. The two searches are read one after the other. The reader must deduce for himself the relationship between them.

Is it not evident that in *Molloy* Beckett is making a disguised statement about human nature, just as was Musil in *The Man Without Qualities?* Virtually all the procedures of the traditional novel are irrelevant to his purpose: characters depicted with recognizable details of person and dress; portrayed in actions logically determined with regard to temperament, character traits, and personal predispositions; and functioning in realistic settings given authority through representative description and accurate reproduction of speech. As Musil has made a statement about character and life by means of complexity and diversity, Beckett has made a comparable statement by employing exactly the opposite means: by reducing everything to the simplest possible terms, by omission of detail, and by stylization of speech and gesture. Clearly, exact notations of times and places and more realistic characterizations would tend to limit Beckett's materials to the observable, the finite, the particular in such a way that universality would be obscured.

The variety of structures that can be invented as skeletons for architectonic novels is limited only by an author's powers of invention. The observations of this chapter would seem self-evident; and yet, so far, very few persons have attempted to apply the concept of spatial construction to literary criticism. An interesting beginning has been made by the French author and critic Michel Butor in four essays: "Philosophie de l'ameublement" ("A Philosophy of Interior Decoration"), "Recherches sur la technique du roman" ("Researches on the Technique of the Novel"), "L'Espace du roman" ("The Space of the Novel"), and "Le livre comme objet" ("The Book as an Object"). Together, these essays comprise an aesthetic of space in literature that is grounded upon the simple assumption that the book itself is but a space to be filled.

Butor first reminds his reader that all fiction embodies an imaginative voyage and that it offers, therefore, invitations to adventure and to forgetfulness that are essentially liberating:

> The physical displacement of an individual—the voyage—will seem to be a specific example of an isolated "territory," as is said, "a magnetic field." Since places are always endowed with an historical dimension—it may be with regard to a universal myth, it may be with regard to the life of an individual—any displacement in space will necessitate a reorganization of the temporal structure, alterations in memories and in plans, in that which comes into the foreground, alterations more or less extensive and momentous.[7]

Butor points out that a new *lieu* not only gives us something novel in itself, but enables us, by separation and consequent contrast, to comprehend more clearly the place we have just left behind. He goes on to explain that the rapidly multiplying number of places available to the modern novelist requires that he locate each more specifically than in the past, that he limit and define meticulously all the objects within the settings he reproduces; for when spaces are treated dynamically (that is, with an awareness of their counterpointing effects and the refracted relationships possible to each one), more and more possibilities for new relationships exist: "The appearance of the rest of the world takes on a particular structure for each place, the actual relationships of proximity possessing the means of being entirely different from those of the original relationships of proximity."[8]

Butor concludes that since technology has made the entire world (past and present) available in minutes or hours, and that since each place implies new and enlightening relationships to all other places, we are now privileged to have at our fingertips virtually unlimited sets of materials for the novel, materials that can be arranged spatially—*must* be—if their full variety and significance are to be realized within the literal space that is provided by the book.

The city constitutes the most popular model for the architectonic novel. It is easy to understand why this should be so, for a city—filled with people of all sorts and composed of all sorts of *lieux*—is a microscopic image of the universe, endlessly rich in symbolic as well as structural suggestions. The variety of novels erected upon the idea of a city is immense. Perhaps the most ambitious is James Joyce's *Ulysses,* a monumental literary and historic synthesis in which Dublin is definitively captured—for the duration of a day, at any rate. An eerie "pop" mythology of the modern city is Robert Desnos' *La Liberté ou l'amour!* By wildly combining bizarre elements, Desnos transforms urban incongruity into a scene of nocturnal enchantment. Michel Butor has himself exploited the contrasts provided by the city in his novel *Passing Time (L'Emploi du temps).* Lawrence Durrell's four-volume portrait of Alexandria presents a most unambiguous illustration of how a finite spatial concept may be used by a novelist to contain complementary and sometimes contradictory versions of an ostensibly stable reality.

From the point of view of architectonic engineering, two of the most noteworthy city novels are John Dos Passos' *Manhattan Transfer* and Alfred Döblin's *Berlin Alexanderplatz.* Both novels, as well as Dos Passos' trilogy *U.S.A.,* [9] are based upon the exploitation of the idea of the city as an enclosure for a wide range of attitudes toward personal, social, and spiritual reality, and in both works the treatment of character is but one of many elements arranged by the novelist into a prose approximation of a city, the city itself suggesting that it is but an emblem for a vaster reality —the world. Döblin's novel, like Musil's, contains much that is "unnovelistic" when considered from the traditional point of view. Although there is a simple hero and a simple plot, both are minor elements in a vast prose collage which consists of a great variety of materials that have been arranged haphazardly, it seems, into a chaotic and asymmetric composition.

Berlin Alexanderplatz retains, unlike comparable novels by Dos Passos, a central protagonist whose battle with the city is the framework upon which the action is erected in a series of encounters, defeats, recoveries, and re-encounters. Franz Biberkopf, the "hero," is an unintelligent and inarticulate victim of passions he does not understand and cannot control. This novel is not, however, a narrative account of the hero's life. It is, instead, an assemblage of materials organized in a design that forms a facsimile of a particular section of Berlin.[10]

The novel envisioned as a city is a powerful and effective but nonetheless relatively simple example of literary spatialization.

Recalling that the need for a finite structure is imposed by a desire for "totality of vision," one may easily foresee the development of nonrepresentational, or abstract, spatial ideals for the structure of the novel. One such approach renders into a graceful abstraction the concept of the novel as an approximation of a city. This is Anaïs Nin's *Cities of the Interior,* a work that is thematically conventional, since the author is interested mainly in human personality, but that is extraordinarily original in terms of style and structure. The "cities" are private and symbolic; they exist as objectifications of the psychic states of Miss Nin's characters. Thus, when one important personage, Lillian, comes to Mexico, the reader is told:

> She had landed in the city of Golconda, where the sun painted everything with gold, the lining of her thoughts, the worn valises, the plain beetles, Golconda of the golden age, the golden aster, the golden eagle, the golden goose, the golden fleece, the golden robin, the goldenrod, the goldenseal, the golden warbler, the golden wattles, the golden wedding, and the gold fish, and the gold of pleasure, the goldstone, the gold thread, the fool's gold.
>
> With her first swallow of air she inhaled a drug of forgetfulness well known to adventurers.
>
> Tropic, from the Greek, signified change and turning. So she changed and turned, and was metamorphosed by the light and caressing heat into a spool of silk.[11]

Here Mexico is transformed into a complex and very intensely rendered symbol of Lillian's attempt to evade confrontation with herself and her past life. The references to adventure and metamorphosis are reminiscent of Michel Butor's comparison of a novel and a voyage.

Unlike *The Man Without Qualities* and *Molloy, Cities of the Interior* is unmistakably *about* the characters who are portrayed in its pages. However, in comparison with traditional character presentation and development, Miss Nin's procedures appear perverse. Her characters have no last names. Their faces and their bodies are rarely described, even though their clothing is frequently carefully detailed. The reader often does not know where or with whom they live. Their ages are almost never indicated. These characters possess a fluid quality. One can never be certain when or where they will "turn up," and one never receives any explanation of how or why they have changed one set of life circumstances for another. In short, in Miss Nin's work as in Beckett's, everything that would be carefully explained in a conventional "realistic" novel is ignored or merely summarized. Both authors select for emphasis only those details that pierce the core of any character or situation, and they refuse to acknowledge the claims of any other types of material for expression.

In *Ladders to Fire,* there is a central figure, Lillian; her last name is withheld, not because she lacks identity as does Musil's Ulrich, but because it does not seem important to Miss Nin to "fix" her in terms of social norms. The work has a conventional theme, Lilliam's struggle to liberate her passions and her femininity, but the theme is bodied forth in a series of incidents in which the emphases are highly unusual. After a strong opening description of Lillian, whose "hand bag was always bursting full and often spilled over," [12] Miss Nin gives a summary of a brief unhappy love affair between Lillian and a man named Gerard. This is presented in a few paragraphs, without any explanation of how long their relationship lasted and without any analysis of the moral implications of the affair, which is adulterous. Now comes the first of several important "movements" in Lillian's development: a lengthy and closely analyzed presentation of her friendship with Djuna (who is the featured character in another portion of *Cities of the Interior*). The culminating situation consists of Lillian's prolonged love affair with Jay, who, again, is given no last name and no personal history other than two crucial episodes that explain his temperament. The final movement of *Ladders to Fire* veers markedly and abruptly away from Lillian. She is dropped without explanation, although it is clear that her painful, if instructive, relationship with Jay has come to an end. At this point, a party is introduced. It is the germinating situation for the appearance of new personalities and new relationships. This party provides the crossroad to another "city of the interior."

Miss Nin's unorthodox approach to characterization permits her to ignore everything that the reader can easily infer for himself so as to concentrate her energy and skill at making images based upon the exposure of the characters' inner lives, their fears, desires, and conflicts; these areas are exposed by more conventional novelists only by means of the stream-of-consciousness flow or by some variation upon it such as the *sous-conversation* recently developed by the French novelist Nathalie Sarraute. [13] It is interesting to compare the description of Vienna that Robert Musil has put into the mind of Ulrich (page 8–9) with the description of Vienna that Anaïs Nin has bestowed upon Renate, the main figure of *Collages*. Both passages are on the first pages of the novels in which they appear:

> Vienna was the city of statues. They were as numerous as the people who walked the streets. They stood on the top of the highest towers, lay down on stone tombs, sat on horseback, kneeled, prayed, fought animals and wars, danced, drank wine and read books made of stone. They adorned cornices like the figureheads of old ships. They stood in the heart of fountains glistening with water as if they had just been born. They sat under the trees in the parks summer and winter. Some wore costumes of other periods, and some no clothes at all. Men, women, children, kings, dwarfs, gargoyles, unicorns, lions, clowns, heroes, wise men, prophets, angels, saints and soldiers preserved for Vienna an illusion of eternity. [14]

Whereas it is Vienna that interests Musil, it is Renate who interests Anaïs Nin. Renate's vision of the city is intended to reveal the essence of her own personality, which is unfailingly animated and creative, as well as humorous and life-bestowing.

The structure of *Cities of the Interior* is even more suggestive of the freedom that can be discovered by the adventurous novelist.

Cities of the Interior is a collection of distinctly separate but related works of novella length with individual titles: *Ladders to Fire, Children of the Albatross, The Four-Chambered Heart, A Spy in the House of Love,* and *Seduction of the Minotaur.* It is described by Miss Nin as a "continuous novel." The various characters, who are often artists, appear and reappear, now one and now another occupying the central position. The order of the component parts of the "continuous novel" does not at all affect one's comprehension of the whole. The individual novellas can, each one, stand quite alone; as parts of a larger entity, they are interchangeable. This is partly because specific chronological references have been avoided and partly because the transitions linking the novellas are so graceful and so fluid that the reader never feels that anything has come to a definitive end.

The structure of *Cities of the Interior* coincides perfectly with the fluid concept of personality which is reflected in the novel's characters and events. In this dynamic idea of being, the focus is always on the process of becoming, on the Bergsonian notion of personality as constant change. Therefore, the ever-developing and self-modifying structure of the "continuous novel" is the ideal "enclosure," for in effect, it destroys the very idea of enclosure. In such a novel, neither a definite beginning nor an irrevocable ending is implied. New "cities" can always be prefixed, inserted, or added whenever and wherever the author desires. The shape of this novel is never final: it cannot be final within the author's lifetime. The result of the organic quality of *Cities of the Interior* is a fiction that is at once extremely abstract and intensely personal, for insofar as it reveals, in a depth highly unusual for psychological fiction, the various phases of sexual being, it is theoretical; but insofar as it creates memorable personages, it is descriptive and evocative. Here a balance is maintained between the general and the specific, each enhancing the other, as, indeed, Miss Nin herself claims they ought to do:

This personal relationship to all things . . . I found to be the core of individuality, personality, and originality. The idea that subjectivity is an impasse is as false as the idea that objectivity leads to a larger form of life. A deep personal relationship reaches far beyond the personal into the general.[15]

Cities of the Interior brings the novel to the boundaries of representational literary spatialism. For although the structure of this "continuous" work may be likened to that of a tree, it may also be envisioned as an abstract conception. It demonstrates one sort of architectonic skeleton. But for the literary spatialist there exists almost unlimited structural variety. Beyond those representative replicas, of which the journey and the city are the most widely used, is the whole range of geometric shapes and relationships. For example, bipolarity has been emphasized in this chapter, but circularity might just as well have been chosen. And beyond the more familiar geometric shapes lie the possibilities of all sorts of composite structures having no models in reality. Virginia Woolf's novel *The Waves,* for example, is a series of prose panels, monologues of varying lengths; each panel is related to a different position of the sun in the sky from sunrise to sunset. This structure suggests nothing more strongly than those modern sculptures that consist of arrangements of undulating sheets of metal whose appearance and apparent relationships change, depending upon how the sheets are illuminated by a moving source of light. The desirability of breaking up linear succession has even led some novelists to the invention of mobile forms, some of which will be examined in the final chapter of this study.

Regardless of the nature of the shape that is adopted by the novelist, his essential spatial orientation to time and reality again and again demonstrates the aspiration described by John Hawkes as "totality of vision." Totality: what better way is there to approximate it than to erect a replica of a world, to colonize it, to put up towns and villages, and to endow this world with a language, a culture, a set of ethics, and even an aesthetic? Although many of the *Ficciones* of Jorge Luis Borges reflect the preoccupations of the literary spatialist, none does so more explicitly than "Tlön Uqbar, Orbis Tertius," [16] a piece that is architectonic both in substance and manner. There are no "characters," only the impersonal voice of a highly learned man who recounts a detective story for intellectuals: the tale of how a group of thinkers conspired early in the seventeenth century to perpetuate the ostensible existence of a country named Uqbar in a nation called Tlön in a "third" universe. Bit by bit, the narrator uncovers pseudohistorical documents that describe the culture of Tlön; it constitutes a practical demonstration of philosophical idealism. Eventually, however, the boundaries between historical time and present time, between the invented and the scientifically verifiable, between fantasy, hoax, or art and reality, are thoroughly obscured. The narrator himself is present at the discovery of an artifact of Tlön, a piece of metal engraved with the image of a divinity worshiped only in "orbis tertius." Thus, imagination has animated and then proved the reality of its own invention.

At once the "real" world submits to the now-verified "imaginary" world, its inhabitants impressed largely by the appeal of its orderly, consistent philosophy. Borges' narrator states that reality is, in fact, eager to yield. At the end of the story, this ostensibly unperplexed narrator predicts that the entire world will soon "become Tlön," but he himself continues to work in isolation on his own project, a scholarly translation into archaic Spanish of Sir Thomas Browne's "Hydriotaphia, Urne-Buriall." This conclusion projects into the past a phenomenon that the discovery and imitation of Tlön has projected into the future: the question to what extent the ideal forms the real.

"Tlön, Uqbar, Orbis Tertius" is highly relevant to the architectonic novel not only because it is a perfect demonstration of literary spatialism, but also because it implies a distinction between the single exclusive perspective and the multiple comprehensive perspective that is applicable to two broad types of architectonic novels. The first displays a closed structure and is independent, as is Tlön, Uqbar, Orbis Tertius, of the laws and restrictions of ordinary, mundane reality. This sort of novel generates its own perfectly consistent realm of being, which does not necessarily have much to do with "reality." The second type of novel displays, by contrast, an open structure and an acceptance of reality, as well as of competing "realities." The authors of novels with open structures reject the clarity provided by the aesthetic frame and deliberately seek a "mixed" reality which incorporates a variety of perspectives. The novel with an open structure is analogous to that stage in Borges' story at which Tlön and the "real" world are beginning to become indistinguishable from one another. In the final analysis, however, both the closed- and open-structured novel seek totality of vision: the one by emphasizing the imaginary as the complement of the real; the other by fusing both in a composition that aspires toward the illusion of an absolute approximation of reality by means of simultaneously projected multiple perspectives.

Notes

1. John Hawkes, "Interview," *Wisconsin Studies in Contemporary Literature*, VI (Summer, 1965), p. 149.
2. José Ortega y Gasset, *The Dehumanization of Art and Other Writings on Art and Culture* (New York, 1956), p. 21. "La Deshumanización del Arte," *Obras completas*, III (Madrid, 1947), p. 366: "El arte de que hablamos no es sólo inhumano por no contener cosas humanas, sino que consiste activamente en esa operación de deshumanizar."
3. Robert Musil, *The Man Without Qualities*, translated by Eithne Wilkins and Ernst Kaiser (New York, 1965), p. 3. *Der Mann Ohne Eigenschaften* (Berlin, 1952), p. 9: "Autos schossen aus schmalen, tiefen Strassen in die Seichtigkeit heller Plätze. Fussgängerdunkelheit bildete wolkige Schnüre. Wo kräftigere Striche der Geschwindigkeit quer durch ihre lockere Eile fuhren, verdickten sie sich, rieselten nachher rascher und hatten nach wenigen Schwingungen wieder ihren gleichmässigen Puls. Hunderte Töne waren zu einem drahtigen Geräusch ineinander verwunden, aus dem einzelne Spitzen vorstanden, längs dessen schneidige Kanten liefen und sich wieder einebneten, von dem klare Töne absplitterten und verflogen."
4. Hugh Kenner, "Art in a Closed Field," *Virginia Quarterly Review*, XXX (Autumn, 1962), p. 600.
5. *The Dehumanization of Art*, p. 35. "La Deshumanización del Arte," p. 376: "Si ahora . . . lo invertimos, y volviéndonos de espaldas a la presunta realidad tomamos las ideas según son—meros esquemas subjectivos—y las hacemos vivir como tales, con su perfil anguloso, enteco, pero transparente y puro—en suma, si nos proponemos deliberadamente realizar las ideas—habremos deshumanizado, desrealizado éstas. Porque ellas son, en efecto, irrealidad. Tomarlas como realidad es idealizar—falsificar ingenuamente. Hacerlas vivir en su irrealidad misma es, digámoslo así, realizar lo irreal en cuanto irreal. Aquí no vamos de la mente al mundo, sino al revés, damos plasticidad, objetivamos, *mundificamos* los esquemas, lo interno y subjetivo."

6. See the interview with Cortázar in Luis Harss's and Barbara Dohmann's book *Into the Mainstream: Conversations with Latin American Writers* (New York, 1967).

7. Michel Butor, *Répertoire*, II (Paris, 1963), p. 96: "Le déplacement physique d'un individu, le voyage, apparaîtra comme cas particulier d'un 'champ local,' comme on dit un 'champ magnétique.' Les lieux ayant toujours une historicité, soit par rapport à l'histoire universelle, soit par rapport à la biographie de l'individu, tout déplacement dans l'espace impliquera une réorganisation de la structure temporelle, changements dans les souvenirs ou dans les projets, dans ce qui vient au premier plan, plus ou moins profond et plus ou moins grave."

8. Butor, p. 49: "La présence du reste du monde a une structure particulière pour chaque lieu, les relations de proximité effectives pouvant êtres toutes différentes des voisinages originels."

9. Chapter 5 contains an analysis of John Dos Passos' experiments with perspective in the form of the Newsreels and the Camera Eye sections of *U.S.A.*

10. Chapter 8 contains a structural analysis of *Berlin Alexanderplatz* and a brief comparison of this work and *U.S.A.*

11. Anaïs Nin, *Seduction of the Minotaur* (Denver, 1961), pp. 5–6.

12. Anaïs Nin, *Ladders to Fire* (Denver, 1959), p. 7.

13. The technical significance of *sous-conversation* will be discussed in Chapter 4.

14. Anaïs Nin, *Collages* (Chicago, 1964), p. 7.

15. Anaïs Nin, *Realism and Reality* (New York, 1946), p. 22.

16. Jorge Luis Borges, "Tlön, Uqbar, Orbis Tertius," translated by Alastair Reid, *Ficciones* (New York, 1962). *Ficciones* (Buenos Aires, 1956).

These queer mental worlds do turn out to describe the familiar world after all, but from an angle the existence of which we should never have suspected.

—Hugh Kenner [1]

2.

Closed

Structures

There are several possible approaches to the novel that displays a closed structure. Tied loosely to the romance and to the Gothic novel of the past and to the comicbook and the science-fiction tale of the present, this type of novel is often characterized as "Surrealistic," "Expressionistic," or "Kafkaesque." Indeed, many *are* Surrealistic in the strictest sense, having arisen from the ideals of the movement and having been written by its adherents. Such are *Hebdomeros, Aurora, La Liberté ou l'amour!, La Nuit du Rose-Hôtel, Au Château d'Argol, Tête-de-Nègre,* and *Babylone.* Others, like John Hawkes's *The Cannibal,* seem to have more in common with German Expressionism than with Surrealism, and Djuna Barnes's *Nightwood* has an ancestor in *Wuthering Heights* but a still nearer one in T. S. Eliot's poem, *The Waste Land.* One might conclude that there is an element of the bizarre in novels with closed structures and wonder, consequently, what is the connection between grotesque subject matter and structure. It is true that most works with closed structures *do* emphasize the extraordinary; they do project, as Hugh Kenner has said, "queer mental worlds." But this is not necessarily the case. For example, both Anaïs Nin's *House of Incest* and Edoardo Sanguineti's *Capric-*

cio italiano are erected upon closed structures and depict the unconscious lives of normal persons. The structures of Gertrude Stein's works are closed; the substance is mundane, even homely. The works of Alain Robbe-Grillet, as well, demonstrate the closed structure while dealing with relatively ordinary topics such as appear in any daily newspaper. Nonetheless, it is true that the closed structure is perfectly suited to the erection of a weird or marvelous tale and that most of the novels in which it is found are in some sense "offbeat."

The closed structure derives its essential features from the fact that only one perspective is permitted as a point of view upon the subject. According to *Webster's Dictionary*, perspective may be "the aspect of an object of thought from a particular standpoint." If only one standpoint is allowed, then the consequent view is bound to be distorted, since but one is inadequate to a complete exposure of the subject. And if the one perspective that *is* permitted is oddly placed—let us say in the mind of a madman —then the resulting world that is revealed will be, indeed, "queer." It is important to keep in mind the possibility that perspective may be indistinguishable from narrative point of view; this occurs in books in which everything is perceived and related by a first-person narrator. But narrative point of view is but one of several possible modes of perspective, and a book that does not have a first-person narrator may, nonetheless, embody but a single perspective. This occurs when every representation of a character, an action, or a theme is projected in the same intellectual, emotional, judgmental, and atmospheric light, or when every character, action, and theme in the book bears upon the same point, as in, for example, *La Liberté ou l'amour!* Structurally, the latter procedure is comparable to the musical development of a composition by means of variations upon a theme. The use of the single perspective precludes the possibility of contrast, which implies analysis, for contrast is possible only among the elements of the composition. In novels with closed structures, these have usually been selected for their homogeneity.

Even the contrast that inevitably exists between the reader's perspective and that embodied in the book is counteracted to some degree by the restriction to a single perspective. This is so because of the very high intensity of focus that is a natural result of the restriction of perspective and the avoidance of patterns calling for analysis by the reader. It is easy to imagine the importance of intensity to the novelist who wishes to evoke a fantastic, grotesque, or supernatural world.

A second consequence of the restricted perspective, one that may be even more important than intensity, is autonomy. Depending upon where the single perspective is located, novels with closed structures may claim near-total freedom from the laws of reality. They are the "closed fields" of which Hugh Kenner has written, and their inventors, having chosen a subject and a perspective, need obey only those principles of characterization, of space and time—in short, the dictates of "reality"—that are attendant upon the restricted point of view that they themselves have selected. There is no need for characters conceived and portrayed according to the principle of verisimilitude and provided with believable motives for their actions, no need for conventionally measured approximations of time and space, for dialogue that reproduces actual speech patterns, or for actions and themes that reflect the lives of ordinary men.

Novels with closed structures may project worlds in which the purely arbitrary laws of nonsense are sovereign, as do *Alice in Wonderland* and *Impressions d'Afrique*. They may evoke worlds of pure fantasy, as do *La Liberté ou l'amour!* and *Aurora*. Or they may embody worlds, like those of *Nightwood* and *Second Skin*, in which fantasy and reality are so deeply intermingled that a fusion is attained, a fusion that is intended to represent an expanded—in fact, a more comprehensive and, therefore, a more accurate reality—than that usually encountered in a work of fiction. The author of a novel with a closed structure wishes to create something similar to a painting by Paul Klee, of whom Bonnard said, " 'He produces a closed world, a picture which is in the nature of a book and carries its interest with it wherever it goes.' " [2]

Some secondary traits of the novel with a closed structure follow naturally upon the restriction of the perspective. If an eccentric first-person narrator is employed, there exists spontaneously the justification for an odd or ornate style, as is found, for example, in Anaïs Nin's *House of Incest,* in John Hawkes's *Second Skin,* and in Michel Leiris' *Aurora.* In any case, the unified perspective necessitates a more or less uniform style throughout, and often the novelist, wishing to intensify the atmosphere of his book, will deliberately use language that is heavily metaphorical, rich with descriptive adjectives, and that builds into rhapsodic and lyric passages. Moreover, novels with closed structures, as perfect vehicles for eccentric points of view, frequently are grotesquely funny. They are filled with that special combination of the tragic and the ludicrous that has come to be known as "black humor." In terms of theme, these novels often, but by no means exclusively, deal with the unnatural, the monstrous, or the marvelous, with the perverse and the perverted. Both for this reason, and because of its freedom from the conventions of time and space, the novel with a closed structure often is indebted to the liberating powers of dream and of the unconscious mind. The dream provides this type of novel with an appropriate source not only of images and of techniques for organizing the various elements of the tale by means of free association, but also with an approximation of a spiritual dimension. In discussing the relevance of the dream to modern art, Roger Shattuck has explained how, "Without relying on the existence of a 'higher' or spiritual world apart from our own inner being, dream can endow ordinary experience with an aura of ritual and the supernatural."[3] Although the resources of the dream may, as in *Tête-de-Nègre* and *Aurora,* be used to evoke and to sustain a vision of spiritual metamorphosis, they may also, as in *Capriccio italiano,* be put to the relatively more conventional purpose of approximating the dream portrait of an ordinary man who is intended to be representative of a large group of men. The suggestiveness of the dream appears inexhaustible.

But when one considers the novel with a closed structure within the general frame of reference of this critical study, one must stress the complementary nature of the single restricted perspective. The deliberate emphasis that one usually finds in this type of novel on the extraordinary ought to be regarded not as a denial of reality, but as an intentional emphasis on a dynamic and long-neglected aspect of reality. Novels with closed structures constitute an aesthetic insistence that the fantastic, the bizarre, the marvelous, the irrational, the hallucinatory, and the horrifying no only exist, but constitute highly important and too often overlooked dimensions of reality. In these books the reader is being offered deliberately restricted, closed—and, therefore, highly intense—complementary perspectives on reality that are intended to correct the more nearsighted focus of the traditional "realist."

Since each novel with a closed structure embodies a single exclusively maintained perspective, each is a self-sustaining creation, free from outside influences (except for the perspective of the reader), from the "laws" of logic and causality, and from what is usually called "credibility." It is not surprising that each comprises a unique and original world, complete in itself. Novels with closed structures are good examples of Michel Butor's contention that the novel is an invitation to a voyage of discovery and that the voyage itself is a removal of perspective from which one sees more clearly the place from which he came. The author of *Nightwood* has conjured up a "black" café society whose members obsessively haunt the dingy bars of Berlin, Paris, and Vienna. Some of the most terrifying closed worlds in modern fiction are those created by John Hawkes. *The Cannibal* portrays the absurd, pathetic, and dangerous little world of Spitzen-on-the-Dein, whose citizens embody the collective unreconstituted and unregenerated psyche of nazism. *The Beetle Leq* reproduces the bleak myth of the American West. *The Lime Twig* presents a curious marriage between the desolate boardinghouse aura of England during World War II and the violent glamour of a criminal-infested racetrack. In *Second Skin,* Hawkes evokes all the tawdriness of Greyhound bus stations from Maine to California but leaves his protagonist, finally, peacefully at home on a "floating island" in the Pacific Ocean. Raymond Roussel's Africa resembles a carnival freak show jammed with spectacular acts and unprecedented marvels. Of a country, there is scarcely a trace. For *Aurora,* Michel Leiris has magically created the haunting landscape of an uninhabited world—a world filled with vast desert wastes, lonely stretches of beach, polar ice fields, underground caverns, and once-elaborate but now-sunken cities—all of which constitute crucial points along an inward journey toward the nameless narrator's creation of his secret self. In *Tête-de-Nègre* Maurice Fourré has evoked a landscape as eerie as, but much more benign than that of *Aurora*. His hero is a real hero, who journeys from a comically provincial picture-book town, Château-Gontier on the Mayenne River, deep in the awesome and beautiful woods of Brittany, to fulfill his preordained mission. Each of these fictional worlds is portrayed with great intensity of language, tone and atmosphere in order the more powerfully to hold the reader within its magnetic field. In most cases, it is necessary for the author of a novel with a closed structure to dispense entirely with conventional logic. He may operate with complete freedom in drawing his characters and in organizing events in time and space.

In novels with closed structures, character may be ruthlessly subordinated to theme. When this takes place, a character may amount to little more than a forceful gesture, an appetite, a life stance of an incredible or perverse nature. The personages of the novels to be examined in this chapter are generally outlandish. The Corsaire Sanglot is a "pirate"—in modern-day Paris—in high-heeled boots! Robin Vote is a woman who is literally transfixed by Djuna Barnes at the instant of transmigration into the form of a dog! Stella Snow is a ferocious old woman who leads a brigade of housewives armed with brooms and shovels to put down a riot in a mental hospital! Tête-de-Nègre is a ninety-three-year-old Baron who wanders about a moldy château with a black mask on his head! It is not surprising that conventional readers complain that such characters are not "real." But, as J. H. Matthews has insisted in his book *Surrealism and the Novel*, "the argument that such personages, ceasing to be 'characters,' become purely 'one-dimensional' loses its force when we understand that, conceived in desire, these beings appeal, outside the realm of naturalistic authenticity, to needs within us without which no exchange is possible between the author and his public." [4]

Each novel with a closed structure proposes its own concept of character as an embodiment of an idea or a force. Verisimilitude is, then, beside the point, just as much so as in Samuel Beckett's *Molloy*. The subordination of character to a total vision spatially conceived is well demonstrated by John Hawkes's novel of 1949, *The Cannibal*, a "black comedy" projection of the basic instincts and perceptions of German fascism between 1914 and 1945. Most of the book's characters are endowed exclusively with symbolic value; these are Cromwell (an English traitor who helps Germany organize for wartime industrialization); Leevey (an obviously Jewish member of the American occupation forces); a foolish Census-Taker; Herr Stintz (a one-eyed schoolteacher who stays up all night to play his tuba); Ernst Snow (a satirically inverted version of the "student prince," who, passive and underdeveloped physically, easily exchanges his passion for dueling for an even more fervent passion for collecting wooden crucifixes); and a Duke who is literally a cannibal. Throughout the novel he is chasing a small boy up and down the twisted dirty streets of Spitzen-on-the-Dein and into the woods where he eventually kills him, dismembers him, and takes him home where he makes soup from the child's remains.

There are two groups of characters, between which Stella Snow provides the thematic and temporal link. The first are associated with the rise of Prussia in 1914; they are all members (however improbable this may seem) of Stella's family. Her father is a totally senile old general, who, unable to pronounce her name, calls her "Stool." Her brothers are twin boys in full-dress uniform and boots who are constantly depicted marching around the house like robots. Her sister Jutta is slack, promiscuous, and permissive, while Stella is upright, demanding, and ferociously proud. Both nourish fascist manhood, Stella by igniting and fanning its ambitions, Jutta by fulfilling its (always perverted) sexual needs. Gerta, the family maid, turns up during the war as a ghoulish and lascivious "V" girl. All of these figures are contained in a house that "was like an old trunk covered with cracked sharkskin, heavier on top than on the bottom, sealed with iron cornices and covered with shining fins." [5]

In order to give *The Cannibal* its vitality as a sustained nightmare, Hawkes has deliberately violated logic at several levels of construction. His characters do highly "unbelievable" things. For example, it is hardly reasonable that a woman as desirable and as intelligent as Stella would fall in love with the skinny, crippled, and clearly mad Ernst Snow. At the same time, it is not possible to believe that the soft and corrupt Jutta could have been a brilliant architecture student while still in her early teens. But Hawkes's most decisive departure from logic concerns his handling of his first-person narrator Zizendorf, the editor of the town paper who leads an "uprising" against the Allied occupiers by ambushing a Jewish dispatch rider. At once Zizendorf establishes himself as the new *Führer*. Employing "I," Zizendorf simply moves in and out of the narrative at Hawkes's pleasure. The author never troubles himself with the fact that Zizendorf could not possibly have been present at all the events he is narrating. He uses Zizendorf's personal voice when he wishes and drops it when he wishes. The result of this alternation between personal and impersonal narrative voices is that one feels he is in the presence of that special lucid sort of madness, that mode of cheerful and banal evil that is so often associated with nazism. All of Hawkes's characters, including Zizendorf, are energized aspects of German political and psychic ambitions. Intentionally, they are animated clichés—and only that. To have examined them more fully, to have explored their motives and passed sentence upon their actions, would have entailed a violation of the boundaries of the closed field, from which the expected has been deliberately banished in order that the reality of the hallucinatory may be more starkly illuminated.

Two of the most interesting phenomena of characterization in novels with closed structures are, first, the reduction of all the characters to their respective functions in the mind of the narrator, or in the perceiving mind through which the book is expressed; and, second, the existence of fluid and double-natured characters whose identities change as the work progresses. Both of these imaginative approaches to characterization may be found in Anaïs Nin's "prose poem," *House of Incest*, written in the 1930s. The book is a dream portrait of a nameless woman who must be regarded as archetypal, since her struggle, portrayed entirely through the imagery of dreams, is to free the healthy, sensuous, loving aspect of herself from the emotional tyranny of impossible or harmful relationships. Apart from the speaking "I," the dreamer who seeks the liberating birth and the cosmic awakening, there are no "characters." Although several of the book's seven movements do project two other women, Sabina and Jeanne, their only significance is as aspects of the personality of the dreamer: the one, Sabina, represents a sexual freedom and recklessness which the dreamer envies; the other, Jeanne, signifies the restricting and ultimately narcissistic loves that are collectively symbolized as "incestuous." Sometimes the dreamer imagines that she is one of these women; sometimes, the other; meanwhile, she herself is passing through a metamorphosis based upon the revelatory and purgative powers of nightmare. She emerges, having achieved at least a brief experience, a promise of the freedom and harmony which she seeks:

> And she danced; she danced with the music and with the rhythm of the earth's circles; she turned with the earth turning, like a disk, turning all faces to light and to darkness evenly, dancing towards daylight.[6]

A similar totally subjective dream novel appeared some thirty years after Miss Nin's: *Capriccio italiano* by Edoardo Sanguineti. Its single perspective, like that of *House of Incest*, is restricted to the content of the narrator's dreams. Genuine existence is denied to every other person who appears in the dreams of Sanguineti's Edoardo, except to Luciana, the wife whose pregnancy is the source of his anxiety. With humor, Sanguineti exposes the narcissism of the ego when it is relieved by sleep of the obligations of sociability. Every "character," besides Luciana, is no more than a symbolic aspect of Edoardo's emotional life.

E, a male often shown trying to seduce Luciana, represents the narrator's own lasciviousness. C, whom he frequently desires, appears to symbolize the corresponding sexual aspect of Luciana (the two women are cousins). A crippled boy often appears; he is associated with Edoardo's fears that his unborn son will not be normal and with the familiar terror of castration. A painter, B, relates a dream he has had of his own birth; this reflects Edoardo's preoccupation with birth in general, with its ambiguous blend of fear and joy. B and R are opposing forces acting upon Edoardo; B consistently leads him toward disclosures of frightening experiences (castration, cuckolding, or the death of his wife); R (a sexually provocative young girl, the daughter of the *portinaia*) is the narrator's guide upon a mysterious Dantesque journey representing a death and a rebirth, a metamorphosis that includes a mystic vision of sexual union and a reassuring revelation of the wholeness of the unborn son, Michele. Both Cintura Nera ("Black Belt") and the Martian are comic symbols of masculine potence (and brutality), while A ("quella grassa") and R are perhaps deliberately trite representations of eroticism.

Aurora provides a very different but equally interesting example of what may be achieved by placing the entire action and all the personages of a novel within the mind of a single individual. The first-person narrator of Michel Leiris' phantasmagoric novel is its central and only character. It is easy to see how this fact alone serves to restrict the perspective and to close out contrasting perspectives that might, at the very least, weaken the imaginative impact of the events that are narrated by this single individual. Not only is the single point of view the natural one when an enclosed, restricted, and even a distorted perspective is desired, it is the one that most readily allows for a total imaginary embroidery of events by means of a rich style. In the opening pages of *Aurora*, Leiris' nameless—and wholly faceless and featureless— narrator rouses himself to the point of breaking out of his self-imprisonment in an attic room of an uninhabited and isolated château. At first, he is self-deprecating and self-loathing. He refers to himself as "I who am only an odious esthete. . . ." [7] But as soon as he has taken the first, and perhaps most difficult, step in the attainment of his freedom by bursting through the front door of the strange château, his ego begins to become gigantic. He announces that he will drop the impersonal third-person pronoun and henceforth use only the first person. His consciousness and his imagination begin to swell to grandiose proportions (a warning to the reader that he has entered a wholly subjective realm). And eventually, this narrator is nothing but an immense sensitivity let loose upon events and perfectly capable of wrenching reality into the shapes of its desiring: "I move on," he boasts, "and it is not I who change my position in space, but space itself that is changed by my movements." [8]

In *Aurora*, no less than in Anaïs Nin's and Edoardo Sanguineti's dream compositions, each of the "characters" is but a projection of the narrator's desires. Indeed, once this narrator has begun to experience himself as aggressive, even ferocious, and, most important, as omnipotent in the creation of fantasy, new "characters" begin to be introduced. Automatons all, their common origin in the narrator's imagination is betrayed by the fact that all are explorers or billboard heroes. The first to appear is a dapper and suave man in a smoking jacket who is associated with an advertisement for American whiskey. He is described as a stone man, a petrified man; he recalls the movie heroes created by the late Humphrey Bogart. This man goes along on Aurora's wild ride through the desert which has its apotheosis in her sexual mutilation atop a revolving pyramid. At this rite, he is an observer, a silent, respectful communicant, a worshiper.

The next variation upon the thematic figure of the explorer is a young man who has been washed up in a small cove where he undertakes a fascinated exploration of an underwater palace. The motif of the hunt which was established by the narrator in the book's first pages is here carried forward by the young man's boots; they have been made from the skins of wild animals. This voyager is said to be an Anglo-Saxon (and, therefore, presumably closer to the primitive type than would be a typical Latin). He is the author of two books whose titles unite the two major thematic strains of *Aurora:* "Jesus-Christ masochiste" and "Mère Patrie et Tante Patrie, roman pornographique." What he discovers in the castle is an even more potent example of the perfected hero than the "stone man," the terrifying confessions of Damoclès Siriel, the former king of the castle and its surrounding ruins. His name is part of a recurrent pattern of images connected with knives and scissors.

As Aurora is the perfected essence of woman, so is Siriel the perfected male principle. He despises human beings. He loves only the earth itself in its most vast and inhuman forms. He adores the abstract, "géometrie sans limites," the intangible, the limitless, the eternal. Like the Corsaire Sanglot, he is haunted by death; he hates everything that lives because of the inevitable reminder contained in life of its certain loss. Damoclès Siriel's confessions recount sadistic crimes against both men and women, but the most horrible of all is the fact that he destroyed his entire kingdom by opening a dike and creating a disastrous flood. Siriel subsumes the identities of the narrator (who has created him) and of the "stone man" and the Anglo-Saxon explorer alike, for he is their superior in cruelty. Aurora is a deity of changing aspects. "Or Aura" signifies the revelatory and the redemptive; "or aux rats" alludes to her magical aspect and especially to the "anneau de fer" which has rats carved upon it; and "Horrora" is a clear assertion of the terror of the sacrifice she has willingly made of her body. Damoclès Siriel is the fitting consort for such a goddess.

As Leiris has wrought from the processes of the daydream the substance, atmosphere, tone, and structure of *Aurora,* so Maurice Fourré has adapted similar processes to the creation of another ritualistic novel in which the characters are quite explicitly said to be the inventions of the author's imagination. Fourré himself, "Le Monsieur Anonyme," is to *Tête-de-Nègre* what the unidentified narrator is to *Aurora:* both, in fact, after having lavished their energies upon the creation of their fantasies, disappear. Perhaps they even die; after all, in the first part of *La Liberté ou l'amour!* Robert Desnos makes an announcement of his own death. Is this not the ultimate act of excluding perspective to a single point of view? The author, once his closed field has been energized, must cease to exist in order to eliminate even his own complex and perhaps contradictory point of view on the world he himself has just created.

John Hawkes animates clichés and moves them about on the surface of a nightmarish landscape. Both Robert Desnos and Michel Leiris fuse admittedly autobiographical first-person narrators with fantastic characters that resemble life-sized paper dolls, and Maurice Fourré, like Djuna Barnes, creates a ludicrous idea by blending the spiritual and the comic and personifies it by turning it into a personage with a distinct and decidedly eccentric voice. Such are the "characters" to be found in novels that are based upon the single perspective.

The central work in any consideration of the novel with a closed structure must be Raymond Roussel's *Impressions d'Afrique,* not only because it was perhaps the first book to display several characteristics that have become widespread, but also because it remains one of the most fascinating displays of pure imaginative power in fantastic literature. In 1910, before any of the writers discussed in this chapter had published a novel, and fourteen years before Surrealism officially came into being, Roussel published *Impressions d'Afrique* at his own expense. Twenty-five years passed before the first printing had been depleted. But the radical nature of *Impressions d'Afrique* has proved highly compatible with the spirit of modernism, and today the book is widely admired.[9] The manner in which it was written provides an example of Hugh Kenner's theory of how the "closed field" may function in literature. Roussel composed some of his works according to the principles of an original, personally invented system for combining words and figures of speech. Although its assumptions are absolutely arbitrary, this system is complicated and internally consistent. Roussel has described it and shown how it worked in an essay called "How I Wrote Some of My Books." [10]

The particular way in which Roussel limited his perspective in *Impressions d'Afrique* also deserves notice. Although the events of the book are ostensibly narrated by a shipwrecked European, this man is utterly self-effacing and totally impersonal. He functions exactly as would a motion-picture camera, to record impartially objects, persons, and situations, delivering their surfaces, their appearances, and their dimensions, totally without emotional coloring or moral judgment. In short, at least ten years before other writers had begun to experiment with the perspectives of the camera, Roussel had provided a model of the view which could be obtained by approximating its objectivity. Closely connected to the matter of the camera perspective is the dominant position occupied in *Impressions d'Afrique* by objects. As if sensing that the motion-picture camera would become the perfect medium for portraying *things* and man's relations with them, Roussel made groups of objects and persons the subject of his book. His "characters" have no human dimension whatsoever. As the objects are presented in contexts that have been stripped of all affective elements, so are the people. As a result, they possess visual reality only; they seem to be immense, flat cutouts, like paper dolls: brightly colored, marvelous, and a little terrifying. Surely, Roussel's gigantic blonde huntress in jodhpurs is the first "pop art" character in literature.[11]

Still another authorial liberty exercised by Roussel in the construction of *Impressions d'Afrique* is the book's independence of limitations in time and space. It gives, in fact, the effect of being free-floating. Its essential nature as a marvel show does not demand any chronological orientation. Since the events of the book do not occur in "real" time, they might take place at any time at all: past, present, or future. The spatial orientation that is provided by Africa is somewhat more significant, but not much more so. India, China, Japan, or Lapland would have served as well as Africa, for the location of the book is irrelevant except as it helps remove the reader from his habit of skepticism by plunging him into an exotic atmosphere in which he may the more easily "suspend disbelief." Africa is a metaphor for a state of mind: imaginative, playful revelry arising from free associations of objects and persons.

Impressions d'Afrique consists of two extended series of highly detailed visual descriptions of the "acts" or displays that have been gotten up by a group of shipwrecked Europeans to amuse and please their captor, an African king named Talou, and to win their release. All of the excitement of the shipwreck and the rescue by the Africans, highly exploitable material for a conventional adventure story, is briefly summarized in a few sentences. Besides Talou, the major "characters" are the narrator, a European; a second, or "inner," narrator, an African who recounts in perfect French the dynastic history and struggles of Talou's court; an immense blonde huntress and inventor, the former mistress of Talou's rival; her equally fantastic brother; and Talou himself. When first encountered, the black emperor is wearing a wig of blonde curls and a woman's dress. He is practicing a falsetto rendition of Daricelli's "Aubade," which he will sing on coronation day. All of this is reported without astonishment by the narrator. The book's "characters" are portrayed just as are the objects: in a measured prose that is barren of qualitative words and renders flat descriptions that serve largely to designate relationships in space among the people, statues, and machines on display in the Place des Trophées.

At once, without any explanation whatsoever, the reader is transported into the midst of an astonishing scene on the Place des Trophées. Here he is entertained by such sights as a statue made of corset whalebones and mounted on a rolling platform; a miniature model of the Paris Bourse; a series of gaudy late-Victorian paintings depicting one Flora and a Sergeant-Major Lécurou, and many equally surprising objects and demonstrations. To the reader's surprise and disappointment, about halfway through the book the narrator embarks upon an explanatory account of the shipwreck, and this leads to the second "inner" narration of the black emperor Talou's rise to power. For a time, the fun seems to be over. But this relatively conventional portion of *Impressions d'Afrique* is merely an interval, a form of "comic relief" that serves by contrast to render even more amusing and astonishing the second series of marvels that are to be performed on the day of the Europeans' release and departure for home. Among the "acts" is a demonstration by a Hungarian musician who is teaching a worm to play a zither; another is an attempt at flight by the emperor's son, who has mounted a board that has been glued to the feet of an enormous bird. Eventually, the day of liberation arrives, and the Europeans are led back to the shore, from which they set sail for their ordinary countries and dull homes.

The spatial and temporal liberty of the novel with a closed structure may be demonstrated by an examination of the similarities and differences between two books that are concerned with the opposing aspects of the same deity—love. Both regard with intensity the relation between liberty and love. And both are constructed by means of the principle of juxtaposition. The two books are Robert Desnos' *La Liberté ou l'amour!* and Djuna Barnes's *Nightwood*. Both novels take their stand in the dubious lands of the perverted: in the one case, sadism; in the other, homosexuality. Neither author is even remotely interested in the psychological reasons for, or the sociological complications created by, these aberrations from the sexual norm. Each is using a sexual modality as a metaphor for a condition of the human soul. In the tradition of the Marquis de Sade, Desnos proposes the possibility of total personal liberty as it may be pursued through total sexual license, a form of liberty that is wholly un-limited except by death itself. In *Nightwood*, Miss Barnes is less interested in liberty than in love, and not at all in sexuality. Through the aspirations and the agonies of her characters, she implies, in fact, that liberty and love are irreconcilable and that very few people, indeed, desire the former, while the pursuit of love is the common cause of human suffering. If *Nightwood* is a form of the Christian message of love in disguise, *La Liberté ou l'amour!* is a litany for a black mass in which every piety is inverted and in which license is enshrined upon the altar traditionally reserved for restraint and self-control.

Both novels briefly invoke Paris as a setting, but neither Desnos nor Miss Barnes wastes a single word on the re-creation of an authentic Paris. Desnos deliberately paints a dense, erotic, night-time city as a base of operations for his hero, the Corsaire Sanglot, whereas Miss Barnes, who also summons the night, employs Paris merely as one of the European cities in which her expatriate American protagonists wander in search of their ludicrous yet tragic destinies. She is even less interested in the surface features of the cities she chooses as settings for various parts of her tale than is Desnos in the credibility of his Paris. Both *Nightwood* and *La Liberté ou l'amour!* embody disjunct structures erected by means of juxtaposition. However, Miss Barnes's book is closer to what Roger Shattuck has described as the "classical strain of juxtaposition": the elements chosen are relatively homogeneous in nature, and, therefore, the final effect of their combination is one of "stillness" or of circularity.[12] This concept helps to explain why *Nightwood*, whose structure is disjunct, nonetheless gives the reader a final impression of unity and self-containment. This is felt less strongly in the case of *La Liberté ou l'amour!*, whose constituents are relatively less homogeneous than are those of *Nightwood*.

The eight parts of *Nightwood* contain materials that are highly unusual in themselves, but, more important, these ma-terials are presented in an apparently haphazard and irrational manner, without order or sequence among the parts. According to Joseph Frank, who has analyzed the book in detail, "The eight chapters of *Nightwood* are like searchlights, probing the darkness each from a different direction, yet ultimately focusing on and illuminating the same entanglement of the human spirit." [13] "Bow Down," the first part, presents the background of the half-Jewish, half-Christian, phony Baron Felix Volkbein, and gives the reader flashing glimpses of Robin, Nora, and the doctor. The settings are Vienna and Berlin. Quickly condensed into the second part, "La Somnambule," is a very long description of Robin and the story of how the Baron Felix courted and married her, only to have her run away and leave him with a baby son. The disproportion, when the book is regarded in conventional terms, is evident; the first part contains virtually no action, and the second is jammed with potentially exploitable dramatic events, all of which are hastily summarized. "Night Watch," the third part, gives the reader a detailed introduction to Nora Flood, quickly establishes her troubled love for Robin, and hurries over their travels to Munich, Vienna, and Budapest to leave them settled in a house in Paris. As in *Impressions d'Afrique*, there is absolutely no explanation of surprising or even bizarre events or relationships. In part four, "The Squatter," another American woman is introduced, one Jenny Petherbridge, who very easily makes a conquest of the passive and undiscriminating Robin and takes her, at the end of the chapter, to America. At this point the book's "time" begins to slow down and to stand still.

In the fifth part, called "Watchman, What of the Night?," the "action" of *Nightwood* is suddenly transformed into an intense, extremely funny, and extremely ludicrous prolonged dialogue between the novel's two great figures of suffering, Nora Flood and the doctor, Matthew Mighty-grain-of-salt-Dante O'Connor. The setting is the doctor's rented room in a cheap Paris hotel, a room that is in itself so terrifying and ridiculous that it might inspire pages of analysis of its "black comedy." This part ends by marking time, so to speak, at the decisive incident that concluded the break between Nora and Robin: a mysterious and sinister evening at Jenny's house, during the course of which a little girl apparently fell in love with Robin. A "scene" ensued. The doctor was present, and in the fifth part of the novel he describes to Nora what seemed to him to have taken place. The

Baron Felix, who had been dropped in the second chapter when Robin abandoned him, unexpectedly reappears now in "Where the Tree Falls." What surprises the reader is that Felix's son Guido is now ten years old. Up until this point, there has been no reference to the passing of years. Time has not seemed important to the circular movement of this tale of perpetual loss. And yet the information that Nora and Robin must have been together for six or seven, perhaps even eight, years now adds depth to the reader's understanding of Nora's grief. "Go Down, Matthew," is, in fact, a continuation of "Watchman, What of the Night?" The dialogue of sufferers is resumed, this time at Nora's house, but now the emphasis is upon the doctor himself. Although an impassioned analysis of Nora and Robin's love begun in the earlier fifth chapter is continued here, it is subordinated to the doctor's own anguished confession of *his* misery, the counterpart of Nora's. Finally, there comes the book's very short (less than four-page) concluding chapter: "The Possessed." Significantly, the setting is now America, where Robin and Nora originally met by accident at a circus. Here, in a little chapel on Nora's farm, Robin is transformed before the reader's eyes, so to speak, into a dog, while Nora herself either falls unconscious or is struck down by Robin in retaliation for Nora's attempt to "possess" her soul through love.

Nightwood contains violations of virtually every tenet of "good novel-writing." The characters are unbelievable. The plot relates little more than the theft of one person's lover by another. The only "action" takes place at several incoherently and incompletely described parties. Instead of action, this book contains long passages of heavily metaphorical, stylized prose and immensely long "unrealistic" conversations. Yet, through the heightened intensity of its language, which is the medium for the restricted perspective, and through the adroit structuring of its disjunct elements, *Nightwood* leaves the reader with a coherent and powerful impression of spiritual agony. The unified quality of this impression results from certain stable and consistent elements among the portions that are juxtaposed. First, all the characters are suffering because of the selfishness of their conceptions of love. Second, love is, in each case, given a specific religious dimension by Miss Barnes's careful identifications of the Baron with Judaism, Nora with Calvinism, and the doctor with Roman Catholicism. Expatriation is another life condition that is shared by Miss Barnes's characters and is revealed by their drifting from one European capital to another, and from Europe to America and back again. This motif is focused upon Felix, who is an incarnation of the eternally Wandering Jew. Finally, the uniform style that is used in each section, regardless of which character is being treated, tends to endow the elements of the structure with homogeneity.

There are two additional factors that give this "classically" disjunct work its ultimate impression of unity and universality. The first is the novel's spatial model, the "nightwood" which is haunted by those who search for love but misconceive its nature. The nightwood is necessarily timeless and without any definite location in space. If one is lost in it, pursuing his salvation, it hardly matters whether he is in Paris, Vienna, Berlin, or New England, or whether it is 1987 or 1937. The second unifying factor, one that helps to enclose and restrict the point of view and, therefore, to heighten the book's intensity, is the use of the Tiresias-like doctor, Matthew O'Connor, as a central sensibility who undergoes all, interprets it as he must, and yet suffers everything that the others suffer because of his role as scapegoat and prophet. The perspective of *Nightwood* is, thus, at once limited and universal. It is limited to the spiritual aspects of love and suffering, but this condensation of the subject serves effectively to enlarge its universal significance.

Nora Flood's cry that "Love is death, come upon with passion" [14] provides as central an insight into Robert Desnos' *La Liberté ou l'amour!* as into Djuna Barnes's *Nightwood*. The first chapter of Desnos' novel consists simply of these lines:

I. Robert Desnos
Born in Paris on the 4th of July, 1900.
Died in Paris on the 13th of December, 1924,
the day on which he writes these lines. [15]

The work itself is a protest against death, death which is defied not only by the Corsaire's religion of erotic self-indulgence, but in every line of Desnos' prose, which flaunts alike limitations of time, space, and mortality. Like *Nightwood, La Liberté ou l'amour!* is a structure composed from juxtaposed elements, with the difference that in the case of Desnos' book, the elements of the composition are less obviously homogeneous. After the cryptic tomb scripture of "I" comes a wild combination of events whose connections with one another at first seem obscure. Chapter II ("The Depths of the Night") is an odd striptease in which the narrator pursues the heroine, Louise Lame, through Paris at night, drawn on by the fact that she is shedding her clothing piece by piece under her fur coat. Chapter III ("All That One Sees Is Gold") contains, hurled together it seems, these elements: an erotic encounter between Louise Lame and the Corsaire Sanglot in a room whose suggestiveness is heightened by the fact that *Jack l'éventreur* (the Ripper) is supposed to have murdered one of his victims there; the "Pater du Faux Messie," a mock-epic history of Bébé Cadum; and "Le Golgotha," a mad Surrealist rewriting of the Crucifixion. "A Brigade of Pastimes" portrays the Corsaire's exploration of the ocean floor and his arrival at an eerie deserted town where he finds a monument to *Jack l'éventreur*. Prefaced by some description of an exploration at the North pole, Chapter V ("The Gulf of Longing") brings the Corsaire to L'Asile d'Aliénés where he has various experiences that are appropriate to a madhouse. Chapter VI is called "A Lampoon of Death." Without explanation, the reader learns that Louise Lame is dead and hears the mysterious "testimonials" of four deaf-mutes. Since the Corsaire does not appear in this scene, one infers that he does not know of her death.

In Chapter VII ("A Revelation of the Worldly Life") the Corsaire returns to Paris, longing for the heroine. A blend of depression and anticipation characterizes the mood of Chapter VIII ("As Far as the Eye Can See"); the Corsaire, now extremely bored, wanders about the outskirts of Paris where he sees corpses come to life. Back in the city again, he delivers a desperately sad and funny soliloquy before his own image in a plate-glass window. Chapter IX ("The Palace of Shadows") brings the Corsaire closer to Louise Lame, who has been resurrected, and in Chapter X ("The Boarding-School, Humming-Bird Garden"), they are reunited as partners in a maso-sadistic orgy at a girls' school. A great leap is embodied in Chapter XI ("Beat on, Drummers of Santerre!"). The scene is the French Revolution; the event, the execution of Louis XVI. The redoubtable Corsaire is present, along with the Marquis de Sade. The entire passage is a tribute to the Marquis, champion alike of erotic and political liberty.

Equally abrupt is the transition the reader must make back to the time and place of Chapter XII ("Possession of the Dream"). The site is the French Riviera near Nice; the time, the present. The Corsaire is host to a group of glamorous persons aboard his yacht. Louise Lame is there, of course. The day is brilliant. Expectations of pleasure are high. Suddenly a school of sharks attacks. The water begins to run red with blood. And the Corsaire? The reader knows that in the preceding chapter the hero was said to have fixed the day and the hour of his own death at age thirty-nine, less one month. But since his age at the time of the boating party is unknown, one cannot be certain what is meant by this enigmatic and incomplete phrase which ends the book: "It is at this moment that the Corsaire Sanglot . . ." [16] One might argue that since *La Liberté ou l'amour!* opens with the announcement of the author's death, on December 13, 1924, and that since this author is undeniably and admittedly giving freedom to fantasy by creating the Corsaire in one of his own imagined images, that the end of the book is intended to signal the end of the gloriously infamous life of the Corsaire.

"Neither time nor space—nothing—can stand in the way of the perfect relationships," [17] Robert Desnos has asserted in *La Liberté ou l'amour!* He demonstrates this assertion. He covers the world from the poles to the depths of the sea. When it pleases him to do so, he moves back in time to the French Revolution. When he most strongly wishes to demonstrate the power of imagination over reality, he brings back to life his dead heroine, Louise Lame. Thus, an exact conclusion to the mystery of the Corsaire's encounter with the sharks is not necessary. Even if he is killed, the author can always bring his hero back to life. In Desnos' aesthetic creed, the imagination is omnipotent.

The extremely varied elements of *La Liberté ou l'amour!* are fused into a single, unified, emotionally convincing whole by means of two factors. The first is the great energy, the daring, and the omnipresence of the Corsaire. By transporting himself at will from one of the novel's locales to another, he unifies these widely distant *lieux* around the glowing figure of himself. His single most arresting trait is his ubiquitousness. Desnos succeeds in creating the impression, without ever saying so directly, that the Corsaire, like Superman, uses a magic cape. Whoosh!—and he is wherever he wills himself to be!—at the bottom of the sea, in England at Le Pensionnat d'Humming-Bird Garden, near Nice, or exploring deserted towns where monuments have been erected to honor *Jack the Ripper*. It is this supernatural power of movement and the defiance of every conceivable obstacle that give the Corsaire the force with which he unifies all the very scattered elements of the novel into a unique and coherent whole.

The second major unifying factor of *La Liberté ou l'amour!* is the scrupulousness with which Desnos has maintained the single perspective. When closely examined, all of the apparently intrusive elements of the novel—the "Pater du Faux Messie," "Le Golgotha," the "Pamphlet Contre la Mort," the riddles of the deaf-mutes, the dialogues among the inmates at l'Asile des Aliénés—bear upon the same simple point of liberty: upon its importance and upon the right of every individual to seize it and to defy any form of interference with his claim to it. Even more important in this connection is the fact that every action of the Corsaire's is strictly consonant with his ideal of total liberty, not only in motion through time and space, but metaphysically, insofar as he seeks victory over death by determining for himself the exact moment at which he will succumb to it. Finally, the single perspective is maintained by the consistent identification of Desnos himself with the Corsaire; there is no dialogue between them and no conflict. They are interchangeable, the one merely acting out the desires of the other.

The question arises whether the elements of *La Liberté ou l'amour!* are actually homogeneous, as stated earlier, or whether they are, in fact, heterogeneous. From the point of view of theme, the novel is a composition that consists of varying types of expressions of a single, fiercely maintained point of view. It is also true that the Corsaire's great leaps in time and space give this book an air of abruptness, of jaggedness, of flashing, brilliant motion. But in spite of the apparent diversity of the novel's various parts, *La Liberté ou l'amour!* is dependent for the maintenance of its single perspective upon relatively homogeneous elements that are juxtaposed against one another.

There is still a final observation to be made about *La Liberté ou l'amour!* It is utterly lacking in any sort of analysis of its contents. It is an act of insistence, an assertion of belief, a proclamation of faith. This generalization may be extended to other novels with closed structures. In our age, which seems compulsively analytic, these novels embody assertions of various types. Some, like *Aurora, House of Incest,* and *Nightwood,* are not simply acts of insistence but are also claims for the spiritual as a coordinate realm of being with the material. *Aurora* and *Tête-de-Nègre* are rituals. They consist of nothing but the same act committed over and over again. Among John Hawkes's novels, only *Second Skin* invites the reader to question its declarations and to search for the location of its "truth."

Authors who have chosen to work with an exclusive single perspective and to close off their novels from surrounding contexts do not wish to explore their subjects. They wish to enthrall, to capture and to enchant the reader by insistence, by intensity and by prolonged exposure, so as to make him experience the reality of the ostensibly unreal. The "ideal," the "fantastic," the "Surreal," the "imaginative," or the "nonrealistic": each is but a term designating some aspect of life whose veracity is either belied or neglected by the empiricist. For the authors of the novels discussed in this chapter, verisimilitude is beside the point. What is required is intense focus upon a single perspective of a reality that has generally been seen from some other much more common perspective. To see something absolutely, one must necessarily concentrate upon those facets that he has never before allowed to come within his field of vision. In this sense, the novel with a closed structure may be regarded as a corrective to realism. It offers not a rival, but a complementary vision of life.

Notes

1. Hugh Kenner, "Art in a Closed Field," *Virginia Quarterly Review*, XXX (Autumn, 1962), p. 606.
2. G. di San Lazzaro, *Klee, A Study of His Life and Work* (London, 1957), p. 83.
3. Roger Shattuck, *The Banquet Years* (New York, 1961), p. 36.
4. J. H. Matthews, *Surrealism and the Novel* (Ann Arbor, Michigan, 1966), p 9.
5. John Hawkes, *The Cannibal* (New York, 1962), p. 61.
6. Anaïs Nin, *House of Incest* (Denver, 1958), p. 72.
7. Michel Leiris, *Aurora* (Paris, 1946), p. 21: "moi qui ne suis qu'un détestable esthète. . . ."
8. Leiris, p. 39: "Je marche, et ce n'est pas moi qui change d'espace mais l'espace lui-même qui se modifie."
9. See, for example, Jean Cocteau's "Note, en toute hâte," *La Nouvelle Revue Française*, XLI (1933), 464; Michel Leiris' "Introduction" to Roussel's "Comment j'ai écrit certains de mes livres," *La Nouvelle Revue Française*, XLIV (1935), 575–82; and Alain Robbe-Grillet's essay, "Enigmes et transparence chez Raymond Roussel," *Pour un nouveau roman* (Paris, 1963).
10. See note 9, above.
11. Without suggesting direct influence, one wishes to remark upon the similarity among Roussel's characters and Leiris' "stone man" and "moll" and John Hawkes's "poker-faced" portrayals of the brutal and glamorous criminals in *The Lime Twig*, Larry and Dora.
12. Shattuck, p. 337.
13. Joseph Frank, "Spatial Form in the Modern Novel," *Critiques and Essays on Modern Fiction: 1920–1951*, edited by John W. Aldridge (New York, 1952), p. 54.
14. Djuna Barnes, *Nightwood* (New York, 1961), p. 137.
15.

I. Robert Desnos
Né à Paris le 4 juillet 1900.
Décédé à Paris le 13 decembre 1924,
jour où il écrit ces lignes.

The original French chapter headings that are referred to in pages 44 to 45 are as follows:

II: "The Depths of the Night" (Les Profondeurs de la Nuit)
III: "All That One Sees Is Gold" (Tout ce qu'on Voit Est d'Or)
IV: "A Brigade of Pastimes" (La Brigade des Jeux)
V: "The Gulf of Longing" (La Baie de la Faim)
VI: "A Lampoon of Death" (Pamphlet contre la Mort)
VII: "A Revelation of the Worldly Life" (Révélation du Monde)
VIII: "As Far as the Eye Can See" (A Perte de Vue)

IX: "The Palace of Shadows" (Le Palais des Mirages)
X: "The Boarding-School, Humming-Bird Garden" (Le Pensionnat d'Humming-Bird Garden)
XI: "Beat On, Drummers of Santerre!" (Battez, Tambours de Santerre!)
XII: "Possession of the Dream" (Possession du Rêve)

16. Robert Desnos, *La Liberté ou l'amour!* (Paris, 1962), p. 118: "C'est alors que le Corsaire Sanglot . . ."

17. Desnos, p. 100: "Le temps ni l'espace, rien ne s'oppose à ces relations idéales."

To provoke, assume a text that is out of line, untied, incongruous, minutely antinovelistic (although not antinovelish). Without prohibiting the genre's great effects if the situation should require it, but keeping in mind the Gidean advice, ne jamais profiter de l'élan acquis. Like all creatures of choice in the Western world, the novel is content in a closed order. Resolutely opposed to this, we should search here for an opening and therefore cut the roots of all systematic construction of characters and situations. Method: irony, ceaseless self-criticism, incongruity, imagination in the service of one.

—Julio Cortázar [1]

3.

Open
Structures

The novel whose structure is open testifies to its author's architectonic daring, for he, or she, has made an heroic attempt to thrust the reality of the work of art into the surrounding reality of life and to merge the two in an intersecting construct. Although both the closed- and the open-structured types of novels manifest their authors' desire to experiment freely with modes of characterization and with spatial and temporal relations, and although both depend upon juxtaposition as a principle of organization, in all other respects, open- and closed-structured novels represent contrasting approaches to spatial engineering. Whereas novels with closed structures are erected upon a deliberate restriction of perspective to one point of view and are intended to suggest self-sustaining, autonomous worlds, open-

51

structured novels embody multiple perspectives, some of which are actually contradictory, whose purpose is to expose the subject from as many angles as possible—and, ideally, with an impression of simultaneity. If the novel with a closed structure is often an assertion of belief, the open-structured novel may well constitute an intellectual exploration undertaken by a novelist who actually is not certain what he believes about the nature of reality: fact versus fiction, imagination versus observation, feeling versus thought, creation versus reportage, and so on. It is quite common for open-structured novels to contain long passages of undisguised philosophical speculation or argumentation as well as theoretical discussions on the nature of art, of art and reality, and of the creative process. Strictly intellectual and aesthetic perspectives are often included among the multiple perspectives of these novels. Finally, instead of the intensity of focus within the closed field that is desired by the author of the novel with a closed structure, the creators of open-structured works aspire toward the approximation of diffusion; of flux; of constantly forming, dissolving, and re-forming relationships among the elements of the work. These novels have much in common with cubist painting besides their evident intellectuality. It, too, is a "research into the emergent nature of reality, which is constantly transforming itself into multiple appearances, at once fact and fiction." [2]

A few of the most typical novels with open structures are these: *The Man Without Qualities* (*Der Mann Ohne Eigenschaften*); *The Counterfeiters* (*Les Faux-Monnayeurs*); *The Sleepwalkers* (*Die Schlafwandler*); *Berlin Alexanderplatz*; *U.S.A.*; *Hopscotch* (*Rayuela*); *Change of Skin* (*Cambio de piel*); and *Cities of the Interior*. Most of these books display the essential characteristics of open-structured works. Besides experiments with space and time, which will be examined in Chapters 7, 8, and 9, these novels possess three striking characteristics, all of which are attempts to "open out" the novel into life itself, or to project it into reality. The first characteristic is the multiplication of perspectives that has already been mentioned: the perspectives may take the form of a great many narrative points of view focused on the same subject; of experimentation with the perspectives of the camera; or of the great variety of perspectives available through literary quotation, illustration, mixtures of prose and poetry, and typographical variation. The second characteristic is the deliberate rejection of the novel's "frame," of those literary conventions that have traditionally served to distinguish the novel from its surrounding context of reality. Third comes the naked exploration within the novel of the processes through which it came into being.[3] In rejecting the borderline between art and life, the open-structured novel is abandoning one of the traditionally unchallenged conventions of the novel.[4] This is done in an attempt to *fuse* aspects of a total reality that are only apparently distinct from each other.

At its simplest, the refusal of the conventional binding off of the novel from "real" life may be seen in the widespread practice of novelists who are offering their readers "fiction" which is undisguised autobiography, as is *Capriccio italiano,* and ostensible "biography" which is, in fact, pure fiction, as is, for example, *Lolita.* Both practices are attempts to destroy the traditional illusion of the novel as something separate and distinct from life. It is as though certain novelists, fearful that too obvious a "fiction" will be dismissed as inconsequential and perhaps as "untrue," have attempted to endow their works with the authority of the empirically verifiable by insisting that their novels are actually documents, a practice that is as old as the novels of Daniel Defoe. Among such works are those many pseudofictions that are offered to the reader as diaries, memoirs, or confessions: *Lolita; Justine* and *Balthazar; The Tin Drum (Die Blechtrommel); Second Skin; In the Labyrinth (Dans le labyrinthe); Degrees (Degrés)* and *Passing Time (L'Emploi du temps);* and Nathalie Sarraute's *Portrait d'un inconnu.* On the other side are those works whose authors, although they are writing undisguised autobiographies, call them "novels," as though to infuse them with the imaginative and aesthetic powers of the art work as distinct from the report. A few of the best-known writers who do this are Henry Miller, Louis-Ferdinand Céline, Jean Genêt, and Michel Leiris. Their aspiration has been very succinctly stated by Leiris:

From a strictly aesthetic point of view, it was a question
for me, of condensing to an almost crude state a collection
of facts and images which I refused to permit myself to
exploit by letting them work upon my imagination; in
short, the negation of a novel. To reject all plot and to
admit as materials only the verifiable facts (and not only
the facts that seem probable, as in the classical novel),
nothing but the facts and all the facts was the discipline
which I chose for myself.[5]

To reject any sort of invention, to refuse to use any materials
except verifiable facts, to use nothing but the facts, and all the
facts: this ambition seems curious, indeed, for a novelist.

An attractive application of Leiris' ideal may be seen in
the writings of Anaïs Nin. Since she is the author of an immense
diary, parts of which have been published, it is not surprising
to find a complete lack of self-consciousness in her portrayals of
herself in her stories and novels. Her work demonstrates several
procedures common to novelists who wish to eradicate the divi-
sion between the work of art and its source in life. *Cities of the
Interior,* Miss Nin's "continuous" novel, abounds in characters
who strongly suggest some of the prominent artists and intellectuals whom Miss Nin knew when she was living in Paris some
years ago. The central figure in her story "Je suis le plus malade
des surréalistes" is Antonin Artaud; in *Collages,* a woman named
Judith Sands is most probably a representation of Djuna Barnes.
At the same time, one of the most prominent characters in the
works that constitute *Cities of the Interior* is called "Djuna," and
she, it seems, is the thinly disguised presence of the author in
the novel. Sometimes Miss Nin makes it clear that she herself
is a character in one of her stories (as, for example, in "The
Mouse"); at other times ("Birth") she leaves the matter un-
clarified.[6] The reader has no way of knowing whether he is reading about an actual or an imagined experience. It seems clear
that Miss Nin draws no clear distinction between her diaries
and her fictions because she sees no need for such a distinction.
Other authors of autobiography or biography dressed up as
fiction and of fiction presented as biography, or autobiography,

evidently share Miss Nin's assumption that the maintenance of a formal boundary between the novel and its surrounding environment—life—is an anachronistic formality without meaning in our time.

What is curious about this tendency is that it is an exact reversal of the illusion of the closed world that was sought by so many great novelists toward the end of the nineteenth century. The major innovations of Flaubert, James, Turgenev, and Conrad tended to separate entertainment from art in the novel by heightening the illusion of the novel as a closed entity; this was achieved generally by the removal of the overt presence of the author so as to give the impression of autonomous characters involved in dramatic, as opposed to narrated, actions. But this advance from the undisguised author narration of the typical nineteenth-century novel to the subtle dramatic renderings of Henry James had hardly been achieved when a contradictory trend appeared back toward the exposure of the author's participation in the work. This tendency toward deformalization was noted by Joseph Warren Beach in 1932 when he published *The Twentieth Century Novel: Studies in Technique.* But it seems to have begun during the first decade of the century and, therefore, to have overlapped with Henry James's final efforts to close off the fictional world as a self-contained dramatic illusion.

It is useful to return to the comparison, suggested earlier, between the open-structured novel and the cubist painting, for both were developing at about the same time. Perhaps the first, certainly one of the first, novels to embody a deliberate exploration of the relationship between the author and the characters he has created is Miguel de Unamuno's *Amor y pedagogía* of 1902. Cubism was being developed by Georges Braque and Pablo Picasso during the last few years of the first decade of the century. In 1914 Unamuno published *Mist (Niebla)*, which contains an even more elaborate and astute analysis of the motives and processes of novel creation than does *Amor y pedagogía*.[7]

Why should novelists—just when they had made such a gain in techniques for producing the illusion of dramatic self-limitation and autonomy—suddenly turn about and begin putting the uncertainties and confusions of reality right back into their books? Is this not a step backward in terms of aesthetic sophistication—to reject formalistic integrity just when it had been achieved? A very few novelists were responding, as were the cubist painters, to the new concepts of reality that were being proposed by scientists and other creative thinkers. A most cogent explanation of this deliberate confusing of art and reality is found in Gertrude Stein's book, *Picasso,* published in 1939. She gives three reasons why cubism came into existence. All are highly relevant to the novel with an open structure:

> First. The composition, because the way of living had extended and each thing was as important as any other thing. Secondly, the faith in what the eyes were seeing, that is to say the belief in the reality of science, commenced to diminish. . . . Thirdly, the framing of life, the need that a picture exist in its frame, remain in its frame was over. A picture remaining in its frame was a thing that always had existed and now pictures commenced to want to leave their frames and this also created the necessity for cubism.[8]

An important related point, one that is more nearly pragmatic than theoretical, is inadvertently alluded to by Donald Sutherland in a brief comparison of narrative structure to the frame of a painting: "The comparison of narrative structure to architecture is right, insofar as both a story and a building make an arrangement or an enclosed place for living, a field of presence for the mind, by which everything outside of it can be dismissed from concern. It functions like the frame of a picture, to isolate what goes on inside it for complete attention and realization."[9] But when a convention has existed for over a hundred years, it gradually comes to be taken for granted, and then it loses its original power. The frame, or the narrative—after overuse—can as easily serve as a boundary to *exclude* the audience's attention as to focus it on what is *inside* the frame. As Miss Stein said, the twentieth century brought two realizations about reality: that there was very much more of it than we had thought and that all of reality was by no means visible or tangible. How very little,

then, was being included in conventional novels, devoted as they
were to the logical, the comprehensible, and generally, to the
visible. If Miss Stein's propositions are accepted, it becomes clear
that the frame of a painting (and the sequential narrative frame
of a novel) creates an artificial boundary between the art work
and reality. The frame alludes to divisions that are arbitrary, that
reflect no significant truth about reality. Furthermore, to return
to Donald Sutherland's observation for purposes of inverting it,
the old need to direct the viewer's attention inside, within, to
the contents of the frame disappears with the conviction that
various dimensions of reality differ with regard to the *degree*
of their reality—a notion that is vanquished by the expansion of
the "real" beyond the visible and the tangible. The need to
focus the spectator's attention on what is enclosed within the
frame is replaced by the need to call his attention to the inter-
connectedness of all aspects of reality. In some cases, the enclosure of the art work within a frame weakens its potential expressive power. Any aesthetic convention may become an ob-
solescent practice after much use. In the case of the novel, readers
who are long accustomed to the patterns embodied in the various
familiar narrative sequences—to the notorious twelve plots—are
likely to become nearly as well conditioned as Pavlov's dogs.
When this happens, without realizing it, readers withdraw the
deepest layers of their concentration from the work. They respond only superficially to the familiar signs laid out along the
surface. This tendency can be counteracted by a new alignment
of elements: in particular, by the shattering of the "frame" that
allows the contents of the work to spill out into life and that
permits the artifacts of life to flow into the work. This startling
mixture of elements seizes the reader by astonishing him. The
open structure is a demand for the reader's acute concentration,
and sometimes it is a demand, as well, for his active participation in the re-creation of the book.

Gertrude Stein spoke of how "pictures commenced to want
to leave their frames." So did certain novels. In cubist painting
the departure is achieved by the opposed techniques of "bleed-
ing" and by the automatic, apparently arbitrary abandonment
of a composition before it is "finished." In 1910 Georges Braque

deliberately called attention to his painting *Still Life with Violin and Pitcher* as a painting by including at the top of the canvas a naturalistically rendered nail. This act is analogous to a novelist's including in a book a revelation of how it was created. In both cases, the artist deliberately shatters the illusion of the work's autonomy as art and, at the same time, calls attention to its nature as another view of reality, one that has been created by a being who perhaps possesses still other views of that same reality. The artist who does this knows, and wishes to express his knowledge, that the appearance a work of art may give of being "finished" is and was—even in earlier epochs—but an illusion. Now, when time itself seems so drastically speeded up, when historical periods succeed one another with such rapidity, it is apparent to all that every art work is but a fragment, an incomplete and forever tentative statement, partly dependent upon its audience for its meaning. Since the audience is forever changing as the work passes through various cultural environments, the nature of the work itself must be regarded as forever fluid and vulnerable to alterations. It is this interpenetration of the work of art and reality that novelists seek when they employ the multiple perspectives that necessarily open up the structure of the work.

There are some simple attempts to fuse the art work with reality by means of suggested continuity. One example is John Dos Passos' introduction of a new character, Vag, in the very last pages of *U.S.A.* André Gide does something similar when, at the close of *The Counterfeiters*, he reveals Edouard's interest in Caloub Profitendieu, thus instigating an entire new sequence of events magnetized by a new relationship. Gertrude Stein has given her own demonstration of how the novel's frame may be dispensed with; she simply ended *The Making of Americans* when she had proved to herself that it was possible to do what she had set out to do. Besides Unamuno's *Amor y pedagogía* and *Niebla,* the most celebrated attack on the literary "frame" is embodied in Luigi Pirandello's *Six Characters in Search of an Author* of 1920.

For the novel, the work of overwhelming significance in this respect is *The Counterfeiters,* published in 1925.[10] Rich as it is in suggestions for the literary spatialist, this novel contains two major innovations of crucial importance for later novelists. First is the great effect of naturalness, of reality, that can be achieved by destroying both the plot and the conventional mode of creating "believable" characters through constantly frustrating the expectations of the reader. This is the famous refusal to profit "de l'élan acquis," from the impetus that has been acquired. Second is the expanded grasp on reality that can be achieved by mixing elements and materials from all sorts of "unnovelistic" sources in a manner that resembles what Apollinaire in *Les Peintres cubistes,* called the "énumération des éléments." Since *The Counterfeiters* contains, concealed beneath its bewildering and brilliant surface, a conventional novel with a conventional protagonist, the book might be said to be more conventional than it *appears.* This novel is a masterpiece of misplaced emphases, which is just what Gide, judging from his *Journal of "The Counterfeiters,"* intended that it should be.

The treatment of the narration was Gide's first problem in planning *The Counterfeiters.* His original intention to use a first-person narrator was fortunately abandoned in favor of a more complex method that (by employing various instruments such as letters, notebooks, and facsimiles of outmoded literary conventions) enables the subject to be explored from a variety of points of view. Next, continuity of any sort was deliberately done away with, as Gide made clear in his famous statement: "The difficulty comes from this, that with each chapter, I must begin anew. Never take advantage of the impetus that has been acquired. This is the rule of my game." [11]

In the most obvious way, discontinuity is achieved by the distribution of interest among the many characters, by the fragmenting of narrative focus, and by the breaking up of the events relevant to each character into bits and pieces that are presented in an apparently random and chaotic manner. But more revolutionary still than these procedures is Gide's departure from any standard of consistency in creating his characters. Not only is each one unpredictable, his actions incomprehensible in terms of traditional "motivation," each comes from a different substratum of reality. First, there are the more or less traditionally treated characters, such as Bernard and Olivier, whose initiation into life and personal development are being traced. Second, there are the deliberately "stagy" or "literary" characters: Rachael, Sarah, Madame Sophroniska, Strouvilhou, and Lady Griffith, of whom Gide wrote, "The character of Lady Griffith is and ought to remain as if outside of the book." [12] Two of these figures, Madame Sophroniska and Strouvilhou, are employed as mouthpieces for intellectual positions that are the opposites of those maintained by Edouard; they are blatant intellectual foils and have no importance in the book except as antagonists. A third source of characters is life itself. La Pérouse, the pitiful old professor, was closely modeled upon someone whom Gide knew (a fact that troubled the author because it embodied the conventional manner of creating characters in fiction). Fourth—and most surprising—is the undisguised presence in *The Counterfeiters* of an actual person, Alfred Jarry. He appears in the description of the banquet, depicted as a madman brandishing a pistol with which he shoots another poet. The incident is said to have actually occurred.[13] Gide perceived that Jarry had willed himself to become his own creation, Père Ubu—hero of *Ubu roi* and inventor of "Pataphysics"—and that he was, therefore, as truly "fictional" a character as any Gide himself might invent. However, the presence of Jarry requires no such specific justification as this. It is but one aspect of Gide's over-all attempt to fuse levels or modes of reality by bringing together their representatives in a single action. The final complication is the insertion of the author's own voice, making comments in the last chapter of Part II in a droll manner that parodies the intimate style of Anthony Trollope or any other typical nineteenth-century novelist who takes his readers into his confidence.

This blending of the creatures of imagination, of intellect, and of reality is repeated in the choice of materials used by Gide to support his invention—an unframed and endless novel. In the *Journal* he admits that the extremely detailed scene in which Edouard observes Georges Molinier's attempt to steal a book has been transcribed directly from Gide's own experience. What is surprising is not that the author should make use of this incident, but that he should do so without disguising its origin:

that he should deliberately expose his method of working so cold-
bloodedly as to strip away any traces of romanticism from the
creative process. In the time-honored manner, Gide makes use
of letters as narrative devices, and he does so in order to achieve
oblique angles on the situations he is describing. Bernard is
introduced to Laura by way of a letter she has written to
Edouard, and which Edouard has left lying between the pages
of his journal. Olivier, who is less perceptive than Bernard and
more easily manipulated by others, reads a letter relating his
brother's comitragic insanity, but he does not realize that it is
Vincent whom he is reading about. But the most ingenious use
of a document is, without doubt, the counterpoint achieved by
the double notebook: Edouard's and Gide's own. It is Bernard's
illegal possession of Edouard's notebook that opens up his experiences of life, friends, and lovers, for in the notebook he finds
the people he knows (especially Olivier) depicted from a new
and revealing perspective, Edouard's. The notebook serves a
narrative function, for many of the novel's events are portrayed
in its pages. It possesses a pragmatic use as well, for it is subtly
used by Edouard to convey to Georges a warning that he must
alert Strouvilhou to the fact that the counterfeiting activity has
been discovered and that he himself must withdraw from the
circle of small thieves. Edouard's notebook is, thus, at once the
means and the end of Gide's novel; although it is one of the
major narrative devices, a major means of attaining changing
perspectives on the material, it is at the same time a crucial part
of the novel's materials: Gide's views about the artist and the
way the work of art is conceived and brought into existence.

A third important aspect of *The Counterfeiters* is the matter
of misplaced emphases. Viewed from the vantage point of the
traditional novel, Gide's work might at first seem the product
of an amateur. His choices as to what he will treat in detail and
what he will hurry over seem "all wrong." Again and again,
potentially exciting material is thrown away: Vincent's bizarre
relationship with Lady Griffith; Sarah's seduction; and, above
all, Boris' suicide. On the other hand, hackneyed material is
often used: the quarrel and the projected duel; old Molinier's
relations with the chorus girl; Bernard's conversion from the

doctrine of total personal freedom to one of personal responsibility by means of a conversation with (of all things) an angel. Of the several love affairs that might have been described phase by phase with all the traditional suspense, the one that receives the nearest approximation to full treatment is Edouard's tenderness toward Olivier. Here is another unexpected emphasis. Even the literal counterfeiters receive but careless attention. Most puzzling of all is Edouard's avowed intention *not* to explore the suicide of pathetic little Boris, for this is one of the richest and most suggestive of the episodes gathered between the covers of *The Counterfeiters*. And what of the reconciliation between Bernard and his father? It is dryly reported in a few sentences.

Since Gide was writing a novel which was an attack on the novel, he deliberately rejected all easy opportunities for sentiment and all predictable patterns of development and resolution of actions: "Life presents us on all sides with the beginnings of dramas, but it is rare that these beginnings follow their course or take shape in the same way that a novelist usually spins them out into a story. And it is precisely this idea that I should like to give in the book, and which I shall make Edouard express." [14]

The reader of *The Counterfeiters* must wonder, what *is* the subject of this bewildering book, in which everything interesting is dropped as soon as it has been introduced? Perhaps there is no true subject, for did not Edouard write in his notebook: "My novel has no subject"? Yes, but later this statement was amended to read: "My novelist will wish to stray away from reality, but I, I will lead him back to it without ceasing. To tell the truth, this will be the subject: the conflict between the facts proposed by reality and the ideal reality." [15]

The means to the achievement of a record of the struggle between the facts as they are proposed by reality and the ideal reality are instability, discontinuity, perversity, surprise, and the exploitation of every means by which to project the substance of the novel beyond its own boundaries. "Not to establish the progression of my novel in the prolonging of the lines already traced out: that is the difficulty. A perpetual surging forward; each new chapter ought to pose a new problem, to be an overture, a direction, an impetus, a flowing forward against the mind of the reader." [16]

By its very nature, such a book can never end; it will begin over and over again. In addition to the mixing of the sources of characters and materials, there are three ways in which Gide effectively destroys the "frame" of his novel. The first is relatively superficial: the cultivation of instability. At the novel's ostensible close, Gide abruptly raises doubts about the one relationship the reader might have assumed would stabilize itself, that between Edouard and Olivier. This ending suggests that a new cycle will begin: a new set of half-developed, half-aborted relationships. Unanswered questions will remain well after the reader has finished the book. Gide has prevented him from leaving *The Counterfeiters* with the sensation of fulfillment common to readers of traditional fiction, the serenity of knowing just how everything was disposed of once and for all.

The remaining two factors of importance in Gide's leap outside the novel's frame are very closely related. One is the way in which he has forced the reader to take account of the processes of art and their shifting relationships to reality by making Edouard's notebooks treatises on the novel. To return for a moment to the matter of emphases, *The Counterfeiters* emphasizes itself as art. Neither its plot nor its characters but the mechanics of the novel itself constitute its major emphasis, an emphasis that is initiated by the presence of Edouard's notebook and completed by the extension of the novel *outside itself* by the publication in 1927 of Gide's own *Journal of "The Counterfeiters."* This appendage to the novel is a continuation *outside* the novel of Edouard's notebooks. It lays bare the sources of parts of the work in Gide's private experience and in the two newspaper clippings from which he derived the ideas for the boys' counterfeiting and Boris' suicide. Gide's insistence on revealing at every step the processes of the novelist produces the "lutte entre les faits proposés par la réalité, et la réalité idéale" which he so heartily desired to evoke.

A very different sort of open-structured work is Carlos Fuentes' novel, *Change of Skin*. It fulfills the promise, made in the prologue to the first part, of being "an impossible feast." There is the slight suggestion of a plot, or more accurately, a structural model in the form of the familiar journey or quest. Four persons are driving through Mexico on an Easter weekend to visit the Great Pyramid at Cholula, which was sacred to the Aztecs. This simple situation supports a number of procedures that are typical of the open-structured novel: a disjunct time scheme which endows the past with the same credence and vitality as the present; heavy use of the cubist "énumération des éléments" that in this case is designed to fuse past and present, fantasy and reality, the sacred and the absurd; fluid characters whose identities change as they pass through various metamorphoses (thus, the title, *Change of Skin*), the intermixing of "real" characters, like Adolph Eichmann, with imaginary ones; several essays; and, finally, the absence of an unequivocal ending for the novel. Fuentes deliberately creates confusion when the four principals explore the Great Pyramid at midnight. Except for Franz, who dies —one is not certain how—the author declines to dispose definitively of his characters. But the most unusual feature of *Change of Skin,* the one that is of greatest significance in the maintenance of the open structure, is Fuentes' treatment of his narrator as one of the characters. While it is true that Maurice Fourré has done this in *Tête-de-Nègre,* the effect in *Change of Skin* is quite different. "Le Monsieur Anonyme," in spite of his fondness for traveling about France in a small truck accompanied by his girl-friend and in spite of his chumminess with the old Baron, always keeps his distance from the other characters. His role is similar to that played by Unamuno, whose characters must make an appointment and come to his office in order to discuss with him their right to go on living. Fourré plays the part of a more benign deity. Still, he is omnipotent. Fuentes' narrator, by contrast, is as chatty and aggressive as a New York City intellectual and as impudent as a television interviewer. He is himself questioning, vulnerable, involved with the enigmas of love, guilt, and creativity. He is truly one of the characters, and, like the others, he "changes his skin" as the work develops.

Although Spanish novelists have long presented, and sometimes probed, the relationship between the author and the characters he creates and have proposed the possible independence of these characters from their maker, until the twentieth century very few novelists have challenged the author's omniscience.[17] Alongside the philosophical ramifications of this deliberate exposure of the creative act, is a structural factor that is essential to architectonic fiction. Since the most nearly absolute vision of reality is the one that includes as many perspectives as possible, the novelist who aspires toward comprehensiveness and complexity must approximate in his work as many relevant perspectives as possible. Two of the most fascinating of conflicting perspectives are the attitudes of the author toward his characters and those which the characters may, in turn, adopt toward their creator. By abdicating his omniscient and omnipotent position, the author has acknowledged the inadequacy of one sole perspective to account for the totality of even his own personal view. The scope of reality has not so much been abandoned to chaos and irrationality as it has been expanded to include contradictory as well as complementary points of view.

Carlos Fuentes' narrator introduces himself immediately in the epigraph to the first of the novel's three parts. At once he addresses the four protagonists—Elizabeth and Javier, Isabel and Franz—in the second-person plural, as "you." This narrator devotes the overwhelming mass of his comments and short speeches to Elizabeth. One feels that he is perhaps in love with her. In any case, he is deeply involved, indeed. As the four protagonists bump along unpaved roads in Franz's Volkswagen, the narrator rides comfortably in a *turismo* limousine, leafing through travel brochures. When an unidentified person (the narrator?) jams the gearbox of the Volkswagen, the travelers are forced to stop for the night in Cholula. This gives the narrator an opportunity to mingle with them in several curious scenes. Beginning as harsh interviews in which the narrator interrogates sometimes Isabel and sometimes Elizabeth, these scenes end with the narrator's making love to the one or the other. During the action, he has gradually taken on the identity of one of the two men. At this point, it is not clear whether the narrator is being used by the characters for the same purpose the two couples exchange mates: to recapture a lost past, as are Franz and Elizabeth, or to seize a fresh future, as are Javier and Isabel. Certainly, however, the narrator is using the characters as puppets through which he can fulfill unexpressed aspects of himself. At midnight there occurs what seems to be a genuine crisis in the action. Isabel insists that the four protagonists go out to explore the interior caverns of the Great Pyramid.

With the arrival of the "pilgrims" in the bowels of the pyramid, *Change of Skin* begins to become the narrator's book. A mysterious voice (the narrator's?) lures Franz into a dangerous position. There is a rock slide. Elizabeth rushes to his aid, and both are imprisoned in a chamber behind a wall of fallen rocks. Javier and Isabel escape, but his initial joy at the prospect of a new life with her quickly turns into hatred when he realizes that she is simply an incarnation of his wife. In a scene whose "reality" is never established, he strangles Isabel with Elizabeth's black shawl. Not only is this episode imbued with an aura of fantasy, it is immediately superseded by an alternative conclusion to the exploration of the pyramid. In this version, a group of hippies called "Los Monjes" ("the Monks") enter the caves, singing and dancing to the music of the Beatles. They clasp hands, form a circle around Franz, and begin leaping about, shouting and singing. Fuentes makes no attempt to dispose authoritatively of Javier, Elizabeth, and Isabel, though numerous hints and one overt prophecy indicate that Franz has somehow been killed.

The concluding portion of *Change of Skin* is an extended fantastic scene in which the Monks assume the identities of the four protagonists and proceed to hold the trial of Franz. A part of the trial takes place at a house of prostitution amidst a sexual orgy. The book is now entirely the narrator's. He freely admits that he is a writer, apparently verifying the reader's suspicion that he is Fuentes himself. The narrator-author now admits that he does not understand the meaning of what is going on among his characters. Nonetheless, he feels that whatever it is, he should write it down: "I want to write what they have told me, that they have told me enough and more than enough, and to put it down on paper well, cleanly, truly, will be to face all the sand of an endless desert. I will betray them. . . . Every novel is a betrayal, an act of bad faith, an abuse of confidence." [18]

At the close of *Change of Skin,* as in the concluding portions of *Mist* and *Tête-de-Nègre,* there is a struggle between the author and characters. Who shall survive? Or, if all are to survive, who shall be dominant? Fuentes' narrator becomes exhausted by the frenzy, the power, the vehemence of the Monks, for he, after all, is around forty. He begins to savor that calm peaceful moment in the future when he can get rid of them simply by ceasing to envision them. But almost at once he realizes that his characters have begun to seize control of him and that the entire effort of envisioning them and animating them has been designed to achieve his own rebirth. This rebirth necessitates the "betrayal" he has earlier spoken of, a betrayal which consists simply of his setting alongside the Monks' eager condemnation of Franz his own grudging forgiveness. The narrator can complement, and even countermand, the Monks' judgment with his own. But once he has brought his characters into being, he cannot get rid of them. They are there still at the end of the book. Franz, though dead, has received forgiveness. Elizabeth and Javier are given back their past by the author, who leaves them at a tender and hope-filled moment shortly after their marriage, thus allowing them another chance at their own future. Isabel is left sitting at an outdoor café in Cholula with the Monks and the narrator. Elizabeth has rescued a crying baby that was discarded by the Monks in the trunk of their car. She leaves it outside the door of a mental asylum that is situated not far from the pyramid, hoping that the doctors and nurses will find it a home, for Javier will not accept it. Finally, the narrator takes leave of Elizabeth: "So long, Dragoness. Take it easy. Stay loose. And don't forget your ever lovin' Freddy Lambert." [19]

This conclusion is Fuentes' demonstration of "el consejo gidiano" ("the Gidean advice"). Just when the source of reality seems to have been firmly established in the mind of the author-narrator—in that of Fuentes himself—the novelist throws everything into doubt by revealing that the narrator is really someone altogether different, a new character, one Freddy Lambert. The book is a sort of extended love letter to Elizabeth, the "dragona." What this ending does is to explode the illusion of finality and to hurl everything into confusion by posing these questions:

Who is Freddy Lambert? Does he know the truth? If so, can he be trusted to tell it? Finally, to make everything worse, Freddy Lambert is evidently insane. At the same time, since one knows that Freddy Lambert, however mad, represents an aspect of the author who has possessed the imagination to create him, one can settle back again to contemplate the variety of visions of "truth" and life, love, creative work, and of guilt and redemption, which the jaunty, chatty narrator has been capable of projecting onto his fictional puppets.

A brief consideration of Fuentes' use of multiple perspectives reveals how, ultimately, novels with open and closed structures are but variant approaches to a single concept of the novel. Fuentes has arranged a vast spectrum of points of view in *Change of Skin*. First, there are the perspectives provided by the four protagonists, varied in nationality, age, sex, education, ambition, and intellectual and spiritual capacity. There are the perspectives that are provided by the constant interplay among the four dominant *lieux* of the work: Mexico, Prague, New York, and Greece. Additional perspectives are embodied in the historical passages, in the numerous short essays, in the song lyrics, in advertising slogans, and in many references to films, books, and newspaper stories. Still another perspective is that of the artist-narrator, or madman, who is fully aware that he is enjoying changing skins with Javier (and indulging his own negative impulses in artistic failure) as well as with Franz (in whose person he can experience the more keenly his own historical guilt). Finally, the link between the madman and the artist that is implied by the ending suggests two contradictory conclusions: either that everything in the book is but an hallucination (the world as seen from a *very* special perspective) or that the mad are merely the only ones who *do* see reality in all of its complexity and contradiction. The narrator, addressing Elizabeth as "Dragona," has asserted: "And this is the point, Dragoness: the illusion of rationality must be preserved in order to preserve the illusion of life." [20] If a total view of life admits contradictions as part of the truth, then the man who sees completely must necessarily suffer confusion to the point of madness. Freddy Lambert is but another perspective adopted by Carlos Fuentes from which to view the reality of his novel.

The opening out of the fictional structure that is illustrated by *The Counterfeiters* and *Change of Skin* represents an approximation of total, absolute perception, the comprehensive approach to the complete truth about the object of perception: the subject of the novel in question. The open structure makes possible a considerable expansion of the theoretical and technical powers of the novel. It is achieved by a twofold process that involves, first, the destruction of the "frame" of the novel so that its contents are free to spill outside; and, second, the intermingling of the elements of the art work with elements drawn from outside. This second step completes the fusion and makes of the novel a fact, a thing, a mode of experience, an indisputable part of reality. Whereas the traditional ideal of a structure that is definitively and unarguably finished draws its own limits by its very nature, the projection into life itself that is attained by the open-structured novel offers the possibility of unlimited combinations and syntheses of individual perspectives, any one of which is more accurate within the terms of the "new" scientific concept of reality than is the traditionally observed separation between art—a perspective—and reality—its ostensible object. If one means by reality the strictly verifiable, then it, too, is but a mode of seeing.

Jorge Luis Borges has written two *ficciones* that embody speculations upon the nature of the book as a statement of perspective. "Pierre Menard, Author of Don Quixote" is a sly pseudo-defense of a twentieth-century French critic's ambition to reproduce exactly—but not to copy—several pages of Cervantes' seventeenth-century masterpiece. The narrator of the tale is a nameless friend of Menard, perhaps a literary critic himself. He both explains and justifies his fellow critic's ambition: "To be, in some way, Cervantes and to arrive at *Don Quixote* seemed to him less arduous—and consequently less interesting—than to continue being Pierre Menard and to arrive at *Don Quixote* through the experiences of Pierre Menard. (This conviction, let it be said in passing, forced him to exclude the autobiographical prologue of the second part of *Don Quixote.*)" [21] After conducting the reader through two hilarious explications of two absolutely identical passages—the one by Menard, the other by Cervantes—the considerable differences in interpretation resulting solely from the critic's knowledge that each was written by a different man, the critic-narrator comes to the conclusion that Pierre Menard has discovered a new technique of reading. If existing books are imagined to have been written by persons other than their authors, particularly if these persons lived in different cultures and different centuries, then any one book embodies the potential power to represent a vast number of perspectives:

> Menard (perhaps without wishing to) has enriched, by means of a new technique, the hesitant and rudimentary art of reading: the technique is one of deliberate anachronism and erroneous attributions. This technique, with its infinite applications, urges us to run through the *Odyssey* as if it were written after the *Aeneid,* and to read *Le jardin du Centaure* by Madame Henri Bachelier as if it were by Madame Henri Bachelier. This technique would fill the dullest books with adventure. Would not the attributing of *The Imitation of Christ* to Louis Ferdinand Céline or James Joyce be a sufficient renovation of its tenuous spiritual counsels? [22]

One of the most interesting implications of "Pierre Menard, Author of Don Quixote" is the suggestion that a book is never meaningful apart from a consideration of who wrote it, when, and under what circumstances. Thus is revealed the considerable profundity of juxtaposition as a structural principle in modernist works; the book, an apparently self-enclosed entity, is, in fact, dependent for its existence upon a consideration of the identity and life circumstances of its author. A book, then, is not a fixed, but a potentially movable, point of view on reality. The idea complements a related proposition that is examined, along with others equally penetrating and comical, in "The Library of Babel." This tale may be interpreted as a demonstration of José Ortega y Gasset's ideas in "The Doctrine of the Point of View."

In Borges' story, the proposition is advanced that the universe is in actuality a library consisting of an indefinite, perhaps infinite, number of volumes. Each volume contains someone's point of view. Therefore, if all the books ever written were to be collected in one place, this place would become total, complete, and definitive. It would be an Idealist universe. Nevertheless, the narrator of "The Library of Babel" cannot help longing for *the one* perfect book, the "total book" which shall contain the "total truth." He believes it likely that such a book is there in the library, though he himself has never seen it. Another way to achieve the "total book" is suggested, however, by a lady named Letizia Álvarez de Toledo. More practical and less optimistic than the narrator, she lights upon the idea of the encyclopedia as an alternative to the digest sought by the narrator:

> * Letizia Álvarez de Toledo has observed that the vast Library is useless. Strictly speaking, *one single volume* should suffice: a single volume of ordinary format, printed in nine or ten type body, and consisting of an infinite number of infinitely thin pages. (At the beginning of the seventeenth century, Cavalieri said that any solid body is the superposition of an infinite number of planes.) This silky vade mecum would scarcely be handy: each apparent leaf of the book would divide into other analogous leaves. The inconceivable central leaf would have no reverse.[23]

Here we have in the idea of the library a metaphor for the "truth" as it was formulated by José Ortega y Gasset within the terms of the theory of relativity: no longer a vast library, the world, containing an infinite number of volumes, or points of view, but conveniently condensed into a single book whose infinite number of pages contain all possible perspectives upon the nature of being. From the point of view of the architectonic novel, the closed structure corresponds to the digest, whose finality and authority are sought by the narrator of "The Library of Babel," while the comprehensiveness of the open structure is echoed in that of the encyclopedia, the suggestion of a mysterious lady named Letizia Álvarez de Toledo.

Notes

1. Julio Cortázar, *Hopscotch*, translated by Gregory Rabassa (New York, 1966), p. 328. *Rayuela* (Buenos Aires, 1963), p. 452: "Provocar, asumir un texto desaliñado, desanudado, incongruente, minuciosamente anti-novelístico (aunque no antinovelesco). Sin vedarse los grandes efectos del género cuando la situación lo requiera, pero recordando el consejo gidiano, *ne jamais profiter de l'élan acquis.* Como todas las criaturas de elección del Occidente, la novela se contenta con un orden cerrado. Resueltamente en contra, buscar también aquí la apertura y para eso cortar de raíz toda construcción sistemática de caracteres y situaciones."

2. Wylie Sypher, *Rococo to Cubism in Art and Literature* (New York, 1960), p. 270. See Michel Butor's essay, "Le roman comme recherche," *Répertoire,* II (Paris, 1963).

3. One may, indeed, wonder whether the novel with an open structure is not the same thing as an antinovel. If one accepts the definition of Julio Cortázar's novelist, Morelli, which provides the epigraph of this chapter, then he will conclude that the antinovel and the open-structured novel *are,* often at least, identical.

4. With regard to the maintenance of a clear boundary between the work of art and life, the Spanish novel from *Don Quixote* onward is a notable exception.

5. Michel Leiris, "De la Littérature considérée comme une tauromachie," *Les Temps Modernes* (May, 1946), p. 1461: "Du point de vue stricte-ment esthétique, il s'agissait pour moi de condenser, á l'état presque brut, un ensemble de faits et d'images que je me refusais à exploiter en laissant travailler dessus mon imagination; en somme: la négation d'un roman. Rejeter toute affabulation et n'admettre pour matériaux que des faits véridiques (et non pas seulement des faits vraisemblables, comme dans le roman classique), rien que ces faits et tous ces faits, était la règle que je m'étais choisie."

6. These two pieces are printed in *Under a Glass Bell and Other Stories* (Denver, 1948).

7. *Amor y pedagogía* has not been translated into English. *Niebla* has been translated by Warren Fite as *Mist. A Tragi-Comic Novel* (New York, 1928).

8. Gertrude Stein, *Picasso* (London, 1939), p. 12.

9. Donald Sutherland, *Getrude Stein: A Biography of Her Work* (New Haven, 1951), p. 22.

10. Wylie Sypher in his book *Rococo to Cubism in Art and Literature* ana-lyzes *The Counterfeiters* in terms of the aesthetics of cubism.

11. André Gide, *Journal des "Faux-Monnayeurs"* (Paris, 1927), p. 89: "La difficulté vient de ceci que, pour chaque chapitre, je dois repartir à neuf. *Ne jamais profiter de l'élan acquis*—telle est la règle de mon jeu."

12. Gide, *Journal,* p. 94: "Le caractère de Lady Griffith est et doit rester comme hors du livre."

13. See Roger Shattuck, *The Banquet Years* (New York, 1961), p. 224.
14. Gide, *Journal*, p. 104: "La vie nous présente de toutes parts quantité d'amorces de drames, mais il est rare que ceux-ci se poursuivrent et ses dessinent comme a coutume de les filer un romancier. Et c'est là précisément l'impression que je voudrais donner dans ce livre, et ce que je ferai dire à Edouard."
15. Gide, *Les Faux-Monnayeurs* (Paris, 1925), p. 238: "Mon roman n'a pas de sujet." P. 240: "Mon romancier voudra s'en écarter [de la realité]; mais moi je l'y ramènerai sans cesse. A vrai dire, ce sera là le sujet: la lutte entre les faits proposés par la réalité, et la réalité idéale."
16. Gide, *Journal*, p. 95: "Ne pas établir la suite de mon roman dans le prolongement des lignes déjà tracées; voilà la difficulté. Un surgissement perpétuel; chaque nouveau chapitre doit poser un nouveau problème, être une ouverture, une direction, une impulsion, une jetée en avant— de l'esprit du lecteur."
17. See Joseph E. Gillet, "The Autonomous Character in Spanish and European Literature," *Hispanic Review*, XXIV (July, 1956), pp. 179–90.
18. Carlos Fuentes, *Change of Skin*, translated by Sam Hileman (New York, 1967), p. 421. *Cambio de piel* (Guaymas, Mexico, 1967), p. 407: " 'Y yo sólo quiero escribir, un día, lo que me han contado. Bastante es lo que me dicen y escribirlo significa atravesar todos los obstáculos del desierto. Toda novela es un traición. . . . Es un acto de mala fe, un abuso de confianza.' "
19. *Change of Skin*, p. 462. *Cambio de piel*, p. 422: "Adiós, dragona. Y no olvides a tu cuate

(Fdo.) Freddy Lambert."
20. *Change of Skin*, p. 310. *Cambio de piel*, p. 309: "todo es el problema de mantener la ilusión racional para mantener la ilusión de la vida."
21. Jorge Luis Borges, "Pierre Menard, Autor del Quijote," translated by Anthony Bonner, *Ficciones* (New York, 1962), p. 49. *Ficciones* (Buenos Aires, 1956), p. 50: "Ser, de alguna manera, Cervantes y llegar al Quijote le pareció menos arduo—por consiguiente, menos interesante— que seguir siendo Pierre Menard y llegar al Quijote, a través de las experiencias de Pierre Menard. (Esa convicción, dicho sea de paso, le hizo excluir el prólogo autobiográfico de la segunda parte del don Quijote.)"
22. Borges, pp. 54–55. Spanish version, pp. 56–57: "Menard (acaso sin quererlo) ha enriquecido mediante una técnica nueva el arte detenido y rudimentario de la lectura: la técnica del anacronismo deliberado y de las atribuciones erróneas. Esa técnica de aplicación infinita nos insta a recorrer la Odisea como si fuera posterior a la Eneida y el libro *Le jardin du Centaure* de Madame Henri Bachelier como si fuera de Madame Henri Bachelier. Esa técnica puebla de aventura los libros más calmosos. Atribuir a Louis Ferdinand Céline o a James Joyce la *Imitación de Cristo* no es una suficiente renovación de esos tenues avisos espirituales?"
23. Jorge Luis Borges, "The Library of Babel," translated by Anthony Kerrigan, *Ficciones*, p. 88. "La Biblioteca de Babel," *Ficciones*, p. 95: "1 Letizia Alvarez de Toledo ha observado que la vasta Biblioteca es

inútil; en rigor, bastaría *un solo volumen,* de formato común, impreso en cuerpo nueve o en cuerpo diez, que constara de un número infinito de hojas infinitamente delgadas. (Cavalieri a principios del siglo XVII, dijo que todo cuerpo sólido es la superposición de un número infinito de planos.) El manejo de ese *vademecum* sedoso no sería cómodo: cada hoja aparente se desdoblaría en otras análogas; la inconcebible hoja central no tendría revés."

Perspective has thus far been defined in the most simple sense as "the aspect of an object of thought from a particular standpoint." As an example, *Webster's New Collegiate Dictionary* cites "historical perspective" as a particular way of seeing something. A simplistic, but perhaps clarifying, picture of the way in which the term "perspective" is being used in this study is embodied by a circle or by a set of concentric circles. In the center is the subject of the novel, the thing that is being observed. Each circumference about this center point may be said to represent a type of perspective, and each individual point upon that circumference designates a specific standpoint in time and space from which the center is regarded. The number of circles that may be imagined to surround the subject of any novel depends upon how many perspectives are included in the work. The perspective of each character who is given a "point of view" constitutes a separate circle. Still other nonhuman perspectives may be symbolized by other circles having the same center. While the structure of novels like *Nightwood* and *La Liberté ou l'amour!* may be visualized by but a single circumference, along which numerous points of vision may be marked, the structure of a novel like *Change of Skin (Cambio de piel)* may be envisioned by perhaps a dozen or more concentric circles.

The question arises whether the author possesses a perspective of his own, from which he can view simultaneously not only the subject but all of the perspectives he himself has focused upon it. The answer that was given most definitively by José Ortega y Gasset in "The Doctrine of the Point of View" and by Jean-Paul Sartre in a well-known essay on François Mauriac's *La Fin de la Nuit* is a clear "no." The Spanish philosopher asserts that the only false perspective is the one that pretends to be the unique one. Sartre, in a general denunciation of François Mauriac as a novelist, makes it particularly clear that a novelist may not avail himself *at the same time* of the old freedom to imagine himself "inside" his character (and, therefore, privy to his every thought) and of the new freedom to create a seemingly autonomous character whose thoughts and feelings can be known only as they are revealed by his actions and words. Sartre explains why this new freedom is of the twentieth century, while the privilege of the omniscient author belongs to the nineteenth: "He [Mauriac] has tried to ignore, as have most of our authors, the fact that the theory of relativity applies to the world of the novel, and that, in a true novel, there is no more place than in the world of Einstein for the privileged observer." [1]

If the author wishes to include his own perspective, then it must take its place alongside those of his characters to be evaluated, with them, by the reader; it is this new aspect of democracy that renders comic the dialogues of Unamuno and Augusto Pérez and gives light irony to Maurice Fourré's appearance in *Tête-de-Nègre* as a mysterious and perhaps sinister stranger. In the final analysis, however, the author's overt presence or absence is but a convention, as Wayne C. Booth has pointed out in *The Rhetoric of Fiction:* "We must never forget that though the author can to some extent choose his disguises, he can never choose to disappear." [2]

Among the various perspectives that are available to the novelist are three general types: the human, the photographic, and the typographic. The first and most common type includes the representation of the subject as it is perceived, experienced, and evaluated by one or more characters, one of whom may be the author himself, disguised or not. The second type of perspective, the photographic, can be simulated by the novelist; the advantage of the still or of the motion-picture camera is its ostensible objectivity. The author who uses it is provided with a ready convention for the elimination of affective and qualitative elements from his descriptions, whether of objects or of people. The third type of perspective is, in fact, a variety of perspectives arising from the nature of the book itself. Illustrations, variations in typography, the use of colored or textured paper, the organization of words according to the spatial properties of the page, and the practice of reprinting passages from other printed sources all constitute modes of "seeing" the subject. Some, the use of textured paper, for example, can have but a simple relationship to the subject because of their nonverbal nature. But the reprinting of passages from books or newspapers constitutes a perspective that is rich with associations and feelings; this is so because of the great variety of relationships that may exist between the verbal nature of the two texts: that of the novel's subject and that of the quotation that is placed in a particular relationship to it.

As the preceding chapters have indicated, a discussion of perspective without some implicit awareness of its relation to structure is virtually impossible. The closed structure is, in fact, closed because of the limitation of the perspective; the open structure derives its capacity for multiple relationships and its impression of nervous thrust in various directions in space from the great variety of perspectives around and upon which it is constructed. In a more specific manner, perspective sometimes actually determines structure. For example, if the contrast between two perspectives on the same subject seems desirable to the author, then the result may well be a dual structure, such as those of *Pale Fire, The Lime Twig,* or *Molloy.* A first-person narrative seems to lend itself naturally to a loose, episodic struc-

The only thing that can possibly match the enormous volume of our time is the volume of the I or the Self. . . .

—Hermann Broch [1]

4.

*Perspective and
Narrative Point
of View*

For some years, the treatment of narrative point of view has been the focal point of discussions of the evolution of the modern novel. It has been considered the essential feature whose technical refinement distinguishes the serialized and often carelessly written nineteenth-century novel from its more fastidious twentieth-century offspring. The ways in which the illusions of reality that are perpetuated by the novel can be heightened by various narrative approaches were first explored in Henry James's famous Prefaces to the New York edition of his more famous works. Later, in 1921, James's ideas were systematized and further analyzed with reference to their technical possibilities by Percy Lubbock in *The Craft of Fiction*. And since 1921 the many and varied aspects of narrative point of view have been thoroughly explored in such books as *The House of Fiction* by Carolyn Gordon and Allen Tate, *The Modern Psychological Novel* by Leon Edel, and *The Rhetoric of Fiction* by Wayne C. Booth. The discovery of the effects to be achieved by manipulating modes of narrative point of view is closely related to the efforts of Flaubert, James, and Conrad to elevate and dignify the novel as a work of art by endowing it with complexity and subtlety and by enlivening it with the vividness of the drama. The early step that most served to establish the novel's independence from reportage as well as its artistic autonomy was the removal of the author from the narrative flow and the attendant transformation of overt narration into scenic representation of actions, as is done in the theater.

Subsequent refinements in techniques of changing the perspective on the subject by limiting, expanding, or contrasting narrative points of view have been made by Dorothy Richardson, James Joyce, Virginia Woolf, and William Faulkner, to name only the most inventive authors who have experimented with it. In Faulkner's novels, for example, the density that is created by the use of several narrators is further deepened by deliberate mystification regarding the identities of these narrators and their relationships in time, space, and feeling to the events and persons they are describing. This use of mystification that is associated with the novels of Faulkner, as well as his special rhetoric, is found in the works of the French lyric novelist, Claude Simon, and of the German writer, Uwe Johnson. It occurs as well, though with a very different effect, in the novels of Alain Robbe-Grillet and Nathalie Sarraute, where the very mystery as to who is speaking seems to press the reader into a more than usually intense identification with the narrator and, consequently, with the substance of the book.

Research into the uses of narrative point of view is being carried forward by the French novelist and critic, Nathalie Sarraute.[2] She has developed a technique called *sous-conversation* as a tool for expressing a previously unexplored area of the mind: the region of awareness that is conscious, but consists of thoughts that have not yet been censored, edited, trimmed, or made "respectable" enough for use in actual speech. Arguing that dialogue is not an accurate record of thoughts and feelings, Madame Sarraute rejects it; at the same time, she believes that dialogue, or something like it, is the last viable resource of the serious novelist. More abrupt and more brutal than dialogue, on the one hand, and, on the other, more highly organized and clearly focused than the stream-of-consciousness flow as one finds it in the works of Dorothy Richardson or of Proust, *sous-conversation* can, indeed, project areas of personality that were previously untouched by the novel. Madame Sarraute's works—*Tropismes, Portrait d'un inconnu, Martereau, Le Planétarium,* and *Les Fruits d'or*— are fluid structures that are composed from long passages of *sous-conversation* that have been distributed among the characters without clear identifications of "speakers" with their subterranean words. The influence of this particular type of perspective on structure is evident, for each of these novels seems to move in present time, without beginning or ending and without clear lines of demarcation among the parts or movements of which it is composed.

The variety of structures that can be erected upon the basis of a carefully selected perspective or upon sets of perspectives is immense. But among this variety there emerge three predominant patterns. The first entails the exclusive use of a first-person narrator. The second consists of the planned and consistent contrast between two perspectives on the same subject. The third is characterized by the combination of three or more narrative points of view of the same characters and situations; this combination evokes a complex, multifaceted open structure that approximates the spatial and temporal dynamics of Einsteinian physics.

The use of "I" as a narrator is as old as fiction itself and certainly as old as the novel, reaching back to *Moll Flanders* and *Tristram Shandy* in English literature and providing the basic narrative procedure of the French *récit*. First-person narration is a natural, perhaps instinctive, manner of telling a story, for it automatically provides a rope or chain for the narrator's progress from one point to another in the relating of his tale. But a distinction must be drawn between the innocent, unselfconscious use of the first-person narrator and the deliberately ambiguous, complex, and tentative use of first-person narration as it is employed, for example, by Henry James in *The Turn of the Screw* and *The Sacred Fount*, by Ford Madox Ford in *The Good Soldier*, and by Joseph Conrad in nearly all of his works. Before Henry James wrote these masterpieces of calculated ambiguity, novelists rarely exploited the immense opportunity offered by first-person narration for dislocating reality so as to come upon it from an unexpected angle. The author of an "I" narration is perfectly free to evoke as extreme and as self-exclusive a vision of reality as he is capable of depicting. One has only to think of Michel Leiris' *Aurora* to become conscious of the extreme power of the deliberately solipsistic point of view when its obsessions are projected upon every phenomenon that is included within a work.

The three novels whose modes of first-person narration are to be examined here are John Hawkes's *Second Skin*, Edoardo Sanguineti's *Capriccio italiano,* and Marc Saporta's *Composition No. 1.* They have several factors in common. First, unlike many first-person-narrated novels, their narrators are ordinary men. Second, in all three books the particular use to which the first-person narration is put results in an extreme dislocation of reality. Except in the case of Skipper, the protagonist of Hawkes's book, the reader cannot tell in what order things happened to the narrator, nor can he distinguish the exact line between what actually took place and what the narrator imagines took place or desires to take place. In short, the plunge into the narrator's thoughts and feelings takes on the aspect of Bergsonian time: events are related by their content and by their significance to the narrator, unhampered by temporal or spatial orientations. In *Second Skin,* as in Hawkes's other books, the reader can never exactly determine the border between fantasy and reality, and the blending of events in time with memories and wishes in *Capriccio italiano* and *Composition No. 1* makes any precise understanding of what actually happened both impossible to ascertain and irrelevant to the author's intentions. Finally, the readers of all three novels must, by bringing their own perspectives into the book to balance those of the first-person narrators, bear the responsibility for "correcting" the deliberately distorted perspective that is embodied in the narrator's account of things. In the final analysis, there is no such thing as a novel based upon a single perspective; the reader's own perspective always plays its part in the complete apprehension of any novel. Furthermore, many authors actually *depend* upon the reader's perspective when they conceive of their scheme of narration.

Second Skin is a demonstration of an idea that is advanced in *Change of Skin (Cambio de piel)*; the two titles reveal a fascination with metamorphosis. The themes of both novels deal with the possibility that sanity depends upon an inability or a refusal to entertain an accurate vision of reality. For such a vision, even if one were sufficiently intelligent, sensitive, and intuitive to seize it, would drive one mad with its mass of contradictions and mutually negating forms of evidence. Skipper alone, among a cast of characters who are woefully mistreated by fate, maintains a stubbornly sanguine and hopeful attitude toward life. He is a fifty-nine-year-old former naval officer of average intellectual powers, from the middle class, with no particular talents and no astonishing obsessions to set him apart from other men. He is fat, but this does not prevent his thinking himself handsome. The events of his life are tragic: his mortician-father's suicide; secret dishonor due to his failure to oppose a mutiny on his ship during World War II; his daughter's doomed marriage to a homosexual; his wife Gertrude's suicide in a tawdry motel; Fernandez' predictable desertion of Cassandra and her baby, Pixie; Skipper's own gruesome flirtation with an androgynous creature named Miranda; the presumed rape of Cassandra by a middle-aged New England fishing captain and his two sons; the brutal murder and mutilation of Fernandez in a Second Avenue whorehouse; Cassandra's suicide; and Skipper's final attainment of love with a native girl named Catalina Kate on a "floating island." Here he lives with Sonny (his faithful sidekick, a Negro), a funny little nun named Sister Josie, and Big Bertha, a midwife. The final chapter of *Second Skin* celebrates simultaneously the birth of a baby to Catalina Kate and All Souls' Eve. The principals gather together for a feast in an enormous freshly dug grave lighted by candles stuck in skulls.

Skipper's "goodness" reeks with arrogance. He is not at all surprised to have survived all those who in life were cruel to him; the novel closes with this passage:

> And now? Now I sit at my long table in the middle of my loud wandering night and by the light of a candle one half-burned candle saved from last night's spectacle—I watch this final flourish of my own hand and muse and blow away the ashes and listen to the breathing among the rubbery leaves

and the insects sweating out the night. Because now I am fifty-nine years old and I knew I would be, and now there is the sun in the evening, the moon at dawn, the still voice. That's it. The sun in the evening. The moon at dawn. The still voice.[3]

Skipper's is the ambiguous triumph of mediocrity. He can be imperceptive and unfeeling when it is necessary to protect himself from the truth. His "wisdom" is based upon the ignorance of the provincial, and in his case, this ignorance is willfully maintained.

A different sort of average man is portrayed in Edoardo Sanguineti's dream novel, *Capriccio italiano*. This book consists of 111 numbered prose blocks of about two or three pages each, which present in fragments the dreams—or one long dream—of a college professor who is known as "Edoardo." He is the exclusive narrator, and he recounts bits and pieces of situations and events that are—the reader soon realizes—drawn largely, though perhaps not exclusively, from dreams. The fragments gradually fall into patterns that together form a caricature of the unconscious mind of an intellectual who is probably in his late thirties, a lapsed Roman Catholic, the somewhat comical victim of alternating sexual anxieties and compensating fantasies. Since everything in the book has been translated into a fear or a desire and Edoardo is never permitted to intervene as the conscious interpreter of his own dreams, the reader must put the elements of the dreams into a portrait of Edoardo. This task will present no difficulty to anyone who has ever seen films directed by Federico Fellini or Michelangelo Antonioni; Edoardo's conflicts are those of the male protagonists of *8-½* and *La Dolce Vita;* of *L'Avventura* and *Il Deserto Rosso.* Furthermore, these dreams are crammed with familiar Freudian symbols such as eggs, knives, blood, bottles, and experiences of biting, cutting, and drowning, all of which are quickly converted by the reader into proofs of Edoardo's sexual insecurity. In the final analysis, *Capriccio italiano* derives its meaning from the blending of the reader's perspective with Edoardo's. The reader might be said to furnish the conscious mind, Edoardo the unconscious. In this way, the total subjectivity of his point of view is balanced and objectified by the broader, more knowing, analytical, aware, and amused perspective of the reader.

Another unique use of the first-person narrator is found in Marc Saporta's novel, *Composition No. 1*. Although the most suggestive feature of this book, from the point of view of architectonic form, is its structure,[4] the narrative treatment is also original and accounts in large measure for the final ambiguity of the novel. It, too, is "about" a rather ordinary man. Marc Saporta's central figure is known only by an initial, X. He is probably in his late thirties or early forties, is from the upper-middle class, and is well educated. He is unhappy both in his position with a financial firm and in his marriage to a brilliant but extraordinarily neurotic woman. Because of Marianne's illness, X generously does not seek a divorce. To console himself, he has, or daydreams that he has, a lovely mistress named Dagmar. X has fought in the French resistance during World War II, but he has also perhaps raped a young girl, Helga, and he is tempted to steal money from his employer to cover gambling debts. Finally, X is the victim of an automobile accident.

One cannot say that any of these things definitely happened to X, or, if they did, in that sequence. *Composition No. 1* is composed of 150 loose and unnumbered pages, most of which are in the present tense. Furthermore, although it is clear that *someone* is describing the events, situations, and characters of the work as they might seem to X, this "someone" at first seems to be a conventionally concealed author who has simply decided to "see" things as X might see them. But gradually one realizes that the narrator *is* X. The reader must experience the book inside out, so to speak. The narrator is himself the main character, but he is hidden, masking himself behind an ostensibly objective style and refusing to evaluate himself in any way. He never uses the pronoun "I." He never gives himself a name or an age. He simply describes everything as it seems to him, as it seemed to him, or as he would *like* it to seem. The result of this odd technique is a first-person narration in which the narrator is writing about himself, while appearing to write about someone else.

On the one hand, the precision and neatness of the descriptions and the total absence of expressed feelings, moods, and overtly stated desires and fears give one the impression that he is reading a wholly objective narration. On the other hand, Marc Saporta has provided a suggestion for the reader that what he is reading is but a record of the most significant events of X's life as they appear to him in a state of delirium after an automobile accident. In one of the descriptions of a hospital room, this passage appears: "The hospital room is nothing but a mass of memories in disorder. On the white ceiling is inscribed the swarming of scenes in superimposition, as on a strip of film used for several re-takes by a careless photographer." [5] X's delirium, then, accounts for the fragmented and disorganized manner in which he perceives the crucial moments of his life as he lies on his back in a hospital bed, while his confused mind makes of the ceiling a private movie screen on which images come and go haphazardly. The explanation of delirium also provides a justification for the author's refusal to number and bind the pages of the book. Saporta's narrative procedure takes from the dream a rationale for dissolving the conventional distinctions between memory (the past), desire (implying the future), and fantasy (suggesting present being) and for substituting a timeless and preeminently visual mode of organization.

The result of the odd inside-out narrative procedure of *Composition No. 1* is an unusual perspective that is at once subjective and objective. It is as though X succeeds actually in seeing himself as others see him. But since in order to do this he must separate himself from his feelings about what he is observing, he becomes depersonalized in the process. The over-all impression that is left on thé reader of this novel is, in truth, quite "schizy." X seems normal enough. Yet there is something sinister, almost frightening, about him. Both of his "crimes" may be only imagined or planned crimes, and even if he did commit them, they are not, as crimes go, especially heinous. Still, X seems capable of doing something monstrous. This fusion of the banal and the terrifying is in part a success of the fragmented structure of *Composition No. 1,* which tends to make each trivial action assume a grotesque proportion and an irrational quality; and in part a success of the narrative technique, which makes

X simultaneously the examined and the examiner. In the process, X is totally separated from his emotions. Just as the reader must provide Edoardo's conscious mind and, therefore, the analysis of his dreams, the reader must supply for X his own emotions, and by reading with empathy bring to the book the passions that have been stripped from X in his illness.

These works make evident the incomplete nature of the idea that has been advanced in the early pages of this study: that the novel with a closed structure receives its definitive characteristic of enclosure from the restriction of the perspective to a single point of view. This is true if one is thinking only of the book qua book, without a reader. It is clearly untrue if one is thinking of the book as an element in the dynamic process of reading. Novels with closed structures *do,* it is true, incorporate within their pages but one unchallenged view of the subject, but this view always must exist alongside, or in contrast to, the perspective of the reader. Often the reader's perspective is absolutely vital to the novel's coherence.

The at once endearing and repulsive simplicity of Skipper's view of life would lose its double nature and its meaning as well were it not for the contrast provided by the reader's more complex view of things, and especially his view of Skipper himself. In the reader's perspective, Skipper and his attitudes appear as both courageous and contemptible. The reader cannot help but understand much that Skipper refuses to acknowledge: that he has deliberately encouraged his daughter to marry a homosexual in order to maintain her need for her father; that Cassandra herself is hardly the "proud and fastidious" girl whom he loves to distraction; and, finally, that he is partly to blame for his wife's as well as for Cassandra's suicide. Above all, the reader sees what Skipper cannot allow himself to see—his guilt. In just this way, the reader of *Capriccio italiano* brings his own perspective to bear on the obsessions of Edoardo. Unconfined to the dream, as is the narrator, the reader is at liberty to produce the explanations that dissolve the tyranny of those dreams and that reveal their essentially comic aspect.

The entire question of perspective can become incredibly involuted. This was surely part of the point of Jorge Luis Borges' story "Pierre Menard, Author of Don Quixote." Meaningful juxtapositions of all sorts occur without one's being aware of their existence. As Borges humorously shows, not only does the combination provided by the pairing of the author and his book constitute a certain perspective on that book, but the combination, as well, of the reader's and the book's perspectives constitutes yet another mutually illuminating relationship that deeply influences the way in which the book is viewed. Earlier assertions of the exclusive nature of the single perspective on which is grounded the organization of the novel with a closed structure must now be amended to account for the ever-present, fluid, and sometimes unpredictable perspective of the reader. In novels whose structures are dependent upon counterpointed, or upon nakedly conflicting, dual perspectives, the third view of the reader may be indispensable to the book's meaning. In such cases, the reader, because he is possessed of the two conflicting viewpoints, is better able to regard the whole than is either of the original observers.

Bipolar narrative points of view seem to appear less frequently than do both the first-person narrative account and the structure that arises from a group of multiple perspectives. One reason for the relative rarity of the dual system may be the very heavy responsibility that it places upon the reader. The deliberate contrasting of two distinct and usually contradictory perspectives ends in incoherence without the resolution of the opposition that is provided by the third perspective of the reader. In a bipolar narrative structure, then, the bipolarity is only apparent, for inherent in its opposition is a demand for the mediation of a third perspective, the one that is needed to reconcile the contradictions that are contained in the two original perspectives. In all works that are constructed upon patterns of juxtaposition, the spectator or reader must provide the harmonizing and unifying over-all view. It is this third perspective upon which depends the coherence of the other two conflicting ones.

A fine example of the relationship between narrative point of view and structure, and of the role of the reader's reconciling third perspective, is found in *The Lime Twig* by John Hawkes. Displaying the same disjunct narrative sequence as does *The*

Cannibal, The Time Twig presents a devastating encounter between fantasy-ridden lower-middle-class victims and glamorous, godlike criminals in England after World War II. The novel begins with a ghostly and intensely personal prologue narrated by one William Hencher; he recounts the clammy horror of boarding houses during World War II, the death of his adored mother after a fire bombing, and his triumphant exploration of an abandoned fighter plane that has somehow landed in a backyard in London. Now Hencher, after the war, has returned to the boardinghouse in which his mother died and has taken a room with a young couple in their mid-twenties, Michael and Margaret Banks. To them he transfers his dangerous love. Hencher leads Michael into the enactment of an old dream, the theft of an aged champion racehorse to be run under a false name at Highland Green. Hencher dies in the novel's first bona fide numbered chapter, kicked to death by the stolen horse, Rock Castle. The book's eight numbered chapters present in disjunct form the gradual corruption of Michael and Margaret and the transformation of their cozy, if unexciting, life, into a nightmare of betrayal, brutality, and ghastly death.

The mode of narration is that of the concealed author, but each chapter is preceded by an epigraph in the form of a capsule comment by a racetrack journalist named Sidney Slyter. Headed by the phrase "Sidney Slyter Says," these epigraphs begin with two or three curt headlines that pertain to the action of the chapter to follow, and these headlines, in turn, introduce Slyter's slangy predictions of what will happen at Highland Green. These epigraphs do far more than merely establish a tone and allude to the larger social realities that encompass the novel's specific actions. Sometimes Hawkes introduces a character in Slyter's commentary. Furthermore, the book's "plot," the theft of the horse, is virtually condensed into Slyter's column, as he gets wind of it, does some investigating on his own, and asks some crucial questions whose irony and suggestiveness illuminate the novel's theme. For example, the columnist states: "Sidney Slyter wants to know what's the matter with Mr. Michael Banks. . . ." [6] Often, too, the columns are used for prophecy. Slyter reports the murder of Cowles, one of the gang, but the murder is not actually depicted until *after* it has been reported by Sidney Slyter.

The use of Sidney Slyter's columns creates the illusion that the novel's eight chapters are actually narrated by him. The reader is always aware of his mind, at once cold, probing, detached, and unquestioningly committed to the pursuit of entertainment and sensual pleasure. Slyter's is an odd presence, a combination of the godly, the cheap, and the sinister. One feels that he represents the mass aspiration of the English lower-middle class: the desire to turn its daydreams of power and sadism into realities. If Slyter is cold and addicted to pleasure, Hencher is warm, devoted, blindly willing to serve those whom he loves, unquestioningly and undemandingly adoring. The structure of *The Lime Twig* reflects this opposition of narrative presences. Hencher's portion consists only of about thirty pages. It represents the period of World War II. The eight chapters that constitute the book's main portion are given over entirely to the presence of Slyter. They begin with the theft of the horse and end with the deaths of Margaret and Michael. The book's short closing section is *not* introduced by Sidney Slyter; it describes the discovery of Hencher's body by several detectives. The second part takes place after the war, and it extends over a period of only two or three days. The two-part structure, which depends upon the contrasting perspectives of Hencher and Slyter, corresponds in temporal terms to World War II and to the immediate postwar period. When Hencher dies, the values that he represents also perish. Meanwhile, what were formerly daydreams of big money won at little effort and of fabulous sexual exploits have become the ghastly realities of such average men as Michael Banks. However, the responsibility for supplying the connections between Hencher's and Slyter's points of view rests entirely with the reader.

In a more unusual manner, Vladimir Nabokov's *Pale Fire* shows how a novel's structure may be based upon bipolar points of view, with the third perspective, that of the reader, being relied upon to furnish the unifying perspective. *Pale Fire* embodies a total rejection of the principle of narration. The book consists of elements which are not traditionally found in the novel. These are four literary documents: a Foreword; a 999-line autobiographical poem, an unintentional parody of Wordsworth's *The Prelude* in malformed heroic couplets, by John Shade, a university-affiliated American poet; a supposedly scholarly Commentary of more than 150 pages by Dr. Charles Kinbote, alias His Royal Highness Charles II, the exiled king of Zembla; and a totally gratuitous, pedantic, but comic, Index. In the manner of some critical works, Kinbote's Commentary is in effect a rival document in competition with the work on which it supposedly provides a critical text.

The juxtaposition of the poem and the commentary serves to evoke equally "unreal" perspectives on reality and, perhaps more important, to create an overwhelming sense of alienation, not only of the two men from each other, but of the intellectual from the creative life, and of the university life from the "actual" life of a country like Zembla. Kinbote is a madman—prejudiced, contemptuous, salacious, exploitative, and utterly self-deluded— who interprets reality from the point of view of his own private paranoia. John Shade, by contrast ostensibly sane, is as pleasant and as tolerant as Kinbote is presumptuous and irascible. Nonetheless, Shade, too, projects his own parochialism and his own sentimentality—illusions of a different sort—upon reality. One has only to sample his "masterpiece" to understand how inadequate, in a sense different from Kinbote's, is Shade's perspective on reality.

By virtue of the dual structure of *Pale Fire,* Nabokov has forced into relationship antagonistic men and milieus. Both Shade and Kinbote betray faulty vision and complacent solipsistic blindness, resulting in their inadequate ideas of reality. By simply juxtaposing the two rival and contradictory documents, the one representing Wordsmith College, the other Zembla, Nabokov has invited the reader to discover the reality upon which these perspectives have been focused. It is his, the third, perspective that will ultimately resolve contradictions, provide coherence, bind up the broken threads, and find a unity in the rival points of view of Shade and Kinbote. Or will this third perspective, neither representative of art nor of critical thought, constitute merely a third fantasy, coherent and consistent within its own terms, but as lacking in correspondence to the "real" world as those ostensibly under examination? Along with Jorge Luis Borges, Vladimir Nabokov wishes to explore the powers of the mind not only to influence, but also to shape the real and to dictate its being. Writers who are inspired by this essentially metaphysical ambition refuse to distinguish between reality and fantasy and decline to designate at what point in their works the imaginary and the verifiable overlap. For them, each perspective has its own validity. A perspective is but a point of view upon reality. To see the truth, one must see simultaneously from a great many perspectives, or from one ceaselessly moving perspective.

The incorporation of multiple perspectives upon the subject is characteristic of novels whose authors wish to embody within their works philosophic attitudes or clusters of philosophic themes and propositions; multiple perspectives are employed in such traditionally structured novels as Thomas Mann's *The Magic Mountain* (*Der Zauberberg*) and Hermann Hesse's *The Glass Bead Game* (*Das Glasperlenspiel*). The term "polyhistoric" is sometimes used to indicate the intellectual complexity and ambition that are embodied in novels based upon multiple perspectives. A good example of such a book is one already discussed in these pages: Robert Musil's *The Man Without Qualities* (*Der Mann Ohne Eigenschaften*).

The open-structured, polyhistoric, or multiple-perspective novel often includes among its many characters a thinker, an artist, or an individual whose temperament combines the traits of both. Since a clear and whole vision of reality depends not only upon astuteness but also upon a capacity for complex perception, intellectuals and artists are natural "mouthpieces" for novelists who wish to evoke simultaneous multiple perspectives. From the appearance of Stephen Dedalus in 1916 onward, the artist-thinker has been commonly found as the central "persona" of the capacious intellectual type of the modern novel. A few of the more prominent of these figures are Hermann Broch's Virgil and Bertrand Müller; Lawrence Durrell's Darley, Pursewarden, and Balthazar; Julio Cortázar's Oliveira; Thomas Mann's von Aschenbach, Serenus Zeitblom, and Adrian Leverkühn, and the array of intellectual and spiritual antagonists that are portrayed in *The Magic Mountain.*

The act of perception contains the instant of collision between the object and the perceptor. From this instant one derives, in large measure, his apprehension of reality. This is the moment in which chaos is at least apparently banished and in which the flux of being is halted for a moment. The larger reality seems to become, the greater the number of "facts" or "truths" it contains, the greater is the universal need for someone to take a clear look and make sense out of things. Making sense out of the irrational is the function alike of the artist and of the intellectual. The thinker banishes terrors and brings clarity to confusion by explaining *why* things are the way they are. He can dissolve terrors by breaking them down and sliding their components into categories of his own design. In this way, he reduces the power of the inexplicable through the application of analysis, for analysis exposes how things function and identifies their source. What the intellectual shares with the artist is the sharpness of vision, the sensitivity of his eyes, ears, and hands, the mental penetration that enables him to grasp the world quickly and to neutralize it by explaining it before it can exercise its disorder and, as we fear, its destruction. This combination of swift perception and of analytical facility accounts for the presence of the intellectual in much architectonic fiction; he is capable of bringing to the subject a special perspective that is both deep and comprehensive.

But in architectonic fiction the artist is perhaps encountered as frequently as the intellectual. Like the intellectual, he is the donor of a special perspective, and he is endowed with special powers that are even more urgently needed than are those of the intellectual. Most of the major novelists of the age have concerned themselves with the problem of art and of the artist: Joyce, Proust, Mann, Broch, Kafka, Hesse, and Beckett. It is as though the twentieth-century novelist, having been forced into concealment by the technical refinements introduced by Flaubert, James, Conrad, and Ford Madox Ford, is finding a way to assert himself by writing himself back into the novel in disguised form as an artist-character. Although the omniscient novelist can never again be taken seriously by serious, knowledgeable readers, the novelist is finding new ways to make himself part of his own fiction. Two general procedures stand out among those of the many books in which this is occurring: the more common is the appearance of the novelist in the disguise of a character, an artist, but not necessarily a writer; less common is the abandonment of the pretense that the novelist is writing "fiction." Novelists like Henry Miller, Michel Leiris, Louis-Ferdinand Céline, Jean Genêt, and Anaïs Nin write directly about themselves *as* artists, using the first-person pronoun without any attempt at the adoption of a fictional mask.

This interest in the artist and in the processes by which art is created is quite natural when one considers that the artist not only shares the power of the intellectual to produce from heightened perception both coherence and order but possesses as well a further power that the intellectual lacks. Not only can he make sense out of reality, he can extract its form and its meaning, combine these with the attributes arising from his own perspective, and make from the two something new, a third being, a superior one: a metaphor, or, on a grander scale, a work of art, a microcosmic approximation of the originally uncontrollable reality. Because of its formal attributes, the "metaphor" may even be regarded as superior to its model in reality. Whereas reality is constantly in a state of flux, unstable, incoherent, inconsistent, and lacking in pleasing proportions, the reproduction, if it is well made, may be fixed, stable, coherent, internally consistent, and pleasing to the aesthetic sense. When all this has been said, the general fact remains that the most important power of the metaphor is that it holds fused in a condition of stability and synthesis the "truth" that is far too fluid in its natural state to be captured, comprehended, and controlled. For their unusually keen powers of perception, but more especially for their ability to disarm reality and to make it something easily mastered, the intellectual and the artist are the "heroes" of much modernist fiction. Their perspectives ought not be omitted from any novel that aims at totality of vision.

One of the most ambitious and thoughtful of open-structured fictions is Hermann Broch's trilogy, *The Sleepwalkers* (*Die Schlafwandler*). Broch was in fact an engineer and the director until the early 1930s of a Viennese textile firm, as well as a serious student of mathematics and philosophy. From these studies naturally came his desire to make *The Sleepwalkers* as comprehensive as possible a collection of perspectives. As Theodore Ziolkowski has written, "Broch had learned from the theories of modern science that even in the so-called pure sciences cognition is not absolute, but relative. Just as in the physics of Einstein or Heisenberg the phenomenon observed is affected by the position and nature of the observer, so too in the philosophical disciplines every idea is conditioned by the character of the person who thinks it. In order to present an idea, one must at the same time present the personality of the thinker. The subject of observation, as Broch put it, must be projected into the field of observation as an *object* of observation." [7] For Hermann Broch, then, the mutual dependence of perspective and structure, and the urge to create an open form, were not simply unselfconscious responses to something drifting about the intellectual atmosphere. He was fully cognizant of developments and discoveries in science and mathematics and of their implications for philosophy, and he deliberately set out to create novels that would embody the perceptual dynamics of these new developments and discoveries.

The Sleepwalkers is an engineering feat in which the materials of construction are blocks of different sorts of prose. The first novel of the trilogy is *The Romantic (1888)* (*1888 Pasenow, oder die Romantik*). It renders, in a style that subtly parodies that of the German novels of the 1880s, the sole perspective of a young Prussian Junker, Joachim von Pasenow. This volume is nearly wholly conventional in structure and is genteel in style. The abrupt ending, however, introduces the element of the disjunct that is to become the structural principle of the third volume:

IV
Nevertheless after some eighteen months they had their first child. It actually happened. How this came about cannot be told here. Besides, after the material for character construc-

tion already provided, the reader can imagine it for him-self.[8]

The second novel, *The Anarchist (1903) (1903 Esch, oder die Anarchie)*, presents a strongly contrasting perspective, that of "impetuous" August Esch, a bookkeeper of the lower-middle class, a Roman Catholic, and a fervent idealist. Its perspective accounts not only for the substitution of anarchism for romanticism but also of the sophisticated Berlin settings and the opulent country-gentleman atmosphere of von Pasenow's home in Brandenberg by a steamy working-class saloon and the crude ambience of a circus whose main attraction is a knife-throwing act.

However, volume III is not in actuality Huguenau's story at all, though he is ever-present and, at the novel's close, is triumphant over both Esch and von Pasenow. This book consists of a collection of perspectives on reality, each of which is attributed to a different character and expressed in a different style. Thus, the book contains not only a great variety of changing perspectives but a great number of styles as well. This diversity has its structural manifestation in a method that proceeds in a disjunct manner in an evidently random combination of prose fragments, each of which represents some aspect of the perspective of one of the many characters. Broch calls attention to the fragmentation of his method by employing, for the first time in the trilogy, official breaks designated by arabic numbers that separate the various blocks of prose. Each character, like John Hawkes's Skipper, adopts an exclusive perspective in the form of a life value and attempts, by clinging to this perspective, both to maintain his sanity and to fight the growing personal alienation he senses from general moral, social, political, and aesthetic creeds. These perspectives may be identified with transcendent values; they are deified ideas.

Broch has not allowed these multiple perspectives to exist in a condition of autonomy and of total relativity. Despite his structural modernity, he wishes to restore some trace of authorial omnipotence and omniscience. He has, therefore, erected under the chaotic surface of *The Realist (1918)*, the perspective of Dr. Bertrand Müller, an intellectual and a student of architecture. What is curious is not that Broch should have included as a character an intellectual who makes sense out of everything by writing an essay called "Disintegration of Values" ("Zerfall der Werte"), but that Müller is a poet as well as a thinker. Gradually, the reader realizes that he is not only the author of "Disintegration of Values," but also of "The Story of the Salvation Army Girl" ("Geschichte des Heilsarmeemädchens in Berlin"), a romantic ballad that is related in alternating sections of poetry and prose. Next, the reader comes to the inevitable conclusion that Müller is also the author of the novel itself.

Hermann Broch has met the problem of perspective in *The Realist (1918)* simply by employing Müller as a perceptual and intellectual container for all the perspectives of the book. Müller offers alternative procedures for organizing chaotic experiences: the rational method of intellectual analysis and the metaphorical and lyrical method of poetry. "What we have, then, is actually an absolute novel that represents the full extent of Bertrand's mind, with its scope from the rational down to the depths of the irrational." [9]

The structural foundation of *The Realist (1918)* suggests a paradox: the exclusive single perspective that is characteristic of the closed novel is, it seems, but the inverse operation of the comprehensive, multiple perspective. As one sensibility may be capable of entertaining but one perspective, another may be capable of entertaining a great many, notwithstanding their mutually contradictory nature. The individual, particularly if he is a serious thinker or a serious artist, is, after all, capable of sustaining a dynamic perception of reality that consists of multiple perspectives. One must leave to psychology the problem raised by Carlos Fuentes in *Change of Skin:* whether an individual who permits himself to take in the total view is at the same time capable of maintaining his sanity.

There is one perspective still that seems to haunt some novelists who are attracted to the open structure. This is self-perception attained from some point of view *outside* oneself; it is perhaps the ultimate feat of perception, and it is achieved by the superintellectual hero of *The Man Without Qualities* when, standing at a window watching an angry crowd milling through the streets of Vienna, he becomes conscious of his own inactivity in the midst of flowing life. He is both the observer and the observed; in this dual function, he intuitively receives the perfect metaphor for his own being: that of a stone around which everything dynamic moves and streams. A similar desire to "pass through" space to a clearer vision of oneself, or of life, is expressed by Horacio Oliveira, the searching protagonist of Cortázar's *Hopscotch (Rayuela):*

> And so, *de feuille en aiguille,* I think about those exceptional states in which for one instant leaves and invisible lamps are imagined, are felt in an air outside of space. It's very simple, every exaltation or depression pushes me towards a state suitable for
> I will call them paravisions
> That is to say (that's the worst of it, saying it) an instantaneous aptitude for going out, so that suddenly I can grasp myself from outside, or from inside but on a different plane,
> as if I were somebody who was looking at me
> (better still—because in reality I cannot see myself—: like someone who is living me)[10]

Such a yearning as this represents the ultimate ambition of the man who wishes not only to know but to experience everything. Its expression transports one from art into the vaster realm of the metaphysical. The authors of such novels as *The Sleepwalkers, The Counterfeiters, Hopscotch, Change of Skin, The Alexandria Quartet, The Man Without Qualities,* and *The Waves* wish less to transcend the world than simply to reveal it from as many angles of vision as possible. Like the cubist painters, they are determined to shatter the old idea that reality is clear, simple, coherent, and unified. Broch, Gide, Cortázar, Fuentes, Durrell, Musil, and Virginia Woolf all refuse their readers the assurance of easy conclusions and quick judgments. They are asking, instead, that their readers observe and acknowledge that reality is polymorphous, illogical, fragmented, chaotic, and, above all, myriad faceted.

Notes

1. Hermann Broch, quoted by Theodore Ziolkowski, *Hermann Broch* (New York, 1964), p. 19.
2. See *L'Ere du Soupçon* (Paris, 1956). Madame Sarraute attributes the invention of *sous-conversation* to Ivy Compton-Burnett.
3. John Hawkes, *Second Skin* (New York, 1963), p. 210.
4. See Chapter 9 for a discussion of the structure of *Composition No. 1*.
5. Marc Saporta, *Composition No. 1* (Paris, 1962). Naturally, one is unable to provide page references to this novel. "La chambre d'hôpital n'est qu'un amas de souvenirs en désordre. Sur le plafond blanc s'inscrit le grouillement des scènes en surimpression, comme sur une pellicule utilisée à plusieurs reprises par un photographe distrait."
6. John Hawkes, *The Lime Twig* (New York, 1961), p. 124.
7. Theodore Ziolkowski, *Hermann Broch* (New York, 1964), p. 19. Ziolkowski says that in spite of Broch's much-admired essay on James Joyce, he was more deeply influenced in the writing of *Die Schlafwandler* by *The Counterfeiters* and by the novels of John Dos Passos than he was by *Ulysses*. See pp. 20–21.
8. Hermann Broch, *Part One: The Romantic (1888), The Sleepwalkers*, translated by Willa and Edwin Muir (New York, 1964), p. 158. Although the three parts of *The Sleepwalkers* are published in one volume in the English language edition, they comprise three separate volumes in the German. Thus, *"Part One"* is *1888 Pasenow, oder die Romantik* (Munich, 1931), p. 275:

"IV
Nichtdestoweniger hatten sie nach etwa achtzehn Monaten ihr erstes Kind. Es geschah eben. Wie sich dies Zugetragen hat, muss nicht mehr erzählt werden. Nach den gelieferten Materialien zum Charakteraufbau kann sich der Leser dies auch allein ausdenken."

9. Ziolkowski, p. 19.
10. Julio Cortázar, *Hopscotch,* translated by Gregory Rabassa (New York, 1966), p. 334. *Rayuela* (Buenos Aires, 1963), p. 461: "Y así, *de feuille en aiguille,* pienso en esos estados excepcionales en que por un instante se adivinan las hojas y las lámparas invisibles, se la las siente en un aire que está fuera del espacio. Es muy simple,

      toda exaltación o depresión me
   empuja a un estado propicio a
      lo llamaré paravisiones
      es decir (lo malo es eso, decirlo)
      una aptitud instantánea para salirme,

para de pronto desde
fuera aprehenderme, o de dentro pero en
otro plano,
como si yo fuera alguien que me
está mirando
(mejor todavía—porque en realidad no
me veo—: como
alguien que me está viviendo)."

*Refusing all interpretive commentary, it [the
novel] ought not give one something to think
about, but something to see. It exposes reality
at a glance; it multiplies points of view; it
varies appearances; it unmasks what no one
sees, the underside, the upperside, the horizontal and the vertical, the inside and the outside, making the distant seem near-at-hand and
the near seem distant; it amplifies, in a word,
all the variations of incident and the limited
distances of the human visual field, and in doing so, it amplifies the apprehension of the
real.*

—Monique Nathan [1]

5.

*The Perspectives
of the Camera*

In their constant search for ways to bring the technical resources of the novel into consonance with contemporary concepts of time and space, novelists have inevitably sought to discover, often with alarm and envy, ways to attain some of the
powers of the century's new art form, the cinema. The critic
Jean Duvignaud has written: "There are men who shake their
fists at the stairway filmed by Eisenstein in 'Potemkin,' because
they demand to know by what means the art of writing can ob-
tain a similar power. These men are novelists." [2] Although most
novelists have not reacted so violently as to shake their fists, they
have, it is true, ransacked the procedures of the film to see what
they might take from it for their own use.

Critics who compare the relative strengths and weaknesses
of the novel and the film generally conclude that the former is

a temporal medium capable of designating, by changes of verb tenses, from three to five chronological relationships and that it is perfectly suited to the exploration of states of consciousness such as dream, memory, and desire, as well as to the formation of condensed figures of speech. The cinema, on the other hand, is usually regarded as a medium eminently spatial, empowered by the image to move freely in space, but confined necessarily to the impression always of presentness.[3] " 'Pictures have no tenses,' says [Béla] Balázs. 'Unfolding in a perpetual present, like visual perception itself, they cannot express either a past or a future.' "[4] The French critic, Georges-Albert Astre, who has compared the powers of the film and the novel, has expressed the same thought: "Film necessarily exists in a continual present; it confers on the past (indeed, on the future) the authenticity of the actual moment in the present."[5] Because the visual images it projects are precise and unequivocal, the film has a limited capacity to create tropes; therefore, it is less suited than is the novel to the exploration and projection of inner states of consciousness. At the same time, the film has a capacity for clear, powerful, and immediate visualization that attracts inventive novelists. The film offers the novelist a purer way of seeing things, for although the camera does not exactly reproduce the physiological process of vision, it does capture visual realities that are free from the interpretations of the human mind. The filmed image is uncontaminated by feelings and emotions. It offers a perspective that is more nearly "objective" than that intrinsic in the word, and thus it must tempt novelists who are seeking new perspectives on their subjects to invent modes of approximating the perspectives of the camera.

The camera, then, offers the novelist a new way of seeing his materials. Setting aside for the present the question of how space and time are affected by the perspectives of the camera, let us see what may be achieved by a novelist who, striving for the appearance of objectivity, attempts an approximation of the camera's view of things. John Dos Passos was among the first novelists to understand how the simulation of the camera could extend the range of the novel's perspectives. His trilogy *U.S.A.* embodies a combination of perspectival approaches to its subject.

Two of these perspectives are prose approximations of camera techniques: the Newsreel and the Camera Eye. Of the other two perspectives, one is that of the conventional concealed omniscient author who presents his characters without apparent judgment or feeling; the other consists of the Biographies, short presentations of the lives of famous Americans in varied prose styles appropriate to each life. While the conventional novel proceeds throughout the trilogy in a vast network of criss-crossing relationships and sets of ambitions and failures, the work is bodied forth, extended, and expanded by the points of view implied by each of the other three clearly labeled perspectives. The Biographies provide an historical dimension. The Camera Eye sections bring to bear on the events and relationships of the work a highly personal, intense, private, "subjective" set of reactions. The Newsreels, by contrast, are impersonal, terse, and free from emotion. They are an approach to an "objective" point of view.

The Newsreels combine the nutshell vulgarity of American journalism with the swift, fragmented feel of the cinema news report. From time to time, Dos Passos inserts song lyrics among the flashing lines of the Newsreels; the consequent conflict between what is reported and reality, or brutality and sentimentality, produces a bitter irony. Furthermore, variations in typography and in the spatial arrangements of the Newsreels on the page greatly enhance their impact on the reader's mind and eye.

The most striking feature of the Newsreel is its mock objectivity. This results from the total lack of discrimination in the listing of events; the absurd and the serious, the trivial and the tragic are juxtaposed without any attempt to evaluate their relative importance. Thus, the notice about the Grand Prix de la Victoire precedes in order of mention the one truly grave item: the leveling of the Lemberg Ghetto. The very incongruity of the items contained in the Newsreel (Brisbane and beer, Lenin and Trotsky, a whale and a suicide) implies a comment on the public mentality. Not only does the Newsreel as a unit, but each item, alludes to some aspect of American life as well as to some specific aspect of U.S.A. For example, the lines about the auto race refer indirectly to the loose and idle lives of Dos Passos' Americans who have been sent to Paris during World

NEWSREEL XXXV

the Grand Prix de la Victoire, run yesterday for fifty-
second time was an event that will long remain in the
memories of those present, for never in the history of the
classic race has Longchamps presented such a glorious scene

Keep the home fires burning
Till the boys come home

LEVIATHAN UNABLE TO PUT TO SEA
BOLSHEVIKS ABOLISH POSTAGE STAMPS
ARTIST TAKES GAS IN NEW HAVEN
FIND BLOOD ON ONE DOLLAR BILL

While our hearts are yearning

POTASH CAUSE OF BREAK ： ᴶ PARLEY
    MAJOR DIES OF POISONING
TOOK ROACH SALTS BY MISTAKE

riot and robbery developed into the most awful pogrom
ever heard of. Within two or three days the Lemberg Ghetto
was turned into heaps of smoking débris. Eyewitnesses esti-
mate that the Polish soldiers killed more than a thousand
Jewish men and women and children

LENIN SHOT BY TROTSKY IN DRUNKEN
BRAWL

you know where I stand on beer, said Brisbane in seeking assistance

Though the boys are far away
    They long for home
There's a silver lining
    Through the dark clouds shining [6]

War I. Two absurd notices follow the lyrics of a very well-known
war song; the plea to keep the "home fires burning" is set next
to an account of what is really happening at home: an artist
commits suicide, and the materialism of America is guilty ("blood
on one dollar bill"). "Potash cause of break in parley" reveals
what national and international values *really* are (the means to
increased production). Connected to the artist's suicide is the
grotesque comedy of an army officer's accidental death by roach
poison. A piece of amusing wishful thinking is the item about
Lenin and Trotsky destroying each other while drunk. The spoof
on American fear of alcohol is reiterated in the next line about

foreign assistance and beer. But the strongest contrast of the Newsreel (its thematic center) is that between the auto race and the Lemberg Ghetto. The latter is delivered in an inexpresssive prose (the most dramatic word is the weak "awful"), while the former reproduces the hysterical gushiness of American sportscasting. The Newsreel ends on a mocking note by referring to the soldiers' longing for home, for the "silver lining" can only suggest money. Indeed, as "The Big Money" shows, virtually all the returning veterans find waiting for them is the opportunity to become rich. In a sly way, the Newsreels expose the surface of sentimentality and the underlying reality of brutality that typify most forms of journalism in the United States.

Alternating with the apparently objective coverage of the Newsreels are the tightly focused and intensely personal musings of the nameless narrators of the Camera Eye sections. By placing the point of view in contrasting perceptual contexts, Dos Passos achieves a means of expanding and contracting the action and its significance between the poles of the general and the specific. The prose employed in the Camera Eye sections owes much to the opening pages of James Joyce's *A Portrait of the Artist as a Young Man:* punctuation and grammatical connectives are not used; word groups replace sentences; individual words are employed exclusively for their sensuous qualities; relationships in time, space, and narrative identity between the narrator of the Camera Eye passages and the other prose blocks are suppressed. The following passage depicts a contrast to the general rush, excitement, and dazzle of Paris during World War I; here, Paris is perceived as soft, warm, hazy, indolent, even suggestive of hope:

> today is Paris pink sunlight hazy on the clouds against patches of robinsegg a tiny siren hoots shrilly traffic drowsily rumbles clatters over the cobbles taxis squawk the yellow's the comforter through the open window the Louvre emphasizes its sedate architecture of greypink stone between the Seine and the sky
>
> . . . .
>
> Paris comes into the room in the servantgirl's eyes the warm bulge of her breasts under the grey smock the

smell of chicory in coffee scalded milk and the shine that
crunches on the crescent rolls stuck with little dabs of very
sweet unsalted butter

. . . .

that burns up our last year's diagrams the dates fly
off the calendar we'll make everything new today is the
Year I   Today is the sunny morning of the first day of
spring We gulp our coffee splash water on us jump into our
clothes run downstairs step out wideawake into the first
morning of the first day of the first year[7]

In contrast to the Newsreel, the Camera Eye expresses feelings
that are muggy, aromatic, redolent, personal, and private. But
both perspectives are necessary to complete the cinematic quality
of *U.S.A.* The Camera Eye sections are like closeups, and the
Newsreels are like documentary sequences based upon montage
composition, which holds in balance a great many conflicting elements; they are comparable to collages in that their varied elements are set down next to one another without comments or
transitions. The ultimate statement that is made by such a composition depends upon the relationships of contrast and similarity
among the juxtaposed parts.

John Dos Passos has clearly labeled the various perspectives
he has adopted, and it is, therefore, evident that he is attempting
to survey his subject from several angles of vision and that he
has employed two of the powers of the camera in order to do so.
A very different, more subtle and more ambiguous effect, is attained when the novelist eliminates all clues as to what perspective he has adopted and simultaneously treats both himself as a
concealed narrator and his protagonist, the identified perceptor,
as though they possessed the sensibilities of "objective" motion-
picture cameras. This is what has been done by the French
novelist Alain Robbe-Grillet. In addition to his several novels,
he has created at least three full-length films. Ever since the
appearance of his first novel, *The Erasers (Les Gommes)*, in
1953, Robbe-Grillet has been the center of a lively literary debate
focused upon two issues: at what point a novel ceases to be a

novel and becomes an attempt to render in prose an imitation of a film; and the implications of *chosisme,* or the heavy emphasis upon objects that results from his adoption of the camera perspective.

These two issues are inseparable, and they are closely related to the question of what happens in the novel when the perspective of the motion-picture camera is adopted by the novelist. The ability to render objects without any of the distortions that seem inevitably to occur when they are perceived by a human mind is, of course, peculiar to the camera. George Bluestone discusses this particular power of the film at some length in a long essay called "Limits of the Novel and the Film." Quoting V. I. Pudovkin's assertion that "relationships between human beings are, for the most part, illumined by conversation, by words" and his conclusion that the cinema frame is, therefore, a perfect medium for the presentation of relationships between persons and objects, Bluestone concludes: "within the composition of the frame, the juxtaposition of man and object becomes critical." Citing numerous examples from the films of Charlie Chaplin, Bluestone demonstrates how the relationship between the animate and the inanimate may become confused in film, since the inanimate may be animated by the camera. The result is that human beings and objects are equally capable of motion and may become interchangeable. The film, then, has "discovered new ways to render meanings by finding relationships between animate and inanimate objects" [8]

Alain Robbe-Grillet is certainly not the only literary figure to have become interested in rendering objects in order to reveal new relationships and new meanings. In France the term *"chosisme"* has been given to this endeavor, whose foremost practitioners are Robbe-Grillet and the poet, Francis Ponge.[9] Some French critics would name also Michel Butor and Claude Simon. Since Robbe-Grillet has written a number of essays that, published together as *For a New Novel (Pour un nouveau roman),* constitute a theory of language and tragedy, and since his novels actually evolve from a blended perspective that combines the subjective human view of the novelist with the objective, nonhuman view of the camera, his works provide some of the best available examples of how the novel may expand its powers by using the perspectives of the camera.

Like Gertrude Stein, Robbe-Grillet is fascinated by the problem of simple accurate description of objects without subjective contamination, and he has dedicated himself to a procedure of description that is designed to free objects from the distortions of their essential nature that are the result of human projection of emotion and meaning—anthropomorphism. Robbe-Grillet's goal is to minimize the tragedy that results when the nonhuman world (imbued with human terrors and desires) merely seems to confirm a human obsession which, thus strengthened, fortified, endowed with "truth," leads its perceptor to commit a tragic action. Each of his books portrays a character who convinces himself of the reality of his own worst fears by interpreting reality in his own image, and each then acts in accordance with his delusion. Thus, Wallas, the detective-protagonist of *The Erasers,* is betrayed by his theory of a crime he is investigating into actually becoming the murderer; the nameless narrator of *Jealousy* (*La Jalousie*) allows his entire environment to become saturated with his fear of his wife's infidelity; Mathias of *The Voyeur* (*Le Voyeur*) eventually cannot resist committing the sexual outrage of which he dreams. Each betrays himself by creating confusion between himself and the objects around him, that is, by refusing objects their integrity of being. Robbe-Grillet's books are filled with despoiled objects that have been made to symbolize some human preoccupation: a centipede crushed upon a wall, some bits and pieces of string, a cardboard box full of a dead man's trinkets, an unidentified Eurasian girl with a black dog on a leash.

Robbe-Grillet rejects what he calls the "humanist" equation: "le monde, c'est l'homme." [10] He wishes to cleanse the world of objects of their impure and false human associations. Therefore, he shuns attributive adjectives and virtually all metaphors. His task is not to interpret the world but simply to see it fresh, to see it as it might be viewed through the lens of a camera. In order to do this, he abandons conventional description and, instead, enumerates dimensions, surfaces, and relationships among objects in their spatial situations:

> To record the distance between the object and myself, and the distances of the object itself (its *exterior* distances, i.e., its measurements), and the distances of objects among themselves, and to insist further on the fact that these are *only distances* (and not divisions), this comes down to establishing that things are here and that they are nothing but things, each limited to itself. The problem is no longer to choose between a happy correspondence and a painful solidarity. There is henceforth a rejection of all complicity.[11]

Below, from *In the Labyrinth* (*Dans le labyrinthe*), is Robbe-Grillet's description of the painting *The Defeat at Reichenfels* which suggests the various images that eventually *become* the novel:

> The contrast between the three soldiers and the crowd is further accentuated by a precision of line, a clarity in rendering, much more evident in their case than in that of other individuals the same distance from the viewer. The artist has shown them with as much concern for detail and almost as much sharpness of outline as if they were sitting in the foreground. But the composition is so involved that this is not apparent at first glance. Particularly the soldier shown full face has been portrayed with a wealth of detail that seems quite out of proportion to the indifference it expresses. No specific thought can be discerned. It is merely a tired face, rather thin, and narrowed still further by several days' growth of beard. This thinness, these shadows that accentuate the features without, on the other hand, indicating the slightest individual characteristic, nevertheless emphasize the brilliance of the wide-open eyes.

> The military overcoat is buttoned up to the neck, where the regimental number is embroidered on a diamond-shaped tab of material. The cap is set straight on the head,

covering the hair, which is cut extremely short, judging
from its appearance at the temples. The man is sitting
stiffly, his hands lying flat on the table which is covered
with a red-and-white checked oilcoth.[12]

From such passages as these that imitate the objectivity of
the movie camera Robbe-Grillet constructs his own version of
the ancient myth of the labyrinth. The materials of *In the
Labyrinth* consist of a group of images, most of which originate
in the painting described above. Multiple meanings are suggested for all the novel's major images, and multiple identities
are posited for all the "characters." In their various ambiguous
aspects, these images constitute action, plot, and theme of Robbe-
Grillet's novels. The patterns into which they are arranged suggest, by their variety, various possible meanings and relationships, and, at the same time, these patterns form the novel's
structure, a maze through which a dying soldier wanders help-
lessly, clinging to a box of trinkets.

Robbe-Grillet, in this as well as in his other novels, handles
language as though he were himself a camera. He views over and
over again from as many angles and at as many distances as he
desires, the objects and images that are his subjects. It is among
the relationships that he creates in this manner that the reader
must seek the meanings of the novel, for they are literally woven
from the movements of the soldier and the boy in and out and
back and forth among the novel's various settings. The first step,
or action of the camera, is that power spoken of by George
Bluestone: the power of the cinema to animate the inanimate.
Employing a cinematic type of transition, Robbe-Grillet first
animates the elements of the painting, *The Defeat at Reichenfels*.
The following passage illustrates Robbe-Grillet's camera work.
First, he moves in upon the subject with an intense focus that
picks up details. Moving very slowly, he proceeds from detail to
detail until a new object is gradually framed by the lens of his
imaginary camera:

The soldier, his eyes wide open, continues to stare into the
half-darkness a few yards in front of him, where the child

is standing, also motionless and stiff, his arms at his side. But it is as if the soldier did not see the child—or anything else. He looks as if he has fallen asleep from exhaustion, sitting close to the table, his eyes wide open.

It is the child who speaks first. He says: "Are you asleep?" He has spoken almost in a whisper. . . .[13]

With this simple, concentrated detail, the author brings to life the soldier and the boy of the painting by giving them the power of speech.

A second passage from *In the Labyrinth* will serve to suggest how the structural impression of the labyrinth is created from a massing up of repetitions and modifications of passages featuring the same images, just as thematic relationships in films are woven from patterns of visual images, often repeated or relocated in various contexts which serve to modify the meanings. Now the soldier is lying in bed in the improvised military hospital. But he is returned—in memory, daydream, delirium, or in the imagined fantasy of the book's concealed narrator—to the tavern scene originally depicted in *The Defeat at Reichenfels*.

The soldier is lying on his mattress fully dressed, having merely taken off his heavy boots which he has put under the bed beside his leggings. He has wrapped himself up in the two blankets, over the overcoat which he has put under the bed beside his leggings. He has wrapped himself up in the two blankets, over the overcoat which he has simply unbuttoned at the collar, too tired to make one more gesture
. . . .
But the main thing is to be sheltered from the falling snow and the wind.
His eyes wide open, the soldier continues to stare into the darkness in front of him, a few yards in front of him, where the child stands, motionless and rigid too, his arms at his sides. But it is as if the soldier did not see the child— neither the child nor anything else.[14]

From such descriptions as this—repeated, inverted, altered, expanded, or merged with another—Robbe-Grillet gradually builds up a novel from visual "shots" much as a film is built up from the shots registered by the camera.

The unique feature of the perspective employed by Robbe-Grillet is that it is subjective and objective at the same time. Generally, his narrators are either unidentified, as in *Jealousy*, or concealed, as in *In the Labyrinth* and *La Maison de Rendez-vous*. This uncertainty regarding whose perceptions are being described has the effect of pressing the reader into an extremely close and intimate identification with the narrator. Since there is no alternative view of things to provide a comparison, a standard by which the reader may evaluate the "reality" of what he is being told, he must accept it as fact. At the same time, the manner of the descriptions—their precision, their dryness, their lack of qualifiers and of words that evoke feelings—is objective in the extreme. Like Marc Saporta, Robbe-Grillet is presenting an intensely subjective view in an intensely objective manner. The result is a fused, a double, perspective, and it is made possible by the borrowing of camera techniques.

The adaptation of the cinematic perspective to the novel in Robbe-Grillet's work has definite structural implications. Description of a highly visual nature *is* the substance of his books. When a great many passages of description, often of the same objects or of the same persons in relationships with objects, are juxtaposed to create a work as lengthy as a novel, the result is an abstract structure that manifests a spatial, not a temporal, orientation to reality. The double perspective tends to spatialize the subject by reducing time simply to any isolated moment of perception without regard to sequence or to any established "actual" frame of reference. Beginning with *Jealousy*, Robbe-Grillet abandoned the use of any conventional, sequential pattern of ordering events in time. For example, the reader who struggles to establish the relationship in time between A's trip to town with Franck and the evening during which all three of the protagonists are seated on the veranda of the narrator's house will only become more and more confused. There is no chronological sequence; there is merely (as in dreams) the occurrence and reoccurrence in the narrator's mind of the images that convey his fears and desires. Spatial realities, on the other hand, are extremely important in

Robbe-Grillet's books. The key identifying factor in the various image groups that constitute *In the Labyrinth* is space. There is the room with the red drapes, the slippers, and the painting; the tavern depicted in the painting; the snow-filled streets; the military hospital; and the hallway of the apartment where the soldier once finds refuge. These points in space are related to one another by the movements of the boy and the soldier in and out of the novel's various sites. This particular example of the spatialization of time has the effect of turning *In the Labyrinth* into an approximation of a film, for it is, at bottom, a stream of visual images flowing before the eye with the effect of a continual present. This is achieved both by the destruction of temporal relationships and by the basic organizational procedure of juxtaposition.

In film, juxtaposition is called "montage." Since every piece of film embodies a perspective of some sort, montage may be said to embody a combination of perspectives, at least two and often more. The great significance of montage for the novelist is that it provides both an example of the organization of elements without transitions or explanatory passages and an example of the inseparability of perspective and structure. Thus, the concept of montage does much more than suggest the effects that can be attained by running together a list of diverse and contrasting elements, it also exists as a richly suggestive example of architectonic structure.

There are two contrasting ideas of what montage actually is, but they are not incompatible for the novelist, however passionately film-makers may defend one or the other as valid. At its simplest, montage is merely the joining of two pieces of film, or, put another way, the construction of the completed film by means of the splicing together of different shots. The source of argument among film-makers and theoreticians involves the nature of the pieces thus joined and the quality of their relationship to one another. But before this argument is examined, with its implications for architectonic structure, it is sensible briefly to examine the theory of Sergei Eisenstein regarding the origin of the montage principle.

Eisenstein reports that he discovered the principle of montage conflict in literature, not at all surprisingly in that very same scene which perhaps twenty years later suggested to a literary critic, Joseph Frank, that certain novelists were attempting to transform time into space, or to "spatialize time": that justifiably famous scene in *Madame Bovary* which depicts Rodolphe's seduction of Emma against the background of the agricultural fair, Monsieur Derozeray's absurd speech, the mooing of cows, and the grunting of pigs. The Russian director found similar precedents for montage in the *tanka* and the *haiku;* both, incidentally, embody the same structural principle as the Surrealist metaphor, in which the two disparate arms give rise to a third image or concept. Here is Eisenstein's explanation of the same process:

> The point is that the copulation (perhaps we had better say, the combination) of two hieroglyphs of the simplest series is to be regarded not as their sum, but as their product, i.e., as a value of another dimension, another degree; each, separately, corresponds to an *object,* to a fact, but their combination corresponds to a *concept.* From separate hieroglyphs has been fused—the ideogram. By the combination of two "depictables" is achieved the representation of something that is graphically undepictable . . . .
> . . . .
> Yes. It is exactly what we do in the cinema, combining shots that are *depictive,* single in meaning, neutral in content— into *intellectual* contexts and series.[15]

While some contemporary critics of the film and the novel are eager to find the points of contrast between the two and tend to conclude that the essential expressive difference is that between the word (a sign) and the image (a representation),[16] Eisenstein himself denies that the cinema is by nature representative and closer, therefore, to painting than to literature. He strongly rejects the concept of the photographed image as a representation and insists most persuasively on its suggestive, evocative and stimulative nature:

Now why should the cinema follow the forms of theater and

painting rather than the methodology of language, which allows wholly new concepts of ideas to arise from the combination of two concrete denotations of two concrete objects? Language is much closer to film than painting is. For example, in painting the form arises from *abstract* elements of line and color, while in cinema the material *concreteness* of the image within the frame presents—as an element— the greatest difficulty in manipulation. So why not rather lean towards the system of language, which is forced to use the same mechanics in inventing words and word-complexes? [17]

Eistenstein did not wish to use film to "aller, d'un seul trait, au coeur vivant des êtres et des objets," [18] which is, suggests one critic, its great power. He wished to use montage elements, consisting of shots, as though they were words which give rise by the juxtaposition of specifics to the birth of a *third abstract* entity—to a concept. Eisenstein insists, in fact, that montage is the structural principle of *all* the arts. In film, however, where its operation is necessarily obvious, it calls attention to itself and becomes manifest as a central structural process.[19]

Whether Eisenstein is correct in his belief that montage is the universal structural principle of art is a question that goes much beyond the scope of this study. What matters is that the montage procedure by juxtaposition of two or more elements *is* the structural principle of much modernist art and that its prominence must be attributed in part to its constant demonstration in the cinema during the last half century. Roger Shattuck has discussed this very thoroughly in "The Art of Stillness." He seems unique among literary critics in having recognized the great importance for literature of Eisenstein's theoretical writings on film.[20] In short, if montage is not the inadvertent invention of the cinema, it has been brought to our attention in that medium in such a way that its operation and its creative possibilities have become more obvious than ever before.

The essential disagreement about the nature of montage concerns the question whether the participating elements are to be relatively similar to one another, so that their ensemble provides an impression of harmony, or whether they are to be relatively varied, so that their combination results in contrast, conflict, tension, and explosion. Those who hold the former view argue that montage is essentially the process of film editing: the process by which film shots are cut apart and rearranged into sequences. In such a view, montage would seem to provide the basis for the linear movement of any film in sequences spliced together from beginning to end. It is, in short, related to animation, or to serial production, which results in a moving image composed from a great many individual shots of the same subject.

Eisenstein was himself vehement in his denials that the simple process of linking shots constitutes the essence of the montage principle:

> The shot is by no means an *element* of montage.

> The shot is a montage *cell*.

> Just as cells in their division form a phenomenon of another order, the organism or embryo, so, on the other side of the dialectical leap from the shot, there is montage.

> By what, then, is montage characterized and, consequently, its cell—the shot?

> By collision. By the conflict of two pieces in opposition to each other. By conflict. By collision.[21]

As Eisenstein made films, taught, and observed the procedures of the other arts, he gradually developed larger areas and types of conflicts that expanded the explosive possibilities of montage: "If montage is to be compared with something, then a phalanx of montage pieces, of shots, should be compared to the series of explosions of an internal combustion engine, driving forward its automobile or tractor: for, similarly, the dynamics of montage serve as impulses driving forward the total film." [22]

On the one hand, montage may produce harmony, an impression of unity, of stillness, of circular movement without beginning or end; on the other, cacophony, an over-all feeling of erratic jumpy jaggedness, and of quick asymmetrical movement in any possible direction. Setting aside the question of which is the "true" montage principle, one may easily see that here exist two alternate and perhaps complementary procedures of juxtaposition. What acounts for their different effects in the work of art is the nature of the components in relationship to one another. In fact, to distinguish these two modes of juxtaposition, one of which corresponds to serial production, Roger Shattuck has used the terms "romantic" and "classical." When the juxtaposed elements are heterogeneous, the result is "an explosive, exciting texture in which connectives are actively missed. We are surrounded with conflict and contrast and cannot expect to reach a point of rest or understanding in the conventional sense." "Romantic" juxtaposition is identical to Eisenstein's theory of montage. When the juxtaposed elements are homogeneous, the emphasis is on the similarity of the joined elements. In this case, "Style . . . becomes circularity, a distortion of linear development and direction in the traditional sense. . . ." [23] This "classical" juxtaposition is perhaps not identical with, but is certainly suggestive of, serial production. Both procedures have been employed in architectonic novels. *In the Labyrinth,* for example, with its uniform prose surface and its repetitions and near-repetitions of images and patterned actions, is based upon the principle of "classical juxtaposition." It is possible to suggest that novels with closed structures are more nearly "classical" in their manner of incorporating juxtaposition, whereas open-structured novels are more often founded upon combinations of heterogeneous elements.

Perhaps the most subtle examples of "classical juxtaposition" are found in the works of Gertrude Stein. Like Alain Robbe-Grillet today, more than thirty years ago she wished to invent a method of description from which all affective qualities would be purged. Most of all, she wanted to free description from the associations of memory. She pointed the way to the imitation of the perspectives of the motion-picture camera, which captures exclusively the *present* being of what is photographed. She did this by working out a way of imitating series production of images in prose. The basic structural unit employed by Miss Stein is defined grammatically: whereas Hermann Broch in *The*

Realist (1918) (The Sleepwalkers) juxtaposes portions of several pages each, and Julio Cortázar in *Hopscotch (Rayuela)* arranges units of lengths varying from twenty or more pages to a single sentence, Gertrude Stein juxtaposes in sequence homogeneous words, phrases, sentences, and paragraphs. In "Portraits and Repetition," she acknowledges her debt to the cinema: "Any one is of one's period and this our period was undoubtedly the period of the cinema and series production." The film offered her a method for describing the present existing essence of an object or person without the falsification of any impressions retained by the memory. As she explained it, "By a continuously moving picture of any one there is no memory of any other thing and there is that thing existing, it is in a way if you like one portrait of anything not a number of them." [24] Serial production destroys the distinctions between past, present, and future and thus automatically reproduces the ongoing *presentness* of its subject.

Miss Stein's method is already apparent in "Melanctha," even though this "story" was published before she had fully worked out either her theories or her individualistic style. There is in "Melanctha" only a frail plot based upon the young woman's friendship with her "foil," Rose Johnson, and her baffled love for the severe young doctor, Jeff Campbell. Like most of Gertrude Stein's work, this piece is lacking altogether in "realistic" descriptions. At the same time, its fused style and structure reproduce the aimless and self-defeating patterns of Melanctha's life. "Melanctha" embodies a circular structure that on an inclusive level echoes the circular nature of the prose passages that contribute to its motion. The round movement of the piece begins with the birth, and death soon afterward, of Rose Johnson's baby, and resumes at this point once more near the end. Circling this point of reference are passages upon passages of uniformly wrought, stylistically homogeneous prose that re-create the rhythms of Melanctha's life, in particular of her sometimes dejected and sometimes excited "wandering." Although no attempt is made to approximate Negro speech, the prose contains syntactic suggestions that create the illusion of the patterns of Negro life in a small town. The mode of stylization resides in an exaggerated simplicity. Nearly all the sentences are compound; the vocabulary is simple; contractions are scrupulously avoided; and there is a great deal of repetition of phrases and sometimes of entire paragraphs. Miss Stein said of her procedure in writing "Melanctha": "In that there was a constant recurring and beginning there was a marked direction in the direction of being in the present although naturally I had been accustomed to past present and future, and why, because the composition forming around me was a prolonged present." [25]

Repetition is the definitive feature of this style. Repetition enables Miss Stein to build up an image of a personality much as a gigantic snowball for a snowman is produced by being rolled forward in waves of increasing pressure so that it picks up more and more substance and weight as it moves. In Miss Stein's work, this onward-rolling quality goes far beyond what would be necessary in a conventional narrative treatment of the same subject. It is comparable to certain scenes in films created by the Italian director Michelangelo Antonioni, scenes that seem to the viewer to have been prolonged to the point of anguish or tedium. But afterward, when one leaves the theater, he realizes that he has retained an intensely clear and a powerfully lasting memory of the scenes that have been so prolonged. A deep and enduring impression of the nature of the young woman named Melanctha is the result in Gertrude Stein's work of a similar application to style and structure alike of concentrated duration and insistent repetition.

In most of Gertrude Stein's work, the adaptation of prose style to serial production results in a fusion of style and structure. This is apparent in *The Making of Americans,* a novel that represents an exhaustive effort literally to "make" the portraits of two typical American bourgeois families, the Dehnings and the Herslands and their children, as well as those of various governesses and sewing women who at various periods worked for the Hersland family. The technique of "making" the portraits is avowedly cinematographic: "I was doing what the cinema was doing, I was making a continuous succession of the statement of what that person was until I had not many things but one thing." [26] As in "Melanctha," the resultant circular structure depends upon that style that is so typically Miss Stein's: it is characterized by a total absence of contractions; the nearly constant exclusive use of the present tense; a lack of internal punctuation; and the frequent use of sentences containing three, four, and even five clauses of equal grammatical weight, linked only by commas. This style derives its effect from repetition. Indeed, repetition is the subject as well as the method of *The Making of Americans:*

> Repeating then is always coming out of every one, always in the repeating of every one and coming out of them there is a little changing. There is always then repeating in all the millions of each kind of men and women, there is repeating then in all of them of each kind of them but in every one of each kind of them the repeating is a little changing. Each one has in him his own history inside him, it is in him in his own repeating, in his way of having repeating come out from him, every one then has the history in him, sometime then there will be a history of every one; each one has in her own history inside her, it is in her own repeating in her way of having repeating come out from her, every one then has the history in her, sometime then there will be a history of every one. Sometime then there will be a history of every kind of them every kind of men and women with every way there ever was or is or will be repeating of each kind of them.[27]

This passage is typical of imitated cinematic "insistence" as it is found in *The Making of Americans.* Miss Stein intended that this book convey a sense of movement, for she felt that constant movement is of the essence of the American life and character. Repetition and insistence are not identical. Miss Stein explains that when she was seventeen and studying with William James, she "first really realized the inevitable repetition in human expression that was not repetition but insistence." She explains that "No matter how often what happened had happened any time any one told anything there was no repetition. This is what William James calls the Will to Live. If not nobody would live." [28]

In Miss Stein's work, insistence at the grammatical and structural level constitutes an adaptation of cinema perspective. The perspective is the single one, consisting of shots that have been spliced together in a sequence to create the illusion of movement in present time. This unusual application of the perspective of the camera not only demonstrates what Roger Shattuck means by "classical juxtaposition," it also clarifies the difference between the ways in which V. I. Pudovkin and Sergei Eisenstein envisioned the montage principle as a mode of organizing the perspectives of the motion-picture camera. The manner in which Gertrude Stein invented a "style-structure" consisting of a great many joined sequential "shots" of the subject represents an adaptation to literature of Pudovkin's concept of montage as "splicing."

Examples of "romantic juxtaposition," of the sort of composition that arises from combinations of conflicting perspectives as developed by Sergei Eisenstein, are far more numerous than are those of the "classical" type. One sample of montage in prose has already been examined in the Newsreel reprinted from John Dos Passos' trilogy, *U.S.A.* Others may be found in almost any chapter of Alfred Döblin's book, *Berlin Alexanderplatz.* Here, in an essentially narrative passage, are combined a great variety of elements, concluding with a heavily "poetic" sentence employing alliteration and identical rhyme:

> The proprietor dries his hands on his blue apron. A green prospectus lies in front of the polished glasses, he pants heavily as he reads: Hand Assorted Come-Back Roast Coffee is unrivaled. People's Coffee (second quality and roast coffee); Pure Unground Bean Coffee, 2.29; Santos, guaranteed pure; first-class Santos Household Mixture, strong and economical; Van Campina's Strong Mixture, pure flavored; Mexico Mixture, exquisite, best value in Plantation coffee, 3.75; assortment of merchandise by railroad, 36 pounds minimum. A bee, a wasp, a bumblebee circles up there on the ceiling near the stovepipe, in winter a perfect miracle of nature. Its tribal companions, companions of its own species, sentiment, and gender are dead and gone or else not yet born; this is the Ice Age which the lonely bumblebee endures without knowing how it came about or why this particular bee. But that sunlight which spreads silently

over the table in front and on the floor, divided into two masses of light by the sign: Löwenbräu Patzenhofer, is age-old and makes all else seem perishable and unimportant, when you see it. It comes from over *x* miles away, it shot past the star *y*, the sun has been shining for millions of years, since long before Nebuchadnezzar, before Adam and Eve, before the ichthyosaurus, and now it shines into the little beer-shop through the window-pane, divided into two masses by a tin sign: Löwenbräu Patzenhofer, spreads out over the table and on the floor, imperceptibly gaining ground. It spreads over them, and they know it. It is winged, light, over-light, light-light, from heaven high I come to you.[29]

Nearly forty years after Döblin's novel was published in Germany, the Mexican author Carlos Fuentes may be observed creating his own prose collage, based, like those of Dos Passos and Döblin, on the principle of montage as an arrangement of elements in conflict:

> *In my mind there's no sorrow,*
> *Don't you know that it's so?*

the voices of the young men who like the painted figures of Luca Signorelli garb themselves with testicular elegance and, releasing the constructive aspects of their spirits of destruction, create around them a world as vast, rich, confused, free, ordered as a canvas by Uccello, as piously demonic as one by the Bosch who pays the price of admission to the rites of Satan. And you have read, Dragoness, and you, Isabel, know intuitively, that no one has clearer visions of God than those of the Devil. That is precisely why he stands so aloof from God; he is God's other face and like Him is a succession of contraries, a permanent fusion of antitheses:

> *What am I supposed to do?*
> *Give back your ring to me*
> *And I will set you free:*
> *Go with him* [30]

The meanings of such passages as these cited here from *Berlin Alexanderplatz* and *Change of Skin* are not in the words themselves. They are in the interstices among the phrases and sentences; they are in the various relationships among the elements of the work, and they must be actively sought by the reader if they are to be found. He must move quickly among the various elements in an attempt to supply relationships that are barely implied, and he must be willing to bring to the work the active responsiveness of all his senses. The artist hopes for a total reaction—intellectual, emotional, and sensual. The reader, if he wishes truly to enter into the experience of the book, must transfer to his apprehension of the novel the same high sensitivity and alertness that he has been accustomed to bring to the reading of poetry.

The affective significance of some of the novel's new perspectives, and their inseparability from structure, may be seen by briefly examining Sergei Eisenstein's idea of the "monistic ensemble," a convention of the Japanese Kabuki theater. The monistic ensemble is related to what is today called "mixed media" art; it means simply that, to arouse the desired emotional response in the spectator, the artist may employ a variety of sensory appeals in the same work, or composition. In a review of a performance by Kabuki players on tour in the USSR, Eisenstein describes the use of the monistic ensemble as he had witnessed it in a particular play.[31] A certain character is forced to abandon his castle and the happy life that is associated with it. First, a predominantly rhythmic music is played to indicate his increasing distance from the castle. Next, he is seen actually walking away from it; this is a literal spatial removal. Third, in a representation of the removal, the scenic flat behind the actor is changed. Fourth, a curtain is drawn between the actor and the flat. Finally, music is again employed to heighten the feeling of pain aroused by the actor's leaving his home and to bring to a close the entire action. The sadness that is associated with this action has been expressed in five different ways that embody five different uses of various media. Each of these different forms of expression of the same emotion also represents a different perspective—a different way of seeing the subject. In an art work that embodies multiple perspectives, there is always the possibility that some of the perspectives will consist of the media of some other art, or of approximations of such media.

The use of the monistic ensemble, or the mixed-media approach to expression, requires the demolition of habitual categories of thought. First, it is contrary to the predominantly Western notion that each of the arts makes its appeal to a particular sense through a particular medium. It demands that one think of the various media, with their respective powers, as constituting a large general stockpile of expressive possibilities. These various media are available, then, to any artist, who may choose the ones he wants and bring them freely and spontaneously into whatever combinations suit the expressive needs of his idea. As an example of what may happen when the conventional classifications are broken down, Eisenstein remarked upon the fact that among the "characters" of the Chinese theater is the Spirit of the Oyster. This mixing of the Spirit of the Oyster with human characters is analogous to André Gide's combination, in *The Counterfeiters*, of "realistic" characters with deliberately flat ones and with still another transported directly from life without disguise, Alfred Jarry. The artist who has in mind the freedom and the enlarged capacity for emotional expressiveness that are offered by the idea of the monistic ensemble may apply in a sequence or, if he prefers, simultaneously, all the modes of expression of the same idea which he is capable of mustering for the situation. As Eisenstein very carefully pointed out in his essay on this subject, in the application of the monistic ensemble, the various media are not used as accompaniments to the single basic medium of the art form but are regarded as *coordinate* powers, each of which may serve as a carrier for the emotion which is actually transferred from one medium to another.

The idea of the monistic ensemble has been introduced to provide an analogy that may clarify some of the uses of perspective in architectonic fiction. In a purely intellectual manner, it shows how a combination of perspectives brought into simultaneous play may expand the potential emotional expressiveness of a work. Novelists have been searching for years for ways to heighten and extend the purely affective powers of the novel. This was pointed out, for example, by Howard Mumford Jones when he included in a summary of the major problems confronting contemporary novelists the great difficulty of conveying nonverbal experiences in words.[32] The same problem has been alluded to in a different manner by Michel Butor. In an interview, he said: "More and more, I want to organize images and sounds with words. In this respect, moreover, one can regard the book as a small theatre." [33]

The problem is, how can the novelist, working with a medium whose immediate sensuous capacities are relatively limited compared to those of film, theater, painting, or music, invoke a procedure of expressive flexibility and power that is analogous to that of the monistic ensemble. The answer, thus far, seems to be that variations in the point of view from which the subject is seen offer the greatest possibilities for the attainment of this aspiration. But these changing points of view, perspectives, are of different types. Those that are made possible by experiments with narrative point of view are primarily intellectual in nature and are inevitably colored by the interpretation of the person whose point of view is recorded. The perspectives of the camera are more nearly sensuous by their nature, since they record the exteriors of the images upon which they are focused; beneath these sensuously rendered surfaces, however, are implications of the strongest intellectual sort. Finally, there exist those perspectives that the novelist may find by exploring the basic capacities of the printed word and of the book. In any case, when a wide range of perspectives *arising from different sources* is brought into play in a work, the result is comparable in procedural terms to the application in theater or film of the monistic ensemble: that is to say, of the particular concept of montage composition by means of conflict that was developed and again and again explained and defended by Sergei Eisenstein.

Notes

1. Monique Nathan, " 'Visualisation' et vision chez Virginia Woolf," *La Revue des Lettres Modernes*, V (1958), p. 271: "Refusant tout commentaire interprétif, il [the novel] ne doit pas donner à penser, mais à voir. Il découvre la réalité à la vitesse du regard, il multiplie les points de vue, il fait varier les apparences, il dévoile ce que personne ne voit, le dessous et le dessus, l'horizontal et le vertical, le dedans et le dehors, le lointain comme étant près, le proche comme étant loin; il accroît en un mot de toutes les variations d'incidence et de distance le champ visuel limité de l'homme et, ce faisant, accroît sa connaissance du réel."

2. Jean Duvignaud, "Dialogue ininterrompu," *La Revue des Lettres Modernes*, V (1958), pp. 153–54: "Il existe des hommes qui serrent les poings devant l'escalier filmé par Eisenstein dans le *Cuirassé Potemkine*, parce qu'ils se demandent par quels moyens un art de prose peut obtenir une efficacité semblable avec ses propres moyens d'écriture en prose. Ces gens sont des romanciers."

3. Two excellent discussions of the respective powers and limitations of the two media are Michel Mourlet's "Cinéma contre roman" and Georges-Albert Astre's "Les deux langages." Both may be found in *La Revue des Lettres Modernes*, V (1958).

4. Cited by George Bluestone, *Novels into Film* (Berkeley, California, 1961), p. 57.

5. Astre, p. 143: "Le film est nécessairement un *continuel présent* . . . il confère au passé (voire au futur) la même authenticité qu'à l'instant actuel."

6. John Dos Passos, "Nineteen nineteen," *U.S.A.* (New York, 1930), pp. 295–96.

7. Dos Passos, pp. 296–97.

8. Bluestone, p. 26.

9. The linking of the names of Robbe-Grillet and Ponge in this context ought not to be taken as an indication of their theoretical agreement about "things" and their treatment in literature. While J. Robert Loy searches (in an article called " 'Things' in Recent French Literature," *PMLA* 71, March, 1956) for the common ground between them, Robbe-Grillet himself makes an icy attack on Ponge in his very important statement, "Nature, humanisme, tragédie." The distinction matters insofar as it serves to clarify Robbe-Grillet's intentions; he wishes specifically to dehumanize objects, and he charges that Ponge's attempts to identify with them ("de penser 'avec les choses' et non pas *sur* elles") imply a denial of the integrity of objects: "To assert that he [Ponge] speaks *for* things, *with* them, in their *heart*, comes down, under these conditions, to denying their reality, their opaque presence. . . ." ("Affirmer qu'il parle *pour* les choses, *avec* elles, dans leur *coeur*, revient dans ces conditions à nier leur réalité, leur présence opaque . . . [p. 62]").

"Nature, humanisme, tragédie," *Pour un nouveau roman* (Paris, 1963), p. 62. "Nature, Humanism, Tragedy," *For a New Novel,* translated by Richard Howard (New York, 1965), pp. 68, 69. Michel Butor has also published his defense of *chosisme:* "Philosophie de l'ameublement," *Répertoire,* II (Paris, 1963), pp. 51–60.

10. Alain Robbe-Grillet, "Nature, humanisme, tragédie," p. 63.

11. *Loc. cit.,* p. 72. French original, p. 65: "Enregistrer la distance entre l'objet et moi, et les distances propres de l'objet (ses distances *extéri-eures,* c'est-à-dire ses mesures), et les distances des objets entre eux, et insister encore sur le fait que ce sont *seulement des distances* (et non pas des déchirements), cela revient à établir que les choses sont là et qu'elles ne sont rien d'autre que des choses, chacune limitée a soi. Le problème n'est plus de choisir entre un accord heureux et une solidarité malheureuse. Il y a désormais refus de *toute* complicité."

12. *Two Novels by Alain Robbe-Grillet: (Jealousy) and (In the Labyrinth),* translated by Richard Howard (New York, 1965), pp. 152–53. *Dans le labyrinthe* (Paris, 1959), pp. 28–29: "Le contraste entre les trois soldats et la foule est encore accentué par une netteté de lignes, une précision, une minutie beaucoup plus marquées que pour les personnages placés sur le même plan. L'artiste les a représentés avec autant de soin dans le détail et presque autant de force dans le tracé que s'ils avaient été assis sur le devant de la scène. Mais la composition est si touffue que cela ne se remarque pas au premier abord. Le visage qui se présente de face, en particulier, a été fignolé d'une façon qui semble sans rapport avec le peu de sentiment dont il était chargé. Aucune pensée ne s'y devine. C'est seulement un visage fatigué, plutôt maigre, encore amaigri par une barbe qui n'a pas été rasée depuis plusieurs jours. Cette maigreur, ces ombres qui accusent les traits, sans pour cela mettre en relief la moindre particularité notable, font cependant ressortir l'éclat des yeux largement ouverts.
"La capote militaire est boutonnée jusqu'au col, où se trouve inscrit le numéro matricule, de chaque côté, sur un losange d'étoffe rapporté. Le calot est posé droit sur le crâne, dont il cache entièrement les cheveux, coupés très ras comme on peut en juger d'après les tempes. L'homme est assis, raide, les main posées à plat sur la table que recouvre une toile cirée à carreaux blancs et rouges."

13. *In the Labyrinth,* p. 153. *Dans le labyrinthe,* pp. 29–30: "Le soldat, les yeux grands ouverts, continue de fixer la pénombre devant soi, à quelques mètres devant soi, là où se dresse l'enfant, immobile et rigide lui aussi, debout, les bras le long du corps. Mais c'est comme si le soldat ne voyait pas l'enfant—ni l'enfant ni rien d'autre. Il a l'air de s'être endormi de fatigue, assis contre la table, les yeux grands ouverts.
"C'est l'enfant qui prononce les premières paroles. Il dit: 'Tu dors?' Il a parlé très bas, comme. . . ."

14. *In the Labyrinth,* p. 201. *Dans le labyrinthe,* p. 108: "Le soldat s'est allongé sur sa paillasse, tout habillé, ayant seulement quitté ses grosses chaussures, qu'il, a placées sous le lit à côté des bandes molletières. Il s'est enroulé dans les deux couvertures, par-dessus la capote dont il s'est contenté de déboutonner le col, trop épuisé pour faire un geste de plus.

Mais le principal est de se trouver à l'abri de la neige qui tombe et du vent.

"Le soldat, les yeux grands ouverts, continue de fixer la pénombre devant soi, à quelques mètres devant soi, là où se dresse l'enfant, immobile et rigide lui aussi, debout, les bras le long du corps. Mais c'est comme si le soldat ne voyait pas l'enfant—ni l'enfant ni rien d'autre."

15. Sergei Eisenstein, "The Cinematographic Principle and the Ideogram," *Film Form*, translated by Jay Leyda (New York, 1957), pp. 29–30.

16. See, for example, the articles by Mourlet and Astre already cited in this chapter.

17. Sergei Eisenstein, "A Dialectic Approach to Film Form," *Film Form*, p. 60.

18. Astre, p. 139.

19. For a full treatment of this idea, see Eisenstein's essays, "The Unexpected" and "The Cinematographic Principle and the Ideogram," *Film Form*.

20. Roger Shattuck, "The Art of Stillness," *The Banquet Years* (New York, 1961), p. 334.

21. Sergei Eisenstein, "The Cinematographic Principle and the Ideogram," *Film Form*, p. 37.

22. *Loc. cit.*, p. 38.

23. Shattuck, pp. 337, 338.

24. Gertrude Stein, "Portraits and Repetition," *Lectures in America* (New York, 1967), pp. 177, 176.

25. Gertrude Stein, *Composition as Explanation* (London, 1926), pp. 16–17.

26. Gertrude Stein, "Portraits and Repetition," pp. 176–77.

27. Gertrude Stein, *The Making of Americans* (New York, 1934), pp. 131–32.

28. Gertrude Stein, "Portraits and Repetition," pp. 168, 169.

29. Alfred Döblin, *Alexanderplatz Berlin*, translated by Eugene Jolas (New York, 1931), pp. 102–3. *Berlin Alexanderplatz* (Berlin, 1929), pp. 93–94: "Der Wirt trocknet sich die Hände an seiner blauen Schürze. Ein grüner Prospekt liegt vor den sauberen Gläsern, der Wirt schnauft tief, während er liest: Handverlesener Kehrwieder-Röstkaffee ist unerreicht! Leutekaffee (Fehlbohnen und Röstkaffee). Reiner ungemahlener Bohnenkaffee 2, 29, Santos garantiert rein, prima Santos haushaltmischung kräftig und sparsam im Gebrauch, Van Campinas Kraftmelange rein im Geschmack, Merito-Melange exquisit. . . . Eine Biene, eine Wespe, ein Brummer kreist oben an der Decke neben dem Ofenrohr, ein vollkommenes Naturwunder im Winter. Seine Stammesgenossen, Art-, Gesinnungs-und Gattungsgenoffen sind tot, schon tot oder noch nicht geboren; das ist die Eiszeit, die der einsame Brummer durchhält, und weiss nicht, wie es gekommen ist und warum grade er. Der Sonnenschein aber, der lautlos die vorderen Tische und den Fussboden belegt, in zwei lichte Massen geteilt von dem Schild: 'Löwenbräu Patzenhofer,' der ist uralt, und eigentlich wirkt alles vergänglich und bedeutungslos, wenn man ihn sieht. Er kommt über x Meilen her, am Stern y ist er vorbeieschossen, die Sonne scheint seit Fahrmillionen, lange vor Nebukadnezar, vor Adam und Eva, vor dem Ichthnosaurus, und jetzt scheint sie in das kleine Bierlokal durch das Fensterglas, wird von einem Blechschild:

'Löwenbraü Patzenhofer,' in zwei Massen geteilt, legt sich über die Tische und auf den Boden, rückt unmerklich vor. Er legt sich auf sie, und sie wissen es. Er ist beschwingt, leicht, überleicht, lichtleicht, vom Himmel hoch da komm ich her."

30. Carlos Fuentes, *Change of Skin*, translated by Sam Hileman (New York, 1967), pp. 235–36. *Cambio de piel* (Guaymas, Mexico, 1967), p. 237:

> "in my mind there's no sorrow,
> don't you know that it's so?

> y como los hombres de Luca Signorelli, se visten con el desenfado de una elegancia testicular y desatan los poderes constructivos de su ánimo de destrucción: crean, a su alrededor, un mundo tan vasto y rico y ordenadamente libre y confuso como una tela de Uccello y tan piadosamente demoníaco como los cuadros del Bosco que le paga el precio de admisión a Satanás; tu clásico dice, dragona, y tú lo entiendes sin saberlo, novillera, que el Demonio posee las más extensas visiones de Dios; por eso se mantiene tan alejado de la Divinidad: es el otro rostro del Santo y como él, es una sucesión inmediata de opuestos, una fusión permanente de antítesis,

> what am I supposed to do?
> give back your ring to me
> and I will set you free:
> go with him,"

31. See "The Unexpected," *Film Form*, pp. 18–27.
32. Cited by George Bluestone, *Novels into Film* (Berkeley, California, 1961), p. 46. Howard Mumford Jones's comment was made in a review of Leon Edel's *The Psychological Novel: 1900–1950*.
33. Michel Butor, "Tel Quel," *Répertoire*, II (Paris, 1963), p. 297: "J'ai de plus en plus envie d'organiser des images, des sons, avec les mots. A cet égard, d'ailleurs, on peut considérer le livre comme un petit 'théâtre.'"

There are a thousand natural combinations that have not yet been composed. Men will invent them and put them to a good purpose, composing with nature that supreme art, which is life. These new combinations—these new works of art—they are the art of life. This is called "progress."

—Guillaume Apollinaire [1]

6.

The Perspectives
Provided by
the Book Itself

In "L'Esprit nouveau et les poëtes" of 1918, Guillaume Apollinaire made a number of prophecies about the impact of the new science and technology on the arts. The statement quoted above contains a suggestion as to how the artist, who is confronted with an apparently fixed number of elements constituting a medium that is limited to certain types of expressive powers, might transcend this handicap and fulfill his desire to create something genuinely new. The magical procedure depends upon *combination.* The fact that the components of a work are not themselves new does not deprive it of its originality or of its naturalness, Apollinaire insists, provided that the *combination* is truly a new one. Although Apollinaire's formulation of the concept of mixing art elements in unprecedented ways may not have had any direct influence upon novelists, especially those in England, Germany, and the United States, his predictions as to the course that would be pursued during the following decades by the vast majority of modern poets and by a significant number of adventurous novelists have proved very accurate. However ancient and respected is the tradition of the mixed-media work in the Orient, in the West it is relatively new and somewhat revolutionary, since it necessitates the overthrow of classical ideals of unity at several levels in the process of artistic creation. Nonetheless, it has constituted one of major tendencies of modernist art from the early days of the century to the present.

It is easy to understand how *things* of most any sort can be combined into a perhaps infinite variety of patterns, once one has overcome traditional habits of thinking and has banished from his mind representational models. However, one must ask, what *sorts* of things can the novelist combine into new creations? The most obvious answer is: words. James Joyce made the ultimate advance in this direction in *Finnegans Wake*. This work, however brilliant and fascinating, has not set off a movement in the direction of free composition with the letters and syllables of the English language. One reason may be that *Finnegans Wake* does not sustain itself as *written* literature; it demands oral interpretation if its communicative powers are to be fully realized. Again, verbal inventiveness of the sort that is found in this "work" is impractical, since so few persons possess the capacity to recognize the meaning of the units that have been brought together to form the autonomous and unprecedented composition. The same comments might be made with reference to Gertrude Stein's book, *Tender Buttons*.

The most suggestive means by which the novelist can arrive at the new combinations he needs to express nonverbal experiences and the spatial and temporal subtleties of the age is to leave words themselves intact, so that they retain their recognizability, and to regard as the units that may be arranged freely without loss of coherence those larger units of composition: phrases, sentences, paragraphs, sequences of several pages, and chapters. Examples of how this may be done have already been presented. However, the technology of the book offers a number of additional possibilities for heightening and deepening the affective as well as the intellectual powers of words. Words and grammatical expressions do lend themselves to a great variety of types and intensities of expression, and these may be expanded still further by experimental typography and by other visual devices easily made possible by movable type.

In addition to those modes of changing perspectives and of finding new ones that have been presented in the preceding two chapters is a third that arises, paradoxically, from the book itself, from that same limited medium that imposes upon the novelist the very restrictions from which he is struggling to escape. The novelist in search of means of changing perspectives may plunder the resources of print: more accurately, of everything that can be printed: words, pictures, diagrams, abstract designs, and so on. He then combines these various elements into a composition of his own invention. There are four major approaches to the multiplication of perspectives through the exploitation of the resources of the book itself. Two consist very simply of bringing into the novel literary techniques and types of content that are traditionally assigned to other literary genres, to poetry and the essay in particular. The third approach is more characteristic of modern poetry than of prose and was very likely popularized by T. S. Eliot's immensely influential poem of 1922, *The Waste Land:* this is the practice of literary quotation, with or without citing sources. The fourth approach to perspective that is treated in this chapter is more nearly technological than are the other three: the use of photographs and illustrations; of different textures and colors of paper; and, most important, of variations in typography and the space presented by the page.

The "poetization" of the novel is scarcely a twentieth-century phenomenon, lyricism having constituted a minor strain in the development of the English novel from Lyly's *Euphues* and Sidney's *Arcadia* to *The Waves.* "Poetic" prose is characterized by frequent alliteration and assonance, the appearance of various forms of rhyme, deliberate rhythmic effects, a relatively large number of metaphors, and often by experimentation with syntax and grammar. Its frequent use is a common feature of modern experimental fiction.[2] In German literature, the precedent for poetic prose is easily located, for lyricism has been accepted as a legitimate aspect of fiction from its rise to the present day. In French literature, a precedent may be found in the Symbolist movement; in the literature of the United States, in such isolated "classics" as *Moby-Dick* and the short stories of Poe. James Joyce has had a great influence in making "respectable" poetic prose, both in his refinemtnt of the "epiphany," which usually achieves its revelation through symbolism, and in his labors to extend the suggestive—the nondenotative—powers of language in all of his works, but especially in *Finnegans Wake*. One of the most formidable achievements of lyricism in the novel is Hermann Broch's book, *The Death of Virgil* (*Der Tod des Vergil*), a long novel that is composed in a heavily ornamental rhythmic prose and that includes among its many pages, as does *The Sleepwalkers* (*Die Schlafwandler*), several extended passages of verse.[3]

Poetic prose is sometimes brought into fiction as a perspective. In some works it functions subliminally, its rhythms and sounds affecting the reader without his awareness, to intensify the particular perspective chosen by the author; this is the case, for example, in novels with closed structures in which it is of the utmost importance that the author establish and sustain his chosen "world" with a maximum power of concentrated energy. Novels with closed structures, for example, *Second Skin* and *Aurora*, depend for the very evocation of their world upon the powers of a heavily descriptive and metaphorical prose. This is no less true of *The Cannibal*, whose power arises in part from such grotesque images as this one:

> A farmhouse at a fork in the clay roads, demolished by artillery fire, lay half-covered in leaves and snow. There the Merchant, without thoughts of trade, dressed only in grey, still fat, had died on his first day at the front and was wedged, standing upright, between two beams, his face knocked backwards, angry, disturbed. In his open mouth there rested a large cocoon, protruding and white, which moved sometimes as if it were alive. The trousers, dropped about his ankles, were filled with rust and tufts of hair.[4]

Nightwood was praised for the marvels of its prose by no less an expert than T. S. Eliot. In his Introduction to the novel, he termed its language "Elizabethan."

In works with open structures, the inclusion of lyric passages does not intensify any single perspective, but serves instead, by means of contrast, to indicate relationships among the various perspectives included in the work. Usually, such relationships are essentially ironic, absurd, and—more rarely—tragic. Among the various modalities of feeling projected by *Berlin Alexanderplatz*—cynicism, sympathy, bitterness, mordancy, exaltation—is the ironic bleakness of the crude prose poem that follows the murder of Biberkopf's girlfriend Mieze:

> Now it starts: boom, zoom, without fife or drum. The trees sway right and left. Boom, zoom, boom. But they cannot keep in time. Just when the trees bend towards the left, boom it goes to the left again, and they snap and crack, grate and grind, burst, crackle, and thud down. Boom, mutters the storm, bend over to the left, hoo, hoo, oo, hoo, now back, it's passed, it's gone, it's just a question of watching for the proper moment. Woom, there it is back again, look out, boom, zoom, zoom those are bombs from airplanes, it wants to tear the wood down, to crush the whole wood.
>
> The trees howl and rock, there is a crackle, they break, there's a rattle, boom. Life's at stake, boom, zoom, the sun is gone, tottering weights, night, boom, zoom.
>
> I'm yourn come now, we'll soon be there, I'm yourn. Boom, zoom. . . .[5]

In German this passage possesses the rough beauty of a folk ballad, but its full effect cannot be felt without the contrast provided by its juxtaposition to passages of ridicule and mockery.

Not merely poetic prose but actual poems appear in some architectonic books. Julio Cortázar in *Hopscotch* (*Rayuela*) reprints a short poem by Octavio Paz, as does Carlos Fuentes in *Change of Skin* (*Cambio de piel*).[6] Maurice Fourré's *Tête-de-Nègre*, as part of its controlling structure of doubles, is composed partly in prose and partly in poetry. The poems contain compressed statements of what has already been presented in the preceding prose passages or prophecies of what is to come. Fourré's poems have an obvious visual appeal:

Basilic Affre
you
will slay
Tête-de-Nègre
Baron
de
Languidic
Basilic
you
will murder
your
tender father
the lace-manufacturer
and
your father
adjunctive and complementary
the
Notary
Basilic Affre
you
will assassinate
Jupiter
your
Master-God
and
future
father-in-law

with   with
the left   the right
hand   hand

On behalf of
the conspiracy
of the innkeeper [7]

Very similar to Fourré's poetic practice is that of Michel Butor in *Mobile: Study for a Representation of the United States (étude pour une représentation des États-Unis)*. The "poems" of *Mobile* are simple lists of juxtaposed words or phrases:

The sea.
　　　　　the waves.
the salt.
　　　　　the sand.
the foam.
　　　　　the seaweed.[8]

As poems, they are truly "mobile," for the reader assembles their elements for himself into a whole. He may at any time dismantle any single whole into its components and erect as many others as are possible within the numerical possibilities provided by the total number of elements.

Another architectonic work that is extremely close to poetry is Virginia Woolf's *The Waves*. Here, every literary element including structure has been subsumed by imagery. The characters speak, not dialogue, but poetry:

"The iron gates have rolled back," said Jinny. "Time's fangs have ceased their devouring. We have triumphed over the abysses of space, with rouge, with powder, with flimsy pocket-handkerchiefs." [9]

One critic of the novel, Wayne C. Booth, perceives Robbe-Grillet's *Jealousy* (*La Jalousie*) as an extended poem: "The effect of such a novel is of an extended dramatic monologue, an intense expression of one quality of mind and soul, deliberately not judged, deliberately left unplaced, isolated from the rest of human experience. It is, thus, less closely related to the traditional forms of fiction than to lyric poetry." [10]

It is not difficult to understand why poetry and its powers should be sought by certain experimental novelists. The problem that they face is how to counteract the natural tendency of the novel to consist of a series of flat surfaces arranged sequentially so as to body forth their subject, to endow it with dimension, with spatial substance, to vitalize and to animate it in the sense that sculpture may be said to be animated. Poetry provides an obvious resource for novelists who are trying to endow their vision with the illusion of plasticity. One approach to the fulfillment of this aspiration lies in the heightening of the subject by stronger and stronger appeals to the reader's senses: the inclusion of smells, of sounds, of tactile impressions, of musical effects, and of ever more and more detailed visualizations (for which imitations of camera techniques are excellent). Sensations help to make the novel incarnate; they give it the illusion of fleshliness and, at the same time, endow it with a soaring and transcendental aura.

A complementary approach to the enlargement of perspective through the exploitation of the powers of poetry is the use in the novel of the essay. One recognizes that the "intellectual" novel, like the "poetic" novel, is part of the tradition of the genre; essays are found, to be sure, in *Tom Jones,* in *War and Peace,* and in all the major novels of Dostoevski. Consequently, the architectonic novel very often includes among its perspectives various types of documents devoted to the examination and evaluation of ideas: notebooks, diaries, journals, works in progress, or passages from such documents. "Essayism" is perhaps the best word by which to designate the overt presence in architectonic novels of patently intellectual materials.

Essayism in the novel may take various forms. One unique example is the use of the Biographies in Dos Passos' *U.S.A.* Short and highly colloquial, the Biographies provide both a perspective from which the events of and just after World War I may be viewed in the context of American history and a subtle contrast which dramatizes the past and present ideals and achievements of America's social thinkers with a note of bitterness and resignation. The essay need not be written. It may take the form of a *petite dissertation* delivered orally by one character to another. In *Change of Skin,* the narrator occasionally addresses little talks to Elizabeth on such topics related to the novel's theme as witchcraft, concentration camps, or the cultural ambience of the 1930s. *Hopscotch,* too, is filled with small dissertations delivered by one or the other of the pseudointellectuals and artists who live in

Paris. The overt essayism of *The Man Without Qualities* (*Der Mann Ohne Eigenschaften*) is notorious, providing one of the central issues of controversy among critics who either adore or detest the work. At least a third of Musil's novel is given over to chapters that comprise Ulrich's speculations on various subjects, and Musil makes no attempt to integrate with the other more nearly narrative chapters these purely intellectual portions.

A contrast to Musil's procedure is that of Hermann Broch, who finds some means of justifying in aesthetic terms the presence in his novels of long passages of philosophical and sociological thought. *The Death of Virgil* demontrates one of Broch's solutions; the entire book *is* a sustained internal monologue devoted to the ethical problems of the artist in society. Action and plot come in from time to time only secondarily—to provide background for the drama within the mind of the great poet. In *The Sleepwalkers* Broch is displaying, as does Gide in *The Counterfeiters* (*Les Faux-Monnayeurs*), the process by which a novel comes into being in the many-faceted mind of a single individual. He has concealed the presence of his author-narrator, Bertrand Müller, until the closing pages of the trilogy's third volume; in this way, Broch has preserved the illusion that his is a traditionally narrated novel in which everything is reported by a hidden omniscient author. The presence of Müller as one of the characters serves to justify the inclusion of the long extended essay on the deterioration of values, "Zerfall der Werte." *The Sleepwalkers* provides a model for the aesthetically acceptable (namely the "explained") integration in the fiction of the author's own intellectual preoccupations.[11] The use of an artifice in the form of an intellectual- or artist-protagonist is typical of more traditional novels, whether or not they are considered "architectonic"; the author who follows this procedure wishes to retain the "frame" of the novel and to maintain the idea that it is an illusion of life. The more characteristically modernist alternative involves the abandonment of the pretense that the novelist engages in when he attributes his own thoughts and words to one of his characters, usually an artist or an intellectual. Instead, the novelist simply speaks for himself without any disguise. This occurs, for example, in such open-structured novels as *Change of Skin* and *The Counterfeiters* and in such closed-structured novels as *La Liberté ou l'amour!* and *Tête-de-Nègre*. The notion that the character, whoever he is, who voices the author's ideas possesses an autonomous being is an illusion in the first place. A small number of writers acknowledge this. Consequently, they arrange things so that their novels seem to explode into truth, revealing the overt presence of the author himself as the man who is responsible for everything that is in the book.

Perhaps the most interesting of intellectual perspectives to be found in architectonic novels are those many treatises on the art of the novel or on art in general that are frequently encountered in modern fiction. The reasons for the novelist's obvious interest in the aesthetics of the novel and especially for his desire to make the novel an account of how it came into being have been discussed in Chapter 4. In this context, it is sufficient to indicate that treatises on the artistic process are to be found, for example, in *The Counterfeiters,* both in Edouard's notebooks and in Gide's own *Journal* that was appended to the novel two years after its first publication; in Lawrence Durrell's *Alexandria Quartet* in the observations of the novelist Pursewarden; in *Hopscotch* in the form of the novelist Morelli's always complex statements of his desire to write an antinovel; and in *Change of Skin* in the narrator's open discussion of the question whether he has created his characters or has become their puppet. *In the Labyrinth (Dans le labyrinthe)* may be regarded as a symbolic reenactment of the processes of imagination caught in the midst of creation. The role of Bernard in *The Waves* approximates that of the novelist present in the work. In all these books, the incorporation of passages devoted to the exploration of the creative process constitutes the novel's interiorized comment on its own being. It is as though the novelist, frustrated in his attempts ever to envision himself with total objectivity, from a perspective outside himself, has discovered that the novel may achieve what the novelist may not: the novel may comprehend itself in a sense that is impossible for the human being.

The addition to the novel of the perspective of the intellectual or of the artist is the reverse of the poetic perspective. In

The Death of Virgil the two are, however, compared, contrasted, and thoroughly analyzed, as well as evaluated. If the poetic perspective expands the affective powers of the novel through language applied in a certain manner, the intellectual perspective expands its rational powers through a display of analytical classification. Both constitute approaches toward reality that, although never absent from the novel, have yet never been so nakedly present as in architectonic fiction where their presence is justified by the never-ending search for vistas from which still another aspect of reality may be revealed.

The third manner in which perspectives are found among the resources of printed language overlaps to some extent the two that have already been discussed. This is inevitable. Perhaps the richest mine for printable perspectives is the citation of what has already been printed: lines, paragraphs, or pages from other books; song lyrics; advertisements; newspaper headlines; letters; poems; musical notations; and allusions to well-known myths or to famous works of art. It is evident that such materials may be of an intellectual or an emotional nature: the variety of comments that may be made upon the subject of any book by means of cleverly selected, juxtaposed literary citations is immense, indeed, perhaps unlimited. The procedure of deriving perspectives from quotation deserves treatment in these pages: first, because it is so widespread that even the average reader is not surprised to find a song lyric or an advertising jingle dropped in among the pages of a bestseller; second, because it provides one of the clearest examples of how free combinations of elements may in fiction, as well as in collage or montage, determine the nature of structure.

The history of the novel and of the epic, one of its most important ancestors, provides a precedent for the reprinting of materials from the surrounding environment and especially for lists of various sorts. This is the ancient practice, so prevalent in the *Iliad,* for example, of the epic catalogue. Roland Barthes comments on this fact in an article describing the implications for the book *qua* book of Michel Butor's *Mobile:* "In this respect, *Mobile* is at the same time very new and very old: this great catalogue of America has for its distant ancestors those epic catalogues—gigantic enumerations with a purely denominative function—of ships, of regiments and of captains, which Homer and Aeschylus placed in their accounts to testify to the infinite compositional possibilities of the war and of its power." [12] For his part, Hugh Kenner finds the original suggestion of the possible uses of the list or the catalogue, in the invention of movable type, with its capacity to create such lists *ad infinitum*. He attributes the first novelistic exploitation of the list to Flaubert in *Bouvard et Péchuchet*.[13] Once more, one cannot fail to pay tribute to James Joyce for the brilliance with which he employed quotation in *Ulysses*, nor can one neglect to mention the great influence on novelists, as well as on poets, of T. S. Eliot and Ezra Pound, both of whom employed the device extensively.

A simple list may trigger an explosion of powerful feeling. This one appears in *Change of Skin:*

Belzec.
Majdanek.
Flossenburg.
Lodz.
Stutthof.
Ravensbrück.
Riga.
Monovice.
Piaski.
Mauthausen.
Trostinec.
Oranienburg.
Treblinka.
Auschwitz.
Bergen-Belsen.
Buchenwald.
Dachau.
Rasaika.
Terezin.[14]

In *Hopscotch* Julio Cortázar uses a list to group the names of artists who have been important in the formulation of Morelli's ideal of the antinovel:

MORELLI had been thinking about a list of acknowledgments which he never got around to including in his published works. It had several names: Jelly Roll Morton, Robert Musil, Daisetz Teitaro Suzuki, Raymond Roussel, Kurt Schwitters, Vieira da Silva, Akutagawa, Anton Webern, Greta Garbo, José Lezama Lima, Buñuel, Louis Armstrong, Borges, Michaux, Dino Buzzati, Max Ernst, Pevsner, Gilgamesh (?), Garcilaso, Arcimboldo, René Clair, Piero di Cosimo, Wallace Stevens, Isak Dinesen. The names of Rimbaud, Picasso, Chaplin, Alban Berg, and others had a very fine line drawn through them, as though they were too obvious to be mentioned.[15]

It is true that traditionally oriented novelists as well as experimenters employ literary quotation; the use of the letter is no doubt the oldest example of such usage in fiction. When "realists" do so, however, they generally wish to create a certain atmosphere or an effect of irony. By contrast, literary quotation in architectonic fiction often becomes an intrinsic aspect of the work's structure, deriving its power from the relationships that are implied by situations of juxtaposition. Any quotation necessarily incorporates a perspective on the subject of the book in which it is cited. Everything that is printed in any novel automatically carries with it a group of associations, and these associations are capable of considerable multiplication: first, when found in any second context replete with its own individual associations; second, when the total complex of associations is colored in some way by the author; third, when it is colored by the interpretation—to some degree necessarily subjective—of the reader; and, finally, when the total complex is further extended by the juxtaposition of more than two contrasting elements or conflicts. Any word or group of words embodies its own comment both upon itself and upon the adjacent words or phrases, even if they are simply listed next to each other as in Butor's "poems." It is clear that if such elements are arranged according to a controlling design of some sort, then they actually lose their individual identities as building blocks and become indistinguishable aspects of the total structure.

In *La Liberté ou l'amour!* Robert Desnos employs frequent references to an advertisement featuring Bébé Cadum—a hero of the capitalist mythology—to sustain a pervasive image of Paris that is at once eerily glamorous and absurd, oddly ancient and up to date, both savage and silly. This ambiguous aura is founded upon the juxtaposition of two cited passages that seem, on the surface, to have nothing whatsoever to do with the Corsaire Sanglot's conquest of Louise Lame. This first is "1. Pater du faux messie." It is a ludicrous genealogy of Bébé Cadum that includes an account of a mock-epic battle fought with soapsuds and rubber tires. The second immediately follows the first; it is "Le Golgotha," a fanciful rewriting of the crucifixion of Christ. Together, these passages constitute the paradoxical essence of Desnos' book, whose themes combine sacrifice with heroic liberty in a mundane city setting that has been raised to the level of a "pop" art Olympus. Another structural adaptation of literary quotation may be found in Michel Leiris' *Aurora*. The novelist adroitly employs a whiskey advertisement as a pivotal point from which to make deft transitions in time and space and to suggest the merging identities of his male figures. The inclusion of several passages from Paracelsus extends the range of Leiris' book by providing a mystical perspective from which the reader is invited to view the ritualistic searches of *Aurora*'s various personages. Marc Saporta in *Composition No. 1* has reprinted on two of the novel's unbound pages the legal consequences of the two crimes ostensibly committed by his protagonist, X.

The considerable degree to which structure may be based upon the carefully planned and consistently maintained use of literary quotation may be seen by referring to a book that has already been discussed, *Pale Fire,* and by examining two others: Julio Cortázar's *Hopscotch* and Michel Butor's *Mobile*. All three of these works sustain themselves in the absence of narration. Although the first fifty-six chapters of *Hopscotch* do constitute a conventional narrative, this narrative is shattered and reconstructed in the second reading that includes the remaining ninety-nine "chapters." *Pale Fire* consists wholly of quotations: four pseudoliterary documents whose meaning lies in what is not printed. Like *The Counterfeiters, Hopscotch* is two books at least: a traditional one and a heterodox version of the former—a novel and an antinovel.

The first fifty-six chapters of Cortázar's novel tell an ordinary enough story. The remaining "expendable chapters," "Capítulos prescindibles," are all made up of quotations of various lengths and drawn from a wide variety of sources. There are, for example, lyrics from American jazz songs, or blues, an Associated Press account of an electric chair execution, a passage from Clarence Darrow's *Defense of Leopold and Loeb,* phrases and passages taken from Antonin Artaud, Witold Gombrowicz's *Ferdydurke,* from the texts of Zen Buddhism, from Meister Eckhart, Lawrence Ferlinghetti, Georges Bataille, Claude Lévi-Strauss, Giuseppe Ungaretti, Anaïs Nin, and Octavio Paz. There are allusions to *The Waves,* to "The Love Song of J. Alfred Prufrock," and to *Under the Volcano;* there is a list of cafés in cities all over Europe; a selection from the diary of Ivonne Guitry; a totally mad plan by one Ceferino for a world government designed along ultra-scientific lines; and there is an explanation by Alban Berg of how he composed his "Chamber Concerto for Violin, Piano and Three Wind Instruments." When these quotations are interspersed among the regular chapters, the structure of the book is necessarily altered (and in a most interesting way that is to be described in Chapter 9). One may indicate at this point that without the "expendable chapters," *Hopscotch* would be a fine, but scarcely a revolutionary, novel. The fact is that Cortázar has employed literary quotation to erect what actually amounts to a movable structure.

Notwithstanding Julio Cortázar's brilliant experiment, the most extreme and wholly consistent example of the use of quotation is to be found in Michel Butor's *Mobile.* Neither a novel nor a travel book, *Mobile* consists entirely of quotations; it is made up of "lists of names, of fragments from dreams, of captions, of tastes, of colors, or of simple names of places; the sum total depicts the constructibility of the new continent." [16] The verbal fragments that are the materials of *Mobile* are arranged into a variety of patterns differentiated by typographical variation and placement upon the page. The result is a free construction that appears to be capable of modification in space, depending upon the angle from which it is viewed. As Roland Barthes has said, the ensemble is not a description of the United States—its subject—but an imaginative representation of the subject.

It is easy to see the possible uses to which literary quotation may be put, especially when this procedure is regarded as a factor that is potentially capable of influencing structure. Furthermore, since the sources from which quotations may be taken are unlimited and are multiplying every day, and since the author is wholly free to organize them as he wishes, the ultimate inventive powers of reprinted materials are theoretically enormous. These are the most flexible and the richest, in terms of verbal associations, of the elements that may be combined, as Apollinaire suggested, to make fresh new compositions.

The fourth major technical resource of the book that is to be examined in this chapter as a mode of changing perspective is visualization: the use in the novel of illustrations, of drawings, of varied types of paper, of typographical variation, and of the placement of words on the page in terms of its spatial properties. Visualization has its suggestive source in the old-fashioned use of illustrations in the novels that were so often serialized in magazines during the nineteenth century. These illustrations simply helped readers "see" what they were being told. They were aids to the imagination. For a variety of reasons, today it is rare to find illustrations included in novels for adults. At the same time, the general striving to augment the expressive powers of the novel and the use of multiple perspectives as a means of doing so have led to some interesting attempts to develop the nonverbal, or purely visual, resources of the book. We have already seen how with the printing of the simple name of Freddy Lambert, Carlos Fuentes destroyed his readers' easy assumptions about the identity of his narrator and, consequently, threw into doubt and uncertainty the entire sense of secure reality about the nature of *Change of Skin.*

Other examples of visualization go back to the 1920s when experimentation in the novel was at its peak. The original edition of Dos Passos' *U.S.A.* was filled with line drawings. Gertrude Stein sometimes wrote her works on colored papers and used colored inks. Döblin's *Berlin Alexanderplatz* contains the reproduction of two pages of street signs, indicating all the diverse activities of the city. In his *Babylonische Wandrung* he included his own drawings. All of Anaïs Nin's books include art: photomontages, reproductions of engravings by Ian Hugo, of collages, and of art works by Jean Varda. In *La Liberté ou l'amour!* Desnos reprints the *calendrier* which bears the magical date of the rendezvous between the Corsaire Sanglot and Louise Lame. Among the most original uses of visual devices are the photographs that André Breton printed in *Nadja;* they buoy outward the magical aspects of the book and endow its mystery with a tangible, a verifiable dimension that achieves the "surreal" by wedding mystery and realistic detail. According to Sir Herbert Read, an icon is "a plastic symbol of the artist's inner sense of numinosity or mystery, or perhaps merely of the unknown dimensions of feeling and sensation." [17] He says that to create icons is the purpose of the great majority of modern sculptors. One might add that this ideal seems to attract a great many writers as well. Such visualizations as those presented here differ markedly from the conventional illustration, which usually serves to provide a picture of the characters and settings described in the text. It is just what its name implies—an "illustration"—and its purpose is to render more concrete visually materials that are descriptive in the first place. The architectonic use of visualization has a different purpose, one that is basically iconographic and is rooted in the power of the symbol to hold in concentrated form the essence of the object for which it stands. Desnos' *calendrier* holds fixed for the reader the ominous beauty of the appointment to which it alludes, both backward and forward in time. It is the same with Döblin's street signs; they embody in capsule form the elemental nature of Berlin, in which the activities of the mass life crowd out the individual with his private burdens and woes.

One of the most interesting aspects of visualization is the use of typographical variation to reinforce or to alter the meanings of words or to create relationships among passages printed in corresponding ways. This procedure is familiar to poetry, having appeared from time to time in English literature in poems ranging from the seventeenth century, by Richard Crashaw, to the twentieth, in a few works by the Welsh poet, Dylan Thomas. In French literature, Apollinaire's *Calligrammes* are probably the best-known examples of *figuration:* the arrangement of the words of a poem into a shape that echoes or contains its verbal content. However, the application of the principle of *figuration* to prose is rare, except for special effects.

Again, one goes back to the work of James Joyce for an early example of still another practice that has attracted numerous experimenters. In *Ulysses,* he employs newspaper headlines in heavy black type, italic type, and the typographical conventions which govern the printing of plays: the centering of the name of the speaker above the passage that records his actual words, while descriptions of the speaker's expression and manner are printed in italics within parentheses. *Finnegans Wake* offers a greater variety still of typographical devices, thus corroborating Huge Kenner's assertion that Joyce was among the first novelists to be aware of the possibilities inherent in the technological aspects of movable type. One finds in *Finnegans Wake* sets of parallel lines placed vertically on the page; various type faces, including a heavy and sustained use of italics; the use of old-fashioned glosses in both right- and left-hand margins; a crude line drawing; a geometric diagram; and occasional footnotes.

Although there has been no general tendency to develop the possibilities of typography as a means of endowing printed language with a visual dimension to complement its aural, intellectual, and emotional qualities, isolated instances of typographical variation do exist to show that a few novelists have been aware of its inherent and largely untapped powers. Again, there is the very suggestive example of the Newsreel and Camera Eye sections of *U.S.A.*, both of which derive their expressiveness as much from their position on the page and the type faces in which they appear as from the words of which they consist. In *Part Three: The Realist (1918) (1918 Huguenau, oder die Sachlichkeit)*, Hermann Broch has utilized different type faces and spatial arrangements, as well as unspaced periods, to give visual power to his demonstration of Stadtkommandant von Pasenow's madness:

Chapter XXXIII
(Leading Article in the *Kur-Trier Herald*
of 1st June 1918.)

THE TURNING-POINT IN THE DESTINY OF THE GERMAN PEOPLE
Reflections by
Town Commandant Major Joachim von Pasenow.

"Then the devil leaveth him, and, behold, angels came
and ministered unto him."—Matthew iv. ii.

Although the change in the editorial policy of this
paper is but a trifling occurrence compared with the mighty
event whose anniversary we may soon be seeing for the
fourth time, yet it seems to me that, as so often is the case,
we must here too regard the smaller event as a mirror of
the greater.
For we too and this paper of ours stand at a parting of
the ways, we too have the desire to take a new and better
path which will lead us nearer the truth, and we nurse the
faith that as far as it is permitted to human powers we
shall . . . .
. . . . [ellipsis is part of citation] . . . .
. . . .
. . . .
where is the devil whom we must drive out from amidst us,
where the angel whom we can call to our aid? [18]

A previously cited passage from Maurice Fourré's *Tête-de-Nègre*
shows how a simple type of poetry can actually serve as a verbal
icon when it receives an air of sanctity and mystery from the
strict cultivation of symmetry. Fourré's passages of verse are like
texts printed above an altar: simple yet stern, transparently clear
yet inexplicable, amusing yet awesome. This unusual quality
results from the way in which typography and spacing have been
coordinated to enhance the actual words used by the author.
Julio Cortázar has made a tentative attempt to employ visualization by means of typographical variation to heighten the de-
notative and connotative capacities of language. Chapter XXXIV
of *Hopscotch* is an exercise in simultaneity. Oliveira is reading

a novel that was left behind by his former mistress, and at the same time he is meditating on her reading tastes. A few lines will suffice to give the general idea:

> IN September of 1880, a few months after the demise of my
> AND the things she reads, a clumsy novel, in a cheap edition
> father, I decided to give up my business activities, transfer-
> besides, but you wonder how she can get interested in things
> ring them to another house in Jerez who standing was as
> like this. To think that she's spent hours on end reading
> taste-[19]

The effect on the reader is really not so great as it might have been. The idea is a good one, but the difficulty of reading seven pages printed as are the above lines undermines its potential effectiveness. C. D. B. Bryan, in a review of *Hopscotch* called "Cortázar's Masterpiece," [20] commented on the printing of this chapter in alternating lines. One feels that he is right in his view that this procedure would have worked well if the printer had used different type faces for the two sequences. But the idea, though imperfectly rendered, is captivating and is suggestive of the various effects that might be achieved by means of experimentation with typography.

This discussion of typographical variation was intended merely as an introduction to the topic. A thorough and sustained consideration of the idea has very far-reaching ramifications and profoundly affects the essential concept of the book—what it is and what it is capable of becoming. Thus far, only Michel Butor and Hugh Kenner seem to have displayed an awareness of how movable type and the spatial properties of the page may be exploited on the behalf of the evolution of the book into a new and different medium. But this speculation upon the nature of the book as it has been almost imperceptibly changing during the past forty or fifty years is the subject of Chapter 7, and it is there that the rather extensive suggestions of Michel Butor will be presented.

These brief paragraphs on the visual qualities of typographical variation bring to an end this extended discussion of the perspectives of architectonic fiction. In itself, a perspective is simply the standpoint from which any object of reality, or any thought, is regarded. But since the technology of the century has made possible the nonhuman or "objective" perspectives of the still and the motion-picture camera, and since the resources of movable type and of the book itself make available still other types of perspectives, the modern novelist has at his command a far greater choice of ways in which to "see" his subject than had the novelist of the past. If he is a realist, he will make an attempt to perceive and to render his subject as completely as possible, that is, from a variety of points of view either simultaneously focused or arranged along a moving spectrum. The choices that he makes in terms of perspective influence and sometimes even determine the structure of the work that will result from whatever arrangement of perspectives he decides upon. Construction in architectonic fiction becomes the arrangement of repeated versions of the same perspective or of different perspectives into a structure that inevitably approximates a plastic concept of one sort or another. The process of organizing various perspectives into structures provides the subject of Part III.

Notes

1. Guillaume Apollinaire, "L'Esprit nouveau et les poëtes," *Mercure de France* (December 1, 1918), p. 16: "Il y a mille et mille combinaisons naturelles qui n'ont jamais été composées. Ils les imaginent et les mènent à bien, composant ainsi avec la nature cet art suprême qu'est la vie. Ce sont ces nouvelles combinaisons, ces nouvelles oeuvres de l'art de vie, que l'on appelle le progrès."
2. See Ralph Freedman, *The Lyrical Novel: Studies in Hermann Hesse, André Gide and Virginia Woolf* (Princeton, 1963), and Walter H. Sokel, *The Writer in Extremis: Expressionism in Twentieth-Century German Literature* (New York, 1964).
3. Waldo Frank's *New Republic* review of *The Death of Virgil* was called "The Novel as Poem" (August 20, 1945), pp. 226–28.
4. John Hawkes, *The Cannibal* (New York, 1962), p. 94.
5. Alfred Döblin, *Alexanderplatz Berlin* (New York, 1931), pp. 491–92.

Berlin Alexanderplatz (Berlin, 1929), p. 408: "Wumm macht der Sturm, nach links musst du. Huhhuah, uu, huh, zurück, das ist vorbei, er ist weg, man muss nur den rechten Moment abpassen. Wumm, da kommt er wieder, Achtung, wumm, wumm, wumm, das sind Fliegerbomben, er will den Wald abreissen, er will den ganzen Wald erdrücken.

Die Bäume heulen und schaukeln sich, es prasselt, sie brechen, es knakkert, wumm, es geht ans Leben, wumm, wumm, die Sonne ist weg, stürzende Gewichte, Nacht, wumm wumm.

Ich bin deine, komm doch, wir sind bald da, ich bin deine. Wumm wumm."

6. *Hopscotch* (New York, 1966), p. 437. *Rayuela* (Buenos Aires, 1963), p. 618. *Change of Skin* (New York, 1967), p. 370. *Cambio de piel* (Guaymas, Mexico, 1967), p. 365.

7. Maurice Fourré, *Tête-de-Nègre* (Paris, 1960), pp. 166–67:

BASILIC AFFRE
tu
tueras
Tête-de-Nègre
Baron
de
Languidic
BASILIC
tu
feras mourir
ton
TENDRE PERE
de
L'Industrie Passementière
et
ton Père
Adjonctif et Complémentaire
le
NOTAIRE
BASILIC AFFRE
tu
assassineras
JUPITER
ton
MAITRE-DIEU
et
futur
BEAU-PERE

de	de
la main	la main
DROITE	GAUCHE

sur
conjuration
HOTELIERE

8. Michel Butor, *Mobile: Study for a Representation of the United States,* translated by Richard Howard (New York, 1963), p. 16. *Mobile: étude pour une représentation des États-Unis* (Paris, 1962), p. 16:

La mer,

      les vagues,

le sel,

      le sable,

l'écume,

      les algues.

9. Virginia Woolf, *The Waves* (New York, 1931), p. 228.
10. Wayne C. Booth, *The Rhetoric of Fiction* (Chicago, 1961), p. 63.
11. For a discussion of the problem of intellectual materials in the novel, see Wayne C. Booth's remarks on *Mist (Niebla)* and *Remembrance of Things Past (A la recherche du temps perdu)*, *The Rhetoric of Fiction*, pp. 289–92.
12. Roland Barthes, "Littérature et discontinu," *Critique* (October, 1962), p. 829: "Et ici . . . *Mobile* est à la fois très neuf et très ancien: ce grand catalogue de l'Amérique a pour ancêtres lointains ces catalogues épiques, énumérations gigantesques et purement dénominatives, de vaisseaux, de régiments et de capitaines, qu'Homère et Eschyle ont disposées dans leur récit aux fins de témoigner de l'infinie 'compossibilité' de la guerre et de la puissance."
13. See Hugh Kenner, *Flaubert, Joyce and Beckett: The Stoic Comedians* (Boston, 1962).
14. Carlos Fuentes, *Change of Skin* (New York, 1967), pp. 282–83. *Cambio de piel* (Guaymas, Mexico, 1967), pp. 280–81.
15. Julio Cortázar, *Hopscotch* (New York, 1966), p. 302. *Rayuela* (Buenos Aires, 1963), p. 412: "Morelli había pensado una lista de acknowledgments que nunca llegó a incorporar a su obra publicada. Dejó varios nombres: Jelly Roll Morton, Robert Musil, Dasetz Teitaro Suzuki, Raymond Roussel, Kurt Schwitters, Vieira da Silva, Akutagawa, Anton Webern, Greta Garbo, José Lezama Lima, Buñuel, Louis Armstrong, Borges, Michaux, Dino Buzzati, Max Ernst, Pevsner, Gilgamesh (?), Garcilaso, Arcimboldo, René Clair, Piero di Cosimo, Wallace Stevens, Izak Dinesen. Los nombres de Rimbaud, Picasso, Chaplin, Alban Berg y otros habían sido tachados con un trazo muy fino, como di fueran demasiado obvios para citarlos."
16. Roland Barthes, "Littérature et discontinu," pp. 828–29: "Enumérations nominales, des fragments oniriques, des légendes, des saveurs, des couleurs, ou de simples bruits toponymiques, dont l'ensemble *représente* cette compossibilité du nouveau continent."
17. Herbert Read, *A Concise History of Modern Sculpture* (New York, 1966), p. 212.
18. Hermann Broch, *Part Three: The Realist (1918), The Sleepwalkers* (New York, 1947), pp. 418–19. *Die Schlafwandler, 1918 Huguenau, oder die Sachlichkeit* (Munich, 1932), pp. 134–35:

"DES DEUTSCHEN VOLKES SCHICKSALSWENDE
      Betrachtungen von
Stadtkommandant Major Joachim v. Pasenow
      Dann verliess ihn der Teufel
      und sieh, die Engel traten hinzu
      und dienten ihm.
          Math. 4/11.

Wenn auch der Wechsel in der Leitung dieser Zeitung nur ein geringeres Ereignis ist neben dem gewaltigen, dessen Jahrestag wir nun in Bälde zum vierten Male werden begehen können, so dünkt mich, dass, wie so oft, wir auch hier die kleinere Begebenheit als Spiegel des grösseren Geschehens zu betrachten hätten. Denn stehen wir auch mit unserer Zeitung an einem Wendepunkt und haben wir auch die Absicht, einen neuen und besseren Weg einzuschlagen, der uns näher zur Wahrheit führen soll, haben wir auch die Zuversicht, dass uns dies, soweit menschliche Kraft zu ··

··

···
wo ist der Teufel, den es aus der Welt zu jagen gilt, wo die Engel, die wir zur Hilfe herbeirufen wollen?"

19. Julio Cortázar, *Hopscotch*, p. 167. *Rayuela*, p. 227:
     En setiembre del 80, pocos meses después del fallecimiento
     Y las cosas que lee, una novela, mal escrita, para colmo
de mi padre, resolvi apartarme de los negocios, cediéndolos
una edición infecta, uno se pregunta cómo puede interesarle
a otra casa extractora de Jerez tan acreditada como la mía;
algo así. Pensar que se ha pasado horas enteras devorando
20. C. D. B. Bryan, "Cortázar's Masterpiece," *The New Republic* (April 23, 1966), pp. 19–23.

Part III
The Spatialization
of Time

In analyzing the spatial and temporal capacities of the film, the art historian Arnold Hauser restated and demonstrated V. I. Pudovkin's belief that the film is not shot, but is built up, or constructed, by means of the process of editing—montage— which endows it with a time and a space entirely its own. Hauser's discussion, "Space and Time in the Film" ("Raum und Zeit im Film"), contains a careful analysis of the way in which this temporal and spatial freedom is achieved. When events in time are spatially organized according to the techniques of juxtaposition that are employed in montage, they lose both their inevitable, sequential nature and their quality of irreversibility. They may, if the film-maker desires it, take on the appearance of simultaneity. "It is the simultaneous nearness and remoteness of things—their nearness to one another in time and their distance from one another in space—that constitutes the spatiotemporal element, that two-dimensionality of time, which is the real medium of the film and the basic category of its world-picture." [1]

Arnold Hauser briefly, and Joseph Frank, more extensively, have shown how novelists have tried to make the novel reflect the spatial-temporal fusion that occurs naturally in the film because of its technological nature but that does not occur naturally in the book because of its apparent nature as an irreversibly linear, sequential medium. Both Hauser and Frank come to the same conclusion: discontinuity and juxtaposition constitute the novelist's most effective approach to the destruction of linear chronology and to the reconstruction of events into spatial constructs. Writing of books by Proust, Joyce, Dos Passos, and Virginia Woolf, Arnold Hauser has observed: "The boundaries of space and time vanish in this endless and boundless stream of interrelations: all this corresponds exactly to that mixture of space and time in which the film moves." [2]

Joseph Frank has described how the spatialization of time occurs in literature, attributing the first notable example of the phenomenon to the famous fair scene of *Madame Bovary:* "For the duration of the scene, at least, the time-flow of the narrative is halted: attention is fixed on the interplay of relationships within the limited time-area. These relationships are juxtaposed independently of the progress of the narrative; and the full significance of the scene is given only by the reflexive relations among the units of meaning." [3] When an event in time is thus halted for an exploration or exposure of its elements, it has been spatialized.

At its simplest, the spatialization of time in the novel is the process of splintering the events that, in a traditional novel, would appear in a narrative sequence and of rearranging them so that past, present, and future actions are presented in reversed, or combined, patterns; when this is done, the events of the novel have been "spatialized," for the factor that constitutes their orientation to reality is the place *where* they occur. One of the most obvious effects to be achieved by means of this process is simultaneity: the representation of two or more actions in different places occurring at the same moment in time. In this way, a novelist may activate a great many characters in a great many situations that are intended to take place simultaneously, or he may dissolve the distinctions between past, present, and future as they are dissolved in dreams and in the stream-of-consciousness flow. It should be pointed out that not *all* novels that contain disjunct episodes and materials and that are organized according to juxtaposition necessarily mirror an attempt at simultaneity, or even at the spatialization of time. Some, like Hermann Broch's *The Innocent (Die Schuldlosen)* and Alfred Döblin's *Berlin Alexanderplatz,* combine conventional chronology with a structure based upon the shattering and recombining of the constituents. To clarify the difference between these works and those that *do* aim at space-time fusions, it is useful to quote Babette Deutsch's definition of cubist poetry, a definition that captures the purpose of fragmentation and reconstitution in the absence of any avowed experimentation with the dimensions of time and space. She says that cubist poetry "answers to Picasso's description of a painting as 'a sum of destructions,' with the emphasis upon 'sum'. Like a cubist canvas, such poetry breaks down the elements of an experience in order to create a new synthesis and so represent it more truly." [4]

By the multiplication of perspectives that is made possible by experimentation with narrative point of view, by the exploitation of the perspectives of the camera, and by the inclusion in the novel of all sorts of materials capable of being reproduced by printing techniques, the possible varieties of spatial organization are greatly expanded. The resultant variety is greater if the novelist chooses the open-structured novel dependent upon the combination of multiple perspectives. Nonetheless, the novel with a closed structure does display its own mode of spatializing time. The attitude of the single chosen perspective is repeated, or "insisted upon," again and again, but in different ways. With the repetition of this perspective, which might be termed a set of variations upon a theme, temporal relationships are absorbed by and fused with the novel's spatial sites. A few of the many works in which this occurs are *Nightwood, Aurora,* and *La Liberté ou l'amour!* Nonetheless, the existence of many perspectives in any work provides an increased number of elements to be splintered, or fragmented, and, consequently, greater opportunities for variety in their reconstruction.

The additional dimension of movement may be embodied

in certain architectonic structures, depending upon the method chosen by the author to fragment, or to make discontinuous, his materials. For novels erected upon the repetitions of the relationships implied by the single perspective, the suggested movement is nearly always circular, a result, inevitably, of the juxtaposition of homogeneous elements into a composition whose beginning and concluding points may not easily be discerned. This impression of movement is an insinuation, an almost imperceptible revolving motion that is as self-contained, as inward in the thrust of its suggested contacts as is the movement of a gyroscope. Movement of a very different sort is evoked by open-structured novels: it is irregular, jagged, unpredictable, full of unexpected intervals and sudden starts. Such movement will take its specific patterns from the arrangements of perspectives that underlie the structure of any specific work. In a very few special cases, the movement of an architectonic novel may be a *literal* movement. This occurs when the author has given the reader the freedom to arrange the various perspectives as he wishes by means of eliminating the traditionally numbered and bound pages of the novel or of destroying the sequence by some other means.

In all cases, however, architectonic structure is arrived at by means of a twofold process. First, the components of the work —its perspectives—are broken down into tiny parts that are the equivalents of the film's shots. Second, these components are re-organized to form the spatial construct desired by the novelist. The result may be a stable, or a mobile, structure. Both the novel of the closed and of the open structure are capable of expressing movement.

Thus far, nothing has been said about the ways in which constructs based upon organization by juxtaposition and including perspectives such as those of the movie camera, which could not have been known to the novelists of preceding centuries, affect the nature of the book as a physical medium. Surprisingly little has been written about this topic, although much has been conjectured about the comparative powers of the image and the word as media. Perhaps it has been only in the last decade that critics and philosophers of art have begun to be aware of the existence of a crisis with regard to the nature of the book and its capacity to survive as an expressive "envelope" in an age to which it seems so ill-suited for communicating spatial and temporal dimensions. With no pretense at comprehensiveness, the author presents in Chapter 7 a few different theories about the powers of the book. Chapters 8 and 9 deal with various types of architectonic structures insofar as they are conceived as being either stable or mobile. With or without their authors' awareness, each of these works to some degree constitutes by its very existence a challenge to the traditional idea of the book.

Notes

1. Arnold Hauser, "Space and Time in the Film," *The Social History of Art,* reprinted in *Film: A Montage of Theories,* edited by Richard Dyer MacCann (New York, 1966), p. 191.
2. Hauser, p. 192.
3. Joseph Frank, "Spatial Form in the Modern Novel," *Critiques and Essays in Modern Fiction: 1920–1951,* edited by John W. Aldridge (New York, 1952), p. 44.
4. Babette Deutsch, *Poetry Handbook: A Dictionary of Terms* (New York, 1957), p. 42.

7.

The Book as a Medium of Architectonic Structure

A great deal has been written during the past few years about the relative merits of the book and the newer electronic media: the tape recorder, the phonograph record, film, television, and now, sound-and-light shows. The topic is too complex to be resolved definitively by any but a combination of analytical approaches, including a consideration of economic, social, and cultural factors. Confronted with the impossibility of undertaking such an extensive and prolonged study, one might begin by agreeing with those critics who say that the book, challenged by the expressive capacities of the new media, cannot, if it wishes to remain vital, remain the same medium it was during preceding centuries. In evaluating the impact of the film on the novel, French critic Michel Mourlet has said: "Just as photography has, to a certain extent, released painting from the obligation of documentary resemblance and destroyed the art of the portrait, so the cinema—insofar as it concerns itself with the same object as the novel—must without doubt force the novel to take stock of its resources and to re-evaluate itself in terms of this new situation." [2] Challenged, the book as a medium for works of art must respond: it must defend itself or adapt to the conditions that are more swiftly and more easily met by the newer media.

In terms of those spatial and temporal exigencies that have all along provided the intellectual initiative for this study, the survival of the book as a major medium does, indeed, seem problematic. Technologically considered, the book reflects in its structure the sequential chronology of the past. Its numbered pages are held fast in a binding, and they clearly designate a movement from the past toward the future, beginning at a definite point, proceeding through quite a number of intermediary points, and terminating at a final, conclusive point. Does not such a structure naturally frustrate the desires of a novelist who wishes to shatter linear organization into quick, vivid, simultaneous instants of experience, related one to the other by their content, not by the order in which they took place? If the novelist wishes to evoke the illusion of a spatial entity that is imbued with tangibility in space, with dimension and bulk, will not the flatness of the book at every point counteract his ambition? Upon a first consideration, it seems that the book's inherent flatness and its inevitable suggestion of progression are ideally suited to the expression of subjects that require a leisurely development in time and are, consequently, inadequate for the creation of subjects that are rendered instead of developed, animated, called into vivid being with suggestions of simultaneity and plasticity. One must ask whether the book is capable of expressing the *fusion* of space and time, which endows both with meaning; and one must bear in mind the attendant proposition that nothing can be seen fully that is not seen either from a moving point of reference or from a great many perspectives simultaneously focused on the same object of observation and analysis. Does not the physical nature of the book impose a linear, sequential narrative order upon its contents?

Beginning with identical observations about the nature of

the book, persons who have given thought to its capacity for adaptation to the electronic age have arrived at exactly opposed conclusions. In an article in *The Listener,* Bernard Bergonzi has expressed his opinion that the novel will survive, but will no longer occupy a central position. Paying tribute to the inventive genius of Laurence Sterne and Ford Madox Ford, Bergonzi moves along the history of innovations that are relevant to the book qua book from those of Proust to those of Robbe-Grillet. He concludes by agreeing with Marshall McLuhan:

> As McLuhan has insisted, it is the new electronic media, such as radio, television, and the cinema, rather than the old print-based forms with their linear bias, which can most effectively convey the sense of simultaneity or recurrence that faithfully reproduces the nature of recollected experience.

> The end product of his art [the novelist's] will still be a small, hard, rectangular object, whose pages are bound along one edge into fixed covers, and numbered consecutively. No matter how revolutionary a novel's content may become, it is still conveyed by a vehicle that has not essentially changed since the days of Defoe or Richardson. One could, of course, have loose pages and allow the reader an active collaborative role in arranging them to suit himself— I believe this was actually done with one French novel— but I imagine the result would not be very popular with librarians.

Bernard Bergonzi concludes his article with a definitive statement of his position that includes a prediction about the future of the novel: "The novel cannot, in fact, escape from the limitations of lineality and chronology. Although the role of printed prose as a communications medium is certain to decline in the future, it will surely survive in some form or other; so, too, the novel will survive, I imagine, though in a less central position." [3]

A completely different view of the nature of the book is that held by Hugh Kenner. Although he does not address himself directly to the question of the novel's survival, he does reveal that his concept of the novel includes the idea that it has attracted subverters from the beginning and that the flexibility of movable type allows the novel to transcend its original function as a record of an oral account of one sort or another. Kenner's history of the gradual exploitation of the resources of the book by literary "comedians" is found in *Flaubert, Joyce and Beckett: The Stoic Comedians*. He begins by making an important distinction between the novel as a record of narration, or of speech, and the novel as a response to the technical capacities of the book as a medium. He says that "narrative implies that someone is talking. It is an art that unfolds its effects in time, like music." [4] Using Joyce's masterpiece as an example, Kenner argues:

> that the text of *Ulysses* is not organized in memory and unfolded in time [as is narration], but both organized and unfolded in what we may call *technological space:* on printed pages for which it was designed from the beginning. The reader explores its discontinuous surface at whatever pace he likes; he makes marginal notes; he turns back whenever he chooses to an earlier page, without destroying the continuity of something that does not press on, but will wait until he resumes. [5]

Kenner describes the ways in which Joyce—long before the experiments of today—tried "to impede the motions of linear narrative; *Ulysses* is as discontinuous a work as its author can manage; we read it page by page, and once we have got the hang of it we can profitably read pages in isolation. We keep learning to pick up clues, and note them in the margin." [6] Hugh Kenner's position rests upon the conviction that the *apparent* sequential nature of the book has always tempted ingenious and daring writers; he convincingly calls forth as evidence *The Tale of a Tub, Tristram Shandy,* and *Bouvard et Péchuchet;* Flaubert's book could not exist without the example provided by the encyclopedia. Kenner conceives of the book as a spatial phenomenon by its very essence, and as a medium whose spatial properties and capacities are basically different from the unrolling movement of narrative.

Hugh Kenner is not alone in regarding the book as a spatial phenomenon and, therefore, as well suited to its present-day role in the transformation of temporal into spatial relationships. It would be difficult to find a more unequivocal statement of belief in the novel's superiority over the phonograph, the tape recorder, the cinema, and television than the one that provides the epigraph to this chapter. Its author is Michel Butor, who has carefully worked out a list of suggestions showing exactly how the book's technological space may be filled; these are found in an extremely suggestive essay called "Le livre comme objet." Butor begins by asking the question that is beginning to be familiar: whether the book is obsolete, whether it *deserves* to enjoy continued existence. After comparing its strengths and weaknesses to those of the phonograph record, the tape recording, and the film, he comes to the conclusion that has already been cited: "The unique, but considerable advantage not only of the book but of all forms of writing over those means of direct registering [the phonograph, the television camera, the tape recorder, and the like] that are undeniably more accurate, is the simultaneous unfolding before our eyes of that which our ears are able to seize only sequentially." [7] In Butor's view, the book, for purposes of achieving the impression of simultaneity, is superior to electronic media. He continues his argument by defining the space of the book in the most concrete terms: "The book, such as we know it today, is the arrangement of the thread of discourse in a three-dimensional space according to two units of measurement: the length of the line and the height of the page. This arrangement has the advantage of giving the reader a great freedom of rearrangement with regard to the 'unrolling' of the text, a great mobility, which approximates to the maximum degree the simultaneous presentation of all the elements of the work." [8]

The examples provided by Butor to support this theory of the spatial capacities of the book are more interesting than is the theory. He is ingenious in finding methods of exploiting the surface of the page by means of unusual typography. One ought to notice that the relationships which Butor finds possible in the composition of the book very frequently resemble the specific types of montage conflicts that are described by Sergei Eisenstein in his essays and lectures. For example, Butor draws an analogy between the vertical and horizontal thrusts of the book and those of the musical staff. He proceeds to explain that for a composer the horizontal movement represents time: the vertical, the disposition of the various instruments he is employing: "Just as the novelist distributes the different individual stories in a solid that has been divided into various horizontal tiers, the vertical relations among the objects and events can be just as expressive as those between the flute and the violin." [9]

This type of opposition between the horizontal and the vertical planes seems to be similar to Eisenstein's idea of "contrapuntal" montage in which various sets of conflicts create corresponding sets of tensions simultaneously. Butor would like to see print moving across the page vertically and horizontally at the same time. He would like to abolish the conventional orientation of the reader to but one page at a time so as to allow for the left- and right-hand pages to be read as a unit and treated as such by the author and the typesetter. Like Hugh Kenner, Butor is fascinated by lists—an invention of movable type—and he points out how the simple contiguity of two words gives rise to a new entity; this is a fact that Eisenstein pointed out over and over again. Butor studies the lists in dictionaries, encyclopedias, and phone-books. He shows how the eye can be invited to move obliquely across the page by means of asterisks and up and down by foot-note notations: "The more that similar marks are numerous and near to one another, the more they compel my attention, the more they form a dynamic constellation against the background of the page. To two fundamental directional points—from left to right, from high to low—are drawn all those others which run from one to the other of these poles." [10] He discusses the various ways in which margins and marginal glosses may be used and suggests variations in the wording and printing of running titles. He concludes by stating: "One sees that the body of the page is capable of being encircled by a veritable surrounding wall of words, a wall that encloses it, illustrates it, and reinforces it." [11]

The next portion of "Le livre comme objet" contains ideas that go back to those of Mallarmé. Here Butor examines the different ways in which variations in printing can add to the "mobile" capacities of the book's space. He brings the concept of *figuration* up to date by relating it to some of the typographical "gimmicks" of comicbooks and advertisements. He urges the serious, experimental writer to appropriate for his own purposes every type of visualization or other practice that he comes upon in commercial printing: "The question is to take upon oneself all the existing commercial art and to elevate it to such a degree that it is able to compete with the works of former times." [12] He then discusses "la page dans la page," reminding one not only of montage organization, but also of the procedure of quotation that was discussed in Chapter 6. Butor assigns the power of this device to its capacity for introducing new tensions into the text. Finally, he briefly demonstrates how an inventive author might use the opposition between the left and right pages (montage, once more); how he might obliterate the conventional center margin and find diverse ways of arranging the running titles found at the tops of pages; and, finally, what uses might be made of visual devices or "appendices" such as maps and genealogies. As in all of his essays, Butor illustrates the ideas of "Le livre comme objet" by referring to the most respectable sources: in this case, the Bible; the *Iliad*; *Gargantua and Pantagruel*; Coleridge's "Rime of the Ancient Mariner"; and works by Balzac, William Faulkner, and Carlo Emilio Gadda. His conclusion is simply the statement that everything that can be done with the page can be done as well with the space of the entire book: "It is not only the body of the page that can be encircled by a wall; it is the body of the work itself. And all of those relationships which we have discovered at the level of the page can be rediscovered at the level of the book's volume.

"All this can be accomplished without changing the exterior appearance of the book or the manner in which it is produced. Certainly, too, it is easy to imagine even more variations [in the

spatial treatment of the book]." [13] Butor has justified his assertion in "Recherches sur la technique du roman" that novels are
"structures mobiles."

One sort of book that might result from an application of
Michel Butor's suggestions for spatial treatments of words is his
own *Mobile: Study for a Representation of the United States
(Mobile: étude pour une représentation des États-Unis).* Its structure is to be analyzed in Chapter 9. Here, it will be useful to
consider the theoretical and conceptual differences between
Butor's idea of a book, as exemplified in *Mobile,* and the traditional idea of a book. This was the crucial issue of Roland
Barthes's review of *Mobile,* "Littérature et discontinu," in which
he provided a very careful description of the traditional notion of
a book. Barthes perceived that the critical hostility with which
Mobile was received in France arose from the fact that the book,
by its nature, proposes at once an attack on the traditional book
and an idea of a new sort of book. He writes that *Mobile* "has
damaged the very concept of the book." [14] Roland Barthes continues to describe the book, as it is traditionally formulated, as
something that runs along in a long file, or a chain, drawing
together ideas which are developed and related one to another,
according to a general plan of organization. Details are secondary
and are left to take care of themselves, since they are but elabora-
tions upon the themes that are being subjected to development:

> What is it that traditional rhetoric dictates? That one must
> construct the book according to large groups and let the
> smaller divisions run along in a series. It pays tribute to the
> idea of a general controlling plan, or plane, and implies a
> scornful denial of the suggestion that the idea can be dis-
> tributed by any other means than paragraph indentation.
> This is why our entire art of writing is based upon the
> idea of development; an idea "is developed," and this de-
> velopment comprises a part of the plane; thus, in a way
> that is firmly grounded, the book is always composed of a
> small number of very well-developed ideas. [15]

But *Mobile* constitutes a denial of this idea of the book in which
"a small number of ideas are very well-developed."

In *Mobile*, there is no general over-all controlling plan of organization. Roland Barthes argues that "the general organization, or plan, is non-existent and detail has been raised to the level of structure. The ideas are not developed. They are distributed." [16] Roland Barthes observes further that in Butor's book, the elements, "cellules," are *combined* without undergoing any internal transformation: that the book's procedure of organization by means of repetition lacks any substantive value and has a strictly and exclusively *structural* function. He asserts that the sort of structural variation that is found in *Mobile* does not imply development, as in musical variation, but simply *variety*. This variety, in turn, results entirely from the manipulation of the book's elements into various combinations whose varying structures do not imply any transformation of the elements beyond their original identities: "Invariable cells are infinitely combined, without any internal transformation. The repetition of the elements manifestly has no psychological value, strictly a structural one. In *Mobile*, there is not variation, but simply variety, and this variety is of a purely combinative nature." [17]

These insights into the concept of the book proposed by Michel Butor, both in his theoretical pieces and in *Mobile*, possess implications of the widest possible significance for the novel. In the first place, the attempt of writers to make the novel a medium for the expression of a plastic structure, possessing dimension and bulk, and extending itself into space, must surely necessitate a shift in the way in which words are used by the novelist. The examples of architectonic structures to be presented in Chapters 8 and 9 will show that words in their various combinations—sentences, paragraphs, and chapters—can be regarded less as containers for meanings than as construction units to be built into the spatial form that is the goal of the novelist. In architectonic books, words bear the same relationship to the whole as do bricks, stones, steel rods, and concrete blocks to a building. This relationship is more accurately structural than expressive. The meaning of the book, then, is no longer *in* the words, but arises, as Sergei Eisenstein explained with reference to montage structure, from the tensions among the elements of the composition in their various juxtaposed arrangements. Within the frame of reference of the books under study, the problem of language becomes not only the difficulty of choosing the best words for what the writer wishes to express, but also how to compose the best combinations by which to evoke the illusion of the sort of structure that is desired.

The second important implication of Roland Barthes's observations in "Littérature et discontinu" concerns structure. The novelist's attempt to shatter the narrative line and, with it, the organization provided by conventional chronology as the essential structural reality of the novel, demands the development of new and compensatory structural conceptions. Upon examination of a wide range of structurally experimental works, one finds that books that incorporate more nearly spatial than temporal approaches to organization are of two types: stable constructs and mobile constructs.

For some novelists, like Marc Saporta and Julio Cortázar, the point is to make the novel express the multiple perspectives of the cubist painting simultaneously with the sensation of movement that was first stated as an ideal of modernist art by the originators of Futurism. The mobile construct demonstrates two types of illusory movement: an inward-directed, intense energy contained in the idea of a ceaseless circle; and a thrust into space that often suggests instantaneous and simultaneous activity. The stable construct is of two types, depending upon whether it has a closed or an open structure. In stable constructs, the area of space is represented as flat, not as three-dimensional, that is, as a surface upon which are located the moments that are recorded in the book. In such works, as in the paintings of *le douanier* Rousseau, space is experienced "as accumulation." [18] To put this idea another way, one might quote the words of Bernard Dort who, in writing of the work of Jean Cayrol, made this observation: "Time has disappeared. There remains this space, the world reduced to a surface which one must traverse." [19] In both stable and mobile constructs, however, time has been "spatialized," for it has been fused with and made to serve the spatial reality which assumes the dominant role as a unit of structural organization.

Notes

1. Michel Butor, "Le livre comme objet," *Répertoire*, II (Paris, 1963), pp. 104–5: "L'unique, mais considérable supériorité que possède non seulement le livre mais toute écriture sur les moyens d'enregistrement direct, incomparablement plus fidèles, c'est le déploiement simultané à nos yeux de ce que nos oreilles ne pourraient saisir que successivement."

2. Michel Mourlet, "Cinéma contre roman," *La Revue des Lettres Modernes*, V (1958), p. 155: "De même que la photographie a pour une certaine part éliminé de la peinture le souci de ressemblance anecdotique et ruiné l'art du portrait, de même le cinéma, en tant qu'il s'attache à un objet voisin de l'objet romanesque, doit-il sans doute obliger le roman à réviser ses valeurs et à se penser en fonction de cette situation nouvelle."

3. Bernard Bergonzi, "The New Novel and the Old Book," *The Listener* (March 23, 1967), pp. 391–92. All quotations are from these two pages. Note the apparent reference to *Composition No. 1* by Marc Saporta.

4. Hugh Kenner, *Flaubert, Joyce and Beckett: The Stoic Comedians* (Boston, 1962), p. 34.

5. Kenner, p. 35.

6. Kenner, p. 59.

7. Butor, pp. 104–5.

8. Butor, p. 107: "Le livre, tel que nous le connaissons aujourd'hui, c'est donc la disposition du fil du discours dans l'espace à trois dimensions selon un double module: longueur de la ligne, hauteur de la page, disposition qui a l'avantage de donner au lecteur une grande liberté de déplacement par rapport au 'déroulement' du texte, une grande mobilité, qui est ce qui se rapproche le plus d'une présentation simultanée de toutes les parties d'un ouvrage."

9. Michel Butor, "L'Espace du roman," *Répertoire*, II (Paris, 1963), p. 48: "De même le romancier peut disposer différentes histoires individuelles dans un solide divisé en étages . . . les relations verticales entre les différentes objets ou événements pouvant être aussi expressives que celles entre la flûte et le violon."

10. Michel Butor, "Le livre comme objet," *Répertoire*, II (Paris, 1963), pp. 115–16: "Plus les signes semblables sont nombreux et proches, plus ils vont forcer mon attention, former une constellation dynamique sur le fond de la page. Aux deux flèches fondamentales: de gauche à droite, de haut en bas, vont s'ajouter toutes celles qui vont courir d'un pôle a l'autre de ces reprises."

11. Butor, "Le livre comme objet," p. 117: "On voit que le corps de la page peut être encadré d'une véritable enceinte de mots, le protégeant, l'illustrant et le défendant."

12. Butor, "Le livre comme objet," p. 120: "Il s'agit d'assumer tout cet art populaire industriel actuel et de l'élever de telle sorte qu'il puisse rivaliser avec les oeuvres d'autrefois."

13. Butor, "Le livre comme objet," p. 123: "Ce n'est pas seulement le corps de la page qui peut être entouré d'une enceinte, c'est le corps de l'oeuvre, et toutes les fonctions que nous avons rencontrées à son niveau peuvent se retrouver à celui du volume.
    Tout ceci sans rien changer à son apparence extérieure, ni à son mode actuel de fabrication. Mais certes il est facile d'imaginer des variantes."
14. Roland Barthes, "Littérature et discontinu," *Critique* (October, 1962), p. 817: "a blessé . . . l'idée même du Livre."
15. Barthes, p. 820: "Que dit la rhétorique traditionnelle? Qu'il faut construire une oeuvre par grandes masses et laisser courir le détail: coup de chapeau au 'plan général,' négation dédaigneuse que l'idée puisse se morceler au delà de l'alinéa; c'est pourquoi tout notre art d'écrire est fondé sur la notion de *développement:* une idée 'se développe,' et ce développement fait une partie de plan; ainsi le livre est-il toujours composé d'une façon fort rassurante, *d'un petit nombre d'idées bien développées."*
16. Barthes, p. 821: "Dans *Mobile,* le 'plan général' est nul et le détail élevé au rang de structure; les idées ne sont pas 'dévelopées,' mais distribuées."
17. Barthes, p. 826: "Des cellules inaltérables sont infiniment combinées, sans qu'il y ait transformation interne des éléments.
    La répétition des éléments n'y a manifestement aucune valeur psychologique, mais seulement structurale.
    Dans *Mobile,* il n'y a pas variation, mais seulement variété, et cette variété est purement combinatoire."
18. This observation was made by Roger Shattuck, *The Banquet Years* (New York, 1961), p. 83.
19. Bernard Dort, "Sur l'espace," *Esprit* (July 8, 1958), p. 79: "Le temps a disparu: reste cet espace, le monde réduit à une surface, qu'il faut parcourir."

8.

Stable
Constructs

In building the stable construct, the novelist proceeds much
as Picasso says he did when he created cubist paintings. First, the
sequential nature of the materials, with their customary relationship to the Renaissance idea of perspective and their implication
of progressive movement from beginning, middle, through end,
must be destroyed. This destruction may be achieved either by
fragmentation or by distortion, that is, by the repression of the
expected emphases and by the exaggeration of those that are unexpected. The materials thus "destroyed" are next resurrected
and animated anew by means of their new positions in the over-all
composition of the work. The apparent freshness of the resultant
composition is, in part, an illusion, for it is unlikely that any new
elements have been included. The newness of architectonic novels,
like that of cubist paintings, is not essential but structural; it is
the result of the artist's desire to reveal hitherto unnoticed
aspects of the subject's reality. As Roland Barthes has written in

"L'Activité structuraliste": "The structuralist takes the real, de-composes it, then puts it back together again." [2]

This process might also be likened to *découpage et agence-ment,* the procedure by which collages are created. In Anaïs Nin's book *Collages,* the collage-maker Varda says, "I'm an artist. I'm only looking for fragments, remnants which I can co-ordinate in a new way." [3] "To cut apart and to re-assemble" is a twofold process. It must not be confused with the traditional method of writing a composition: the stating of an hypothesis and the de-velopment of its ramifications in terms of discursive logic. In architectonic fiction, construction maintains its literal meaning simply conceived as the act of building a structure from arrange-ments of different types of materials: bricks, steel, and concrete. In writing of Butor's book *Mobile,* Roland Barthes said with reference to the word "construction": "In this context, the banal term 'construction' recovers the idea of a design that is very precise and very different from the 'constructions' taught in school." [4] Julio Cortázar's Morelli, theoretician of the antinovel, writes in his notebook: " 'I think in a vague sort of way that the elements I am aiming for are a result of *composition.* The school-book chemistry point of view has been turned inside out. When composition has reached its extreme limit, the territory of the elemental opens up.' " [5] When applied to the architectonic novel, the terms "construction" and "composition" alike signify the second and conclusive action by which the final structure is achieved: the arrangement of perspectives into approximations of spatial entities, either representational or nonrepresentational, stable or mobile.

In a very real sense, the meanings of a novel constructed according to the architectonic procedure are not in the words. They are to be found, instead, in the relationships among the juxtaposed portions of the work, as is the final image or concept that is derived from the collision of elements in Eisenstein's idea of montage composition. The meanings may be said to lie among the interstices of the structure. Joseph Frank uses the phrase "reflexive reference" to explain this phenomenon. He discusses the parallel between the aesthetic procedures of modern poetry and those of the spatialized novel, arguing that "both can be

properly understood only when their units of meaning are ap-
prehended reflexively, in an instant of time." He concludes that
"the reader is forced to read *Ulysses* in exactly the same manner
as he reads modern poetry—continually fitting fragments together
and keeping allusions in mind until, by reflexive reference, he
can link them to their complements." [6] The meaning of an
architectonic novel resides in the relationships among its parts. In
this sense, the whole may be said, as in mathematics, to be
greater than the sum of the parts.

A simple yet revealing example of a stable construct is
Hermann Broch's novel, *The Innocent* (*Die Schuldlosen*). The
work is a "Novel in Eleven Parts" ("Roman in Elf Erzählungen").[7]
Its familiar theme is the immorality of individual nonengagement
in matters of social and ethical importance. This theme is embodied in a series of contrasts between a young Dutch businessman, Andreas, a relativist and opportunist who uses his philosophy to rationalize his ethical sloth; and Zacharias, a schoolteacher of rigid, inflexible, and sterile convictions, whose prejudices and stubbornness constitute just the opposite sort of social
immorality from that of Andreas.

Instead of development of its theme, *The Innocent* demonstrates the presentation of the theme in fifteen disjunct structural
components: a prologue; eleven short stories and three poems, or
Stimmen. The stories are arranged in cycles corresponding to
the decades 1912–1923–1933. The "Vor-Geschichten" contains two
stories: "Sailing with a Weak Breeze" ("Mit Schwacher Brise
Segeln") and "A Methodical Design" ("Methodisch Konstruiert").
The "Geschichten" itself consists of seven stories: "Forlorn Son"
("Verlorener Sohn"); "The Ballad of Imker" ("Ballade vom
Imker"); "The Tale of the Maiden Zerlina" ("Die Erzählung der
Magd Zerline"); "An Easy Parting" ("Eine Leichte Entäus-
chung"); "The Four Discourses of Instructor Zacharias" ("Die
Vier Reden des Studienrats Zacharias"); "The Ballad of the
Match-Maker" ("Ballade von der Kupplerin"); and "The 'Bought'
Mother" ("Erkaufte Mutter"). The "Nach-Geschichten" contains
these two tales: "The Stone Guest" ("Steinerner Gast") and
"Drifting Clouds" ("Vorüberziehende Wolke"). Each group is
introduced by a poem written in a tone that sums up the char-

acter of the decade. But all three movements in the cycle are unified, for each poem is in the *Stimmen* of the old beekeeper who provides the controlling mind and spirit of *The Innocent,* just as Bertrand Müller provides it in *The Sleepwalkers (Die Schlafwandler). The Innocent* itself is prefaced by "Parabel von der 'Stimme,' " a rabbinical story that alludes to the over-all theme and provides clues to the relationships between the stories in which Andreas appears and those in which he does not.

The identity of each of the fifteen constituent parts of *The Innocent* remains integral, self-enclosed, and undisturbed by the unity of the whole. As verified by the separate publication of the original five stories, each one is self-sustaining. At the same time, each gains dimension and complexity from its relationships to the other stories. By itself, the history of escapist Andreas is interesting, but it is neither original nor profound. Apart from their significance in the total context of his life, Andreas' entanglements with the novel's three major women characters might well seem cheap and sensational. But when Andreas' life is placed in juxtaposition with that of Zacharias—and their two lives are seen against the fulfilled and harmonious life of the old beekeeper —the composition has been enlarged and rounded out to provide, not just the presentation of a collection of lives, but a comprehensive image of a universal theme.

The Innocent demonstrates but one of the two stages of architectonic construction. The parts have not undergone fragmentation; they are coherent in their self-containment. But they have been reconstructed in a sense, for their existence in combination with one another both alters and extends their significance by virtue of the new relationships suggested by the arrangement of the final structure.

In *Berlin Alexanderplatz,* German literature provides a more complex example of the twofold process of construction that results in a stable construct. Although this novel is sometimes praised for its stylistic originality, its structure is actually its more interesting and more distinctly "modern" characteristic. *Berlin Alexanderplatz* may be compared to a massive collage; as a novel, it is an assemblage of diverse materials which include a typical Expressionist hero who is good-hearted, but none too bright and none too articulate, and a series of events that do constitute the "story" of Franz Biberkopf's struggle to survive, in every sense, on the streets of Berlin between the two world wars. Here is a list of the novel's other components, each of which contributes a special perspective on Franz and the period of his life that is represented in the novel: a large group of scarcely individuated characters that represent well-known social types; snapshotlike descriptions of street scenes and persons; lyrics from ballads, patriotic songs, and hymns; references to Old Testament tales and to Greek myths; quotations from advertisements, newspaper poems, mathematical formulas, and nursery rhymes; references to contemporary figures such as Erwin Piscator and Gustav Mahler; an occasional vignette such as the one describing the arrival in Berlin of a famous actress; a digression on German politics; passages of lyric prose wrought for their musical qualities; a group of line drawings portraying the various civic activities of Berlin; and chapter heads worded in the jauntily bitter tone that is usually associated with the plays of Bertolt Brecht. For example, one especially mordant chapter heading reads: "Hop, hop hop; the little horsie has to keep on galopping" ("Hopp hopp hopp, Pferdchen macht wieder galopp").

Although Alfred Döblin does not scramble the elements of the actual story of Franz's sufferings in Berlin, he *appears* to do so because he buries the separate movements of this story amidst a mass of printed materials, all of which provide perspectives upon its simple incidents. He may be said to have combined the narrative technique of the traditional novel with the montage organization of film. The result is that the traditional novel is partly concealed under the various elements whose use in the novel serves to approximate the complex organization of the city itself and that, at the same time, captures both the diversity and the monotony of any great city, whose varied surfaces point usually to the same reality of brutality.

The procedure employed by Alfred Döblin results in a structure that is nonlinear, chaotic, ragged, asymmetric; in short, perfect for the representation of a great city. The method is more effective than that used just one year later by John Dos Passos in *U.S.A.* Dos Passos, like Döblin, attempted a representation of a great *lieu*—its sights, sounds, smells, and its babble of voices. The manner in which he brought the perspectives of the camera and the historical perspective of the biography into this trilogy has been discussed in Chapter 5. However effective is its incorporation of various perspectives, *U.S.A.* remains essentially linear in its spatial organization. In *Berlin Alexanderplatz* there is no single fixed system according to which the various perspectives are arranged. Consequently, the ultimate impression is of a massive organic growth that actually occupies space, that has bulk, that extends its mass into the surrounding reality. But *U.S.A.*, despite the ingenuity of its conception, is still a linear creation, moving from one point to another in a straight line consisting of units whose parts are presented in an unvarying number, nature, and order. Dos Passos has shown his subject from many angles of vision, but these serve less to multiply and enrich its implications than to splinter over and over again the fragments of his grand design. The use of changing perspectives does not really *alter* the reader's vision of the subject, as it does in *Berlin Alexanderplatz;* instead, it *amplifies* this vision in breadth (as a wide-angle camera lens amplifies its subject) until the book achieves through mass accumulation of detail the dimensions of epic. Nevertheless, the alert reader quickly catches on to the sequence of narrative, Camera Eye, Newsreel, and Biography passages. And soon, easily able to predict when he will encounter each type of prose, he may sense a monotony, a tediousness, a structural flatness that detract from the work's power, a power that is partly a result of Dos Passos' structural creativity in applying what he observed from the cinema.

A much more complex example of the twofold structural procedure of fragmentation and reconstruction is found in Carlos Fuentes' novel, *Change of Skin* (*Cambio de piel*). Like *Berlin Alexanderplatz* and *U.S.A.*, *Change of Skin* is an assemblage of elements that have been combined into an extremely complicated composition. The temporal and spatial relationships of *Change of Skin* are far more comprehensive than are those of the two earlier novels and far more ambitious insofar as the book's structure posits within itself the possibility of freedom from the evident irreversibility of time.

At a first appraisal, *Change of Skin* appears to be divided into three parts: a conventional prologue, a body, and an epilogue. The rather short opening portion, "An Impossible Feast," is essentially introductory. In it are presented the four characters, the intensely present narrator who addresses them as "you," and a dramatized presentation of Cortes' conquest of Mexico. The conquest is counterpointed against the novel's present action in the Aztecs' sacred city of Cholula. Fuentes recounts Cortes' passages in the present tense and the ostensibly present action in the past tense, thus indicating that the past is quite as alive, perhaps more vivid and pulsating than is the present. Finally, these pages introduce the Monks (Los Monjes), the group of kids, hippies perhaps, who eventually become interchangeable with the four protagonists: Elizabeth, Javier, Isabel, and Franz.

The novel proper, the center portion, occupies pages 25 to 364. The elements of this part display discontinuity in structural terms and constitute violations of logic on several levels. The time is a night near Easter; the settings, two rooms in a shabby hotel in Cholula. Radiating around this center are various other spatial and temporal realities embodied in memories and daydreams. Three other "worlds," or spatial-temporal realities, are introduced in the guise of flashbacks to the childhoods of Elizabeth (located in a poor Jewish section of New York City), of Javier (situated in lower-middle-class Mexico City), and of Franz (evoking music-filled Prague before World War II). The characters change places, as the two women occasionally are being interrogated by the narrator, who gradually assumes the identity in these scenes of the two men. Another dimension of identity is added by virtue of the fact that Elizabeth and Franz are sometimes together, making love and exchanging confessions and dreams, while Isabel and Javier torment each other with ridicule, with accusations, and with perverse embraces. Finally, overlaid upon all of these relationships are others in the form of the perspectives that are suggested by reprinted passages from newspapers, tourist pamphlets, lists of various sorts, song lyrics, passages from Javier's notebook, a lenghty analysis of Brahms's *German Requiem,* and those short addresses that are delivered by the narrator to Elizabeth. From this apparent mess, as from life itself, emerge several themes: the failure of love, the difficulty of achieving creation, the universality of guilt, and the equally universal need for forgiveness. The multiple perspectives which Fuentes employs tend to establish the universality of these themes by placing them in a variety of contexts that are spatially—and therefore temporally—far from one another.

The book's concluding portion elevates the "action" to a transcendental plane. Its wild events tend to render time reversible. In the view of the narrator, Franz can be forgiven his role in the German army during World War II because his subsequent twenty years of decency constitute a hard-earned penance. In seeking to recover his youth and to escape his failures in art and in marriage in a relationship with Isabel, Javier finds in youth a judgment much more harsh than that of his wife, who is over forty. In a vision, Freddy Lambert gives Javier and Elizabeth back the love, youth, and hope of their days in Falaraki just after their marriage. Time *can* be turned back. One *can* change his skin. The structure of *Change of Skin* shows how the architectonic procedure of construction can be used to endow ordinary actions with metaphysical significance by condensing into all times and places the same message and by demonstrating that time can, after all, be made to roll backward.

The ornate texture and the mass of times and places spinning off from this one night in Cholula endow *Change of Skin* with an air of tremendous nervous activity that suggests motion. Nothing, it seems, is fixed. The characters have multiple identities. There is more than one version of every major action. The novel's ambitious open structure subsumes several traditional boundaries: that between past and present; that between one person's intimate secrets and another's knowing curiosity; those limitations of perception that separate from one another any individual's several identities; the line that is conventionally maintained between the work of art and life itself; the demarcations that supposedly exist between dreams and reality and fantasy and action; and, finally, the distinction between supernatural power and the mundane events of daily routine. The power of the supernatural explodes in the third part of *Change of Skin* and brings about "miracles." Still, in spite of the novel's power of internal combustion and its impression of nervous thrust and pulsating tension, it is a stable construct. The three parts of Fuentes' book are clearly not interchangeable, for the prologue and the epilogue definitely circumscribe the materials of the center portion—the novel per se—between historical and supernatural perspectives. Moreover, everything proceeds toward the third part: the exorcism. Full of tensions and of contradictions that suggest activity, *Change of Skin* is nonetheless a stable structure, essentially comparable to *Berlin Alexanderplatz.*

Another novel that is similarly deceptive, seeming upon first examination to be capable of motion, is Edoardo Sanguineti's *Capriccio italiano.* It is the fragmentation of the novel's substance into portions of only a few pages each that conveys the possibility that these fragments might be reorganized and rearranged into a considerable variety of patterns. Upon closer examination, however, one sees that any reorganization of Edoardo's dreams would have no effect whatsoever on their significance to his waking life. Moreover, as in *Change of Skin,* in *Capriccio italiano* one observes a progression of sorts from a clearly established beginning toward an equally definitely established conclusion. Edoardo's nightmares begin with his wife's unplanned conception, and they end—clearly implies Edoardo himself—with the birth of the baby who is, after all, accepted by his parents. The patterns in which the dream elements appear are vulnerable to reorganization within these points in time, but there is nothing to be gained or lost either structurally or thematically from such rearrangements.

What is very interestingly demonstrated in *Capriccio italiano* is the transformation of temporal points of reference, usual in the traditional novel, into spatial points of reference. Although the novel's contents are wholly lacking in chronological coherence within the points established by the conception and birth of Edoardo's third son, they are indisputably attached to various significant recurrent locations in space. These are the *lieux* which appear and reappear in Edoardo's dreams: an *albergo* near a lake, Edoardo and Luciana's apartment in an unidentified city, a mysterious house located near a large fountain at the edge of a deep forest, the bathroom shower, a cathedral, a chicken house, and a large painting that is animated in such a way that it seems to become an outdoor locale. Around these essential spatial realities are patterned all the various emotions that constitute the features of Sanguineti's caricature of Edoardo, the sexually fearful professor.

Stable constructs of a very different sort from *Berlin Alexanderplatz, U.S.A., Change of Skin,* and *Capriccio italiano* are created by Alain Robbe-Grillet. Except for *La Maison de rendezvous,* his novels are based upon the single fused perspective that unites the objective view of the camera with the subjective view of the protagonist, who is also sometimes the narrator. Robbe-Grillet's theory and practice of description—those precise and scrupulously measured passages—enable him to use words as means of etching subliminally upon the sensibilities of the reader a definite impression of a structure. Since he cuts away the substructure of chronological time, he is able to focus on the isolated moment of perception with exceptional force and intensity. As a result, each particular meaningful moment and its accumulation of attached emotion is created for each of Robbe-Grillet's protagonists at the same instant that it is created for the reader, without his awareness, by means of the repetition and manipulation of the descriptive passages. Each important image, for example, the crushed centipede of *Jealousy (La Jalousie)* or the boy with the swirling cape in *In the Labyrinth (Dans le labyrinthe),* is firmly and extensively evoked in a descriptive passage. Next, it is related to other, often similar, images. These are then accumulated, piled up, and related to still others. They are then modified, reversed, lengthened, shortened, and generally woven into a pattern that, little by little, as the novel moves on, comes to *be* the one overriding impression of the novel's central experience. Robbe-Grillet's stark and repetitious manner of handling language as though he were himself a camera has two structural purposes: first, to destroy linear time, to collapse it into isolated and crucial moments (collisions of perceptor and perceived); second, to "draw" with the patterns of the descriptions an abstract shape that bears a specific relationship to the theme of the work.

One feels that, more than anything else, Robbe-Grillet wants, in writing a novel, to build something. "Clearly, he wants his books to have the solidity and independent existence of a statue or a picture, which resists any anecdotal or intellectual summary." [8] But since words cannot be wholly freed from their relationships to observable reality, the novel as an object cannot be Robbe-Grillet's aim, as the finished painting is that of a painter. He is using the novel, much as paints, clay, or collage materials are used, to erect an impression, an illusion, that will exist in an ultimately nonverbal relationship to the reader. Instead of a record made with words, the novel becomes, in this writer's hands, the secondary means to the construction of an independent, abstract entity. If a Robbe-Grillet novel is read swiftly at one sitting, the final impression is of a structure which is itself abstract, although it may consist of minutely detailed parts. When the book is finished, this impression will remain in the reader's mind as the illusion of a form—solid, three-dimensional, architectonic. This abstract form is the ultimate emblem of the novel's central experience, action, or emotion. It has much in common with the "constructs" of Naum Gabo and Antoine Pevsner.

There is, in fact, no better way of summarizing the characteristics of the stable construct than to refer to the major axioms stated in the Constructivist Manifesto issued in 1930. Architectonic novels—be they representational or non-representational, stable or mobile, closed or open in structure—display by the nature of their being the presence of the following assumptions in their conception and construction. These are the four major tenets of Constructivism:

1. To communicate the reality of life, art should be based on the two fundamental elements: space and time.
2. Volume is not the only spatial concept.
3. Kinetic and dynamic elements must be used to express the real nature of time: static rhythms are not sufficient.
4. Art should stop being imitative and try instead to discover new forms.[9]

Notes

1. Pablo Picasso, "Conversations," by Christian Zervos, *The Creative Process*, edited by Brewster Ghiselin (Berkeley, California, 1954), p. 49.
2. Roland Barthes, "L'Activité structuraliste," *Lettres Nouvelles* (February, 1963), p. 73: "L'homme structural prend le réel, le décompose, puis le recompose."
3. Anaïs Nin, *Collages* (Chicago, 1964), p. 71.
4. Roland Barthes, "Littérature et discontinu," *Critique* (October, 1962), pp. 827–28: "Ce terme banal recouvre ici un projet très précis et fort différent des 'constructions' recommandées a l'école."
5. Julio Cortázar, *Hopscotch* (New York, 1966), p. 351. *Rayuela* (Buenos Aires, 1963), p. 488: "Creo oscuramente que los elementos a que apunto son un término de la *composición*. Se invierte el punto de vista de la química escolar. Cuando la composición ha llegado a su extremo límite, se abre el territorio de lo elemental."
6. Joseph Frank, "Spatial Form in the Modern Novel," *Critiques and Essays in Modern Fiction: 1920–1951*, edited by John W. Aldridge (New York, 1952), pp. 44, 46.
7. This ingeniously constructed novel came into being almost by accident. Broch's publisher wished to capitalize on the *succès d'estime* of *The Death of Virgil (Der Tod des Vergil)* and suggested to Broch that he reprint five early stories in a single volume. But when Broch reread the stories, he decided to rewrite them, and then, struck by the unity of their themes, he conceived the plan of combining them in a novel. The five stories that had previously been published (all before 1934) do not appear in a set sequence of any sort, but are scattered throughout the work with the six new stories.
8. J. C. Weightman, "Robbe-Grillet," *Encounter*, XVIII (March, 1962), p. 33.
9. Herbert Read, "Constructivism: The Art of Naum Gabo and Antoine Pevsner," *The Philosophy of Modern Art* (New York, 1953), p. 231.

> *The time experience of the present age consists above all in an awareness of the moment in which we find ourselves: in an awareness of the present. Everything topical, contemporary, bound together in the present moment is of special significance and value to the man of today, and, filled with this idea, the mere fact of simultaneity acquires new meaning in his eyes.*
>
> —Arnold Hauser [1]

9.

creation of a
present continuous

Mobile
Constructs

Many explanations—technological, sociological, and philosophical—might be advanced to account for the twentieth century's love of movement or, perhaps more accurately, for the century's acceptance of the changing orientations toward reality that are made obligatory by movement. Movement necessarily involves the individual in a variety of spatial realities, each of which is infused with its own temporal reality. Consequently, one may ask, what is reality—the sort that can be measured—if it is not the simultaneity of a perhaps infinite number of spatio-temporal sites? Movement need not be valued on its own account. It is, within the frame of reference of Einstein's discoveries about space and time and the consequences of these discoveries for perception, the only means of really seeing anything accurately and completely.

This study of the poetics of space in the novel is based upon the assumption that, in our time, to perceive, comprehend, or apprehend any object, the perceptor must accumulate a variety of perspectives upon that object. He must "see" it from as many points of view as possible. The alternative to the use of multiple perspectives is the use of a moving perspective. As was stated in the Introduction, in modern physics, space is considered as relative to a moving point of reference. With this in mind, one may suggest that a single perspective, if movable, provides just as accurate a mode of comprehensive perception as does a collection of perspectives focused upon the same object. One is assuming for the purpose of clarifying this point, that there is no distortion on the part of the perceptor. But if there *is*—and most persons who are interested in literature are convinced that such distortion occurs—then that is all the more reason why a variety of perspectives is needed to rectify imbalances and projections resulting from the interpretations of various perceptors.

To conclude the argument, the illusion of movement is desirable in the architectonic novel because it can bring the space-time orientation of the "fiction" into a more accurate relationship with reality. It accomplishes this, first, by abolishing the anachronistic linear organization that proceeds from a definite beginning, through a clearly established middle, leading toward a conclusive end. Second, the illusion of movement in the work of art bridges the evident abyss between it and the context of life in which it exists; it is a part of that context, a fact that was implicitly denied by the traditional line of demarcation embodied in the idea of the neat, rounded ending that left no questions to be asked by the reader or answered by the author. In the third place, movement, by energizing or animating the work of art, endows it with one of the characteristic features of life itself and, therefore, heightens its claim to the reader's attention. It was this insistence on the novel as another of life's "real" experiences that Waldo Frank meant when he wrote, "To the incidental character of the novel as a reflection of life we give great care; to its essential nature as a contribution to life we bring ignorance and neglect." [2] And in the fourth place, movement provides an excellent means of spatializing time by destroying the old linear organization and by proposing in its place the simultaneous existence of a variety of spatial realities, each of which is infused with its own dimension in time. Movement is,

then, in architectonic fiction, associated with the idea of the
present, as Arnold Hauser proclaimed in writing of "Space and
Time in the Film" ("Raum und Zeit im Film"), for all perception of reality takes place in present time. This is true even if
some mode of perspective, the book, for example, embodies the
perspectives of the past or suggests the perspectives of the future.

As mentioned earlier, an ideal image for the visualization of
how motion is suggested by architectonic or "constructed" fiction
is the circle; its center must be thought of as representing the
subject of the book; the circumference, the point of view or the
perspective from which it is seen. A work with a closed structure
based upon a single perspective will require only one circle to
indicate the relation between perspective and subject, but a work
with an open structure will require as many circles as there are
perspectives, each wheeling about the same center. With such a
diagram in mind, it is easy to imagine how motion affects perspective. The reiteration of the point of view in a closed structure
may be designated simply by various points marked out upon the
circle that represents the exclusive perspective of the work; the
movement of the viewer in time or space may be captured by
setting in motion the single diagrammatic circle. In a work with
multiple perspectives, the diagram that schematizes structure will
consist of a fixed point around which many circles may be
imagined to rotate at various speeds, depending upon the temporal and spatial patterns and rhythms of the book. Since space
is conceived as relative to a moving point of reference, the points
of rest along each circumference stand for those loci in space and
time at which motion is halted long enough for the act of perception to occur and to be registered. During these points of rest,
time is, as Joseph Frank pointed out, in effect, "spatialized."

It begins to become clear why, in terms of the perceptual
postulates that underlie this study, the motion of contemporary
art is so frequently circular. Roger Shattuck has explained this
phenomenon as a by-product of the rejection in our time of discursive logic, an idea that recalls the definition and description of
the traditional book of Roland Barthes that was presented in
Chapter 7. "Discursive logic is linear," Roger Shattuck reminds
readers of, The Banquet Years, "and moves from point to point.

Art of the modern era, like religious meditation, is circular and revolves around a point whose location is limitless." [3] Circular motion does, indeed, embody a denial of the idea of progress from beginning to end and of the whole notion of development, upon which the traditional concept of structure in prose writing has depended for its ideal of good organization. Circular motion is, instead, an insistence, an intensity, a power directed at deepening and energizing, a power directed inward upon itself. Although circular motion does not provide the only pattern of movement that is found in architectonic fiction, it is perhaps the most common, its emphasis constituting a corrective to the much more usual linear pattern based upon points along a straight line.

The entire question of motion in the novel is necessarily an ambiguous one because the "motion" of which one speaks is an *impression* of motion. By what criterion, then, has one argued that the structures of *Change of Skin* (*Cambio de piel*) and of Robbe-Grillet's verbal constructs, except for *La Maison de rendez-vous,* are "stable"? Might not another critic assert that these books are just as "mobile" as those that are analyzed in this chapter? After all, the concept of motion in the novel is only an illusion in the first place. And, in the second, might it not be argued that *all* fully achieved novels move, are "alive" insofar as they embody a dynamic quality? Perhaps, it might be asserted, a "mobile" work is simply one that is vital in the same way that sculptures are vital. In defining his ideal of Vitalism, the British sculptor Henry Moore wrote, "For me a work must first have a vitality of its own. I do not mean a reflection of the vitality of life, of movement, physical action, frisking, dancing figures and so on, but that a work can have in it a pent-up energy, an intense life of its own, independent of the object it may represent." [4] In Moore's sense, all *good* novels possess a dynamic internalized and autonomously engendered and sustained life energy of their own.

Something different from this quality of the vital is meant by "mobile." There are two characteristics that may be said to endow an architectonic novel with "mobility." One is a literal mobility: the interchangeability of the book's parts. Works that embody such a principle are understandably rare, for to achieve it, an author must virtually invent his own idea of a book and convince a publisher of its merit. Nonetheless, a few such books exist: *Composition No. 1, Hopscotch (Rayuela)*, and *Mobile: Study for a Representation of the United States (Mobile: étude pour une représentation des États-Unis)*. The interchangeability of the parts constitutes a denial of linear chronology and postulates the concept of simultaneous spatial and temporal orientations. The other characteristic of a "mobile" novel is its embodiment of the aspiration of continuous creation. A novel that moves contains the means for the abrogation of its beginning, middle, and end, as well as compensatory suggestions for its dynamic existence in the past and its capacity for projecting itself into an imagined future. In all cases, a structure that is dependent upon juxtaposition is the chief means by which the impression of "mobility" is attained.

Deceptive situations present themselves. For example, *Change of Skin (Cambo de piel)* gives a first impression of tremendous suppressed activity and of a potentiality for movement, but this impression proves, upon examination, to be false. Fuentes' novel is definitively enclosed by its prologue and its epilogue between two points in time. Another book that gives an initial impression of mobility is Edoardo Sanguineti's *Capriccio italiano*. Like Fuentes, Sanguineti has imprisioned his "free" portions between passages that clearly constitute a beginning and an ending. With the birth of Edoardo's son, all is resolved by means of a specific event that occurs at a specific and never-to-be-repeated chronological moment. At the same time, there are novels, like those of Gertrude Stein, that appear static at first glance, but that actually are carefully constructed approximations of circular motion. One finds that in her books "an infinitely long series of details constantly turns back upon itself, [creating] an illusion of movement in stillness." [5]

Among those novels that project their subjects simultaneously into the past and the future by means of insistence upon an intense, timeless present are Michel Leiris' *Aurora* and Maurice Fourré's *Tête-de-Nègre*. Both are reenactments of spiritual quests, and both appropriately incorporate circular structures that are suggestive of ritual as well as of the ever-present urgency of the journeys that occur in these books. In both *Aurora and Tête-de Nègre,* the impression of circularity implies eternality, since the idea of the magic quest is so ancient and so deeply associated with the spiritual anxieties and aspirations of man.

Aurora consists of a series of explorations, metamorphoses, and apotheoses that are modeled upon the supreme sacrifice of Aurora herself atop a magically revolving pyramid. The initial quest that gives the novel its structure is set in motion in the book's opening portion, which brings the timid narrator out of his secluded château and launches him upon a journey toward abasement, death, and eventual resurrection. The second quest is undertaken by the "stone" man in the smoking jacket who is privileged to be the companion of Aurora. After a fierce and wild ride on horseback across a desert in which the (black) man and the (white) woman seek "to discover in the plains of the valleys and in the flowers the course of their destiny," [6] they engage in a ritual that culminates in the novel's central and most excruciating sacrifice. A gigantic pyramid is magically evoked from the wastes of the desert. Aurora mounts the peak, and, by means of copulation with the gradually revolving pyramid that grinds deeper and deeper into her body until nothing remains but her flaming hair, she provides the other figures with a supreme example of pantheistic ecstasy.

The third part of *Aurora* presents another figure in search of metamorphosis: a young explorer who is washed up in a small cove where he undertakes a fascinated exploration of a submerged castle. Here he discovers the confessions of Damoclès Siriel, the former king of the submerged kingdom. The confessions serve to embed one quest within another: Siriel's search for unlimited personal liberty is enclosed by the exploration of the young man. Haunting, eerie, brutal, and strangely lovely is the prose of the opening passages of *Aurora*'s fourth part. Here is depicted metamorphosis on a grand scale. The scene is an underground burial chamber in which bodies that have been chopped into tiny fragments and mixed with the bits and pieces of other bodies are magically transformed first into specters, and later into auras or forms of "miel." Now another voyager is introduced, a young man who is carrying the volume by Paracelsus that provides the "text" of *Aurora*. The narrator breaks in to announce that he is himself assisting at the metamorphosis of Aurora. She is now destroyed all over again by being whipped until her body shatters into pieces. Afterward, she is quickly transformed into a mist that rises toward heaven to be absorbed by a large white cloud.

Part V comprises still another metamorphosis. The reader is presented with a simultaneous version of the immediately preceding transformation as it is envisioned in the fantasies of a vagabond. In this personalized re-creation, Aurora is depicted as an alluring prostitute in a public dance hall. At the same instant that this prostitute dies, a gorgeous mystic column tumbles to the ground. A vast cosmic disturbance is set off. All of nature begins to undergo a series of profound transformations. Little by little, the various metamorphoses assume greater and greater metaphysical scope as creation is torn apart, intermixed, and reconstituted.

At the end of Part V, the vagabond finds himself inextricably placed upon a path that seems to the reader the same one along which the narrator passed when he originally freed himself from the château of the book's opening pages. Now, in Part V, the vagabond arrives at Cigues-Mortes, the town whose image had been tatooed on the body of the prostitute. He appears at the same moment that the narrator himself steps inside an outlying "hangar" to avoid a thunderstorm. Thus, he is observed by the narrator, who, having lost his courage, is now a timid sort of voyeur. He admits that he is still too terrified to submit to destruction, that he shrinks still from metamorphosis, now represented by Aurora in the form of beautiful but deadly lightning bolts. As the narrator looks on, Aurora strikes down the vagabond, splitting him exactly in half. Now various apparitions appear. Among them are the "stone" man and Damoclès Siriel himself. Together, they bury the corpse of the vagabond, placing him head down in the sand so that his legs form a "V" above the surface. Having submitted to the power of Aurora, the vagabond is now, as he had desired, "directed toward a subterranean life." [7]

The narrator's long process toward metamorphosis is now

nearly complete. To weave together the times and distances that loom between the story of the vagabond and that of the narrator, Leiris employs an analogy between the philosopher's stone and the mystic lore of the alchemist Nicholas Flamel, whose secrets are said to be buried among the stones of Nôtre Dame. In this way, Leiris initiates a subtle motion back toward the present, at the same time reinforcing the mystic quality of his theme. Now the narrator is returned to the action and is again placed in a thoroughly contemporary setting; he is a guest at a seaside gambling casino. The place, or *lieu*, then, remains stationary from the scene of the vagabond's burial and resurrection to that of the narrator, for the former's body is still on the beach, in full view of the narrator as he himself now—finally—walks down to the water and fulfills his desired destiny by drowning himself. The fusion of times and the stability of place provided by the beach serve to emphasize the eternality of the spirit of Aurora and to bring to a satisfying close the long wavering motion of the narrator's journey toward death, his passage toward sacrifice and redemption.

In *Aurora* Leiris achieves an impression of timelessness and of cyclical motion by ignoring conventional chronology. He not only disdains any precise location in the present, deliberately creating a narrator who might be of any time; he also moves freely back and forth across the centuries, wildly blending the most ancient and the most glaringly contemporary of images. The pattern of enactment and reenactment provides the sensation of a fluid, circular structure that is quite appropriate to a book of a mystical nature. This impression of fluidity is achieved largely through the detachment of the action from definite points in time. The near-exclusive use of uninhabited and wild natural settings and the magic milieu of the moldy château, where anything can and ought to happen, together create the novel's supreme air of timelessness, of ritualized eternality, of endless significance to the adventurous spirit.

To create *Aurora*'s pervasive sense of "presentness," of scarcely perceptible but continuous motion, Leiris sometimes juxtaposes the ancient and the contemporary to evoke instants of simultaneous action. This is comparable to the way in which

Robert Desnos in *La Liberté ou l'amour!* brings a "pirate" into a Paris that is dominated by the mythology surrounding Bébé Cadum. For example, Leiris makes visual counterpoint of the rape and murder of some black women in Africa by white colonists and the suicide in New York City of a mulatto woman who has been abused by several white men. These events are to be seen as simultaneous, the blood bath and the whiskey bath as symbolically identical. In a similar manner, the pyramid which Aurora mounts is identified with a *gratte-ciel* (skyscraper) which is said to copulate with the sky and in which Aurora is at one time said to be imprisoned. Through these overlays and superimpositions of personages, actions, and symbols, the quality of the eternal is suggested by Leiris. His narrator's quest is endowed with the never-ending, cyclical rhythm that is demanded by the substance of a book that depicts the iconography of intense erotic pantheism. For this substance, the novel's spiraling, coiling, somewhat sinister form, its recurrent images of blades, knives, swords, and scissors, as well as its evocation of gloomy wastes and barren seaside plains, are perfect. *Aurora* is a structural approximation both of the form and the motion of the gyroscope, everything being concentrated, as it whirls, more and more intensively upon its own axes: that is, upon the transcendental submission, suffering, and triumph of Aurora herself that constitute the center of the spinning circles.

A variation upon the idea of the circular structure in ceaseless motion is provided by Maurice Fourré's *Tête-de-Nègre*. It is truly a "mixed" work, not only because it contains alternating passages of prose and poetry cast in the form of a "drame en trois actes," [8] but also because it embodies a combination of the traditional linear with the circular pattern and, finally, concludes with a leap that is designed to break open the novel's closed structure. At first, the line of the "action" appears to be, indeed, a line, for each of the three acts corresponds to a particular ritualized phase in the conventionalized quest of the hero, particularly those associated with the Grail legend; the first comprises the tender and painful parting from his *père nominatif* and from the little town of Château-Gontier on the banks of the Mayenne River. The second phase comprises the hero's arrival in the mysterious wood of Languidic in Brittany, long associated with the Grail legend, at the inn Relais du Monastère. This *acte* represents the stylized preparation of the hero at the hands of his mentor and new father figure, Gildas Le Devéha. The third *acte* presents the often-predicted assassination of the Baron and the celebration of the new reign that is to begin under the mutual aegis of Basilic-Hilaire, the deliverer who is now a prince, and his princess, Feu-Follet. If *Tête-de-Nègre* were an ordinary fairy tale, it would end with the combined funeral and wedding feast.

But this book is, as well as a reenactment of an ancient myth, a reenactment of authorial creation. "Le Monsieur Anonyme," Maurice, the "jeteur de sorts" ("one who gives the evil eye"), all along has been one of the novel's characters. He is judged guilty of the murder of Tête-de-Nègre by a mysterious "TRIBUNAL" and is sentenced to death. Maurice eludes the tribunal by mysteriously disappearing and by voluntarily taking his place in the triple casket of the Baron. With the disappearance of the author, the "omnipuissant Maurice," the continued existence of the characters is thrown into doubt. They all seem to lose their confidence. Basilic-Hilaire understands what has caused the crisis, for he says, "Monsieur Maurice, our late Creator, has dropped the bloody strings of the marionettes." [9] Life, he perceives, is the "surnaturelle liberté." At this point, the theatrical metaphor is dropped. Its existence is referred to as a "nightmare" by the ultimately self-sustaining and mutually sustaining lovers.

Maurice Fourré has brought his novel into the realm of the continuous present by means of several literary procedures. First, in having chosen the ancient and often-repeated pattern of the quest, he implies that what has so often happened must go on happening. He has reinforced this suggestion of a continuous action by scrupulously avoiding in the text of the work any sort of chronological reference; moreover, the only spatial referents are Château-Gontier and the wood of Languidic, both of which are intrinsically timeless. There is no reason to think that Basilic-Hilaire's heroic action has already taken place at any given moment or is destined to occur at any precise moment in the future. There is, instead, the feeling that it has occurred over and over again and must reoccur over and over again.

At the same time, there exists within Fourré's circular pattern—and in those of other works still to be examined—the decided preservation of the progress of human growth from infancy through youth to eventual maturity. In the third *acte* the reader learns that years before Basilic-Hilaire's arrival at the Relais du Monastère, another passerby had appeared who, though well intentioned, had not possessed the strength to carry out the assassination. This was the hero in his youth attempting what he was not yet mature enough to accomplish. His triumph upon his second attempt not only seals his love for Soline, but serves as a metaphysical catapult to launch him into the liberty of the individually sustained life.

The deliberate and sustained ambiguity of *Tête-de-Nègre* has this structural aspect: the undeniably linear pattern that embodies the various phases of the quest is embodied in a larger circular pattern, which, lacking any temporal dimension, establishes the eternality of its movement in a continual present. At the same time, in terms of the work's simultaneous developmental linear pattern, the author has abruptly shattered the carefully built-up illusion of the work as a theatrical entertainment, a "farce . . . provoquée par Maurice," in order to destroy the artificiality of these characters as they existed in the mind of the author and to provide them with an opportunity for individually conceptualized and activated existence in a realm that goes beyond the work of art. In *Tête-de-Nègre,* the circular motion does *not* turn inward upon itself to deepen the quality of its own reality. Instead, it is suddenly broken, as the characters leap out of the "magic" circle into hazardous, unpredictable life.

Circular form, with its accompanying illusion of "presentness," is found in many of the works of Gertrude Stein. In order to see how motion is embedded in the structure of a book like *The Making of Americans* one must first see that, here, the essential structural unit is not the chapter, the section, or even a series of paragraphs set apart from one another by spacing or by numbers, as, it is in the great majority of architectonic novels. Miss Stein conceives of a structural unit as a word group or an individual word. These very small units are organized according to the principle of "classical" juxtaposition whose purpose is—through the "insistence" of cinematic serial production—to evoke the existence of the subject in a continual present from which all impressions from memory have been scrupulously eliminated. Miss Stein states: "My ultimate business as an artist was not with where the car goes as it goes but with the movement inside that is of the essence of its going." [10] This paradoxical movement, that seems not to be movement at all but immobility, can be fully experienced only by reading an entire book by Miss Stein. A single passage may, however, suggest how Gertrude Stein's prose moves slowly forward by means of repetitions and subtle modifications of grammatical groups:

> And so my reader arm yourself in every kind of a way to be patient, and to be eager, for you must always have it now before you to hear much more of these many kinds of decent ordinary people, of old, grown, grand-fathers and grand-mothers, of growing old fathers and growing old mothers, of ourselves who are always to be young grown men and women for us, and then there are still to be others and we must wait and see the younger fathers and young mothers bear them for us, these younger fathers and young mothers who always are ourselves inside us, who are to be always young grown men and women to us. And so listen while I tell you all about us, and wait while I hasten slowly forwards, and love, please, this history of this decent family's progress.[11]

The Making of Americans has a definite beginning in the settlement in America of the Dehnings and the Herslands, but there is no reason, assuming that both families continue to produce children, that their history should ever come to an end. Thus Miss Stein, having set in motion this particular circle, abandoned it once she was certain it would spin on and on by virtue of its own momentum. When she saw that she could do what she had set out to do, she simply stopped writing the book.[12]

Roger Shattuck has described the impression that is created

by Gertrude Stein's approach to the evocation of a continuous present: "This is the structure that produces the effect of monotony and reiteration in their works [those of Erik Satie and Gertrude Stein], movement without advance. An infinitely long series of details constantly turns back upon itself, an illusion of movement in stillness." He concludes that Miss Stein's "poems and narratives do not progress from one point to another, but establish themselves deeper and deeper in a perpetual mode of existence." [13]

The classic example of the novel that insists upon living in a continuous present is *The Counterfeiters*. The first step into present existence is taken by Gide when, instead of settling the relationship between Edouard and Olivier at the end of the book, he abruptly introduces the possibility of a new relationship between Edouard and Caloub Profitendieu. But in terms of structure, this ending is a superficial device, a sort of rope hurled by the novelist from the book to reality in order to bind them together. A similar desperate action was taken by Alfred Döblin when, at the end of *Berlin Alexanderplatz*, he left Franz Biberkopf standing beside a road listening to a travel song that promises adventure, discovery, friendship, and even love. The road stretches out away from the city, far beyond the "Alex," toward freer and fuller vistas. It points *out there*—into space; it is the emblem of the novelist's desire to thrust his character beyond the confines of the book into some state of greatly expanded freedom, into a real life in the world. *U.S.A.*, too, ends with the introduction of a new character. He is a hungry boy named Vag, and he is pictured standing alone at the edge of a highway with a phony leather suitcase in one hand and the thumb of the other stuck out in the gesture of the hitchhiker.

Although the intention of Döblin and Dos Passos alike is clearly to defy the convention of the "rounded-off" ending and to insinuate an action that continues to develop outside, or beyond, the novel itself, the introduction at the end of a new character is merely suggestive, a device without structural authority. Gide has gone much further. By publishing his own *Journal of "The Counterfeiters"* two years after the novel appeared, he actually brought the novel back to life. He extended its being by bringing to its subject an altogether new perspective: that of the author speculating upon the difficulties of making the composition. In this perspective, the reader must see in a new and ever perplexing light those already equivocal ruminations and convictions to be found in Edouard's journal. The struggle between reality and art that Gide wished to evoke is so *successfully* evoked that one is never able to come to any definitive conclusion about the book and its characters in the light of the journal it contains, or of that other one appended to it two years after the publication of the novel. Not being able to distinguish exactly the reality from the art, one is constantly tormented by the urge to find it once and for all in order to dispose forever of the book as art. But Gide has made this impossible. He has succeeded in making his novel live as a continual sense of an irritating problem that cannot be solved.

A different sort of approach to the creation of the continuous present may be seen in Anaïs Nin's *Cities of the Interior*. While the structural unit employed by Gertrude Stein is grammatical—the word, phrase, clause, sentence, or paragraph—Miss Nin puts together novella-length, but not necessarily self-contained, blocks of prose into a "continuous" novel. Because it will not announce its final, concluding portion, *Cities of the Interior* embodies a refusal to locate itself at any point in past time and posits the possibility of its own organic growth at any moment in future time—unexpectedly—with the addition of yet another part. This part might appear anywhere: at the apparent "beginning," most anywhere in the "center," or at the ostensible and tentative "end." The relaxed asymmetry of *Cities of the Interior* creates the impression that it is made of parts that can be arranged in a great variety of structures, but that the parts will, in any position, retain their power of new growth. Since, like *The Counterfeiters*, this novel will not end, will not withdraw its energies from our field of concentration, it *lives*.

Miss Nin's "novel" of 1964, *Collages*, embodies an equally original approach to the spatialization of time in a continuous present. *Collages* demonstrates that circular motion which Roger Shattuck calls "movement without advance," movement that creates an intensification of the book's atmosphere, themes, and images. Consisting of nineteen short, self-sustaining episodes or vignettes, *Collages* draws its varied materials from three sources, all of which manifest considerable variety: settings, characters, and themes. The settings include Vienna; Mexico; Holland; Malibu and Downey, California; and—indirectly, by means of the characters with whom they are associated—Haiti, France, England, Morocco, Acapulco, Japan, Germany during World War II, Russia, and New York City (Third Avenue, Greenwich Village, the sculpture garden of the Museum of Modern Art). The colors and textures of each of these settings are evoked in a richly embroidered yet always lightly comical prose.

The many characters of *Collages* are as diverse as are the settings. None is portrayed in detail. Each is swiftly sketched in a deft vibrant prose that renders his individuality imagistically. There is Leontine, a buoyant black singer whose father was a revolutionary in Haiti; a poignant old man, more a seal than a human being, who finally goes off to die on a rock ledge with the animals he loves; Henri, a fabulous chef who had "invented the Crêpe Suzette for Prince Edward, the charcoal broiled steak for Diamond Jim Brady"; exotic Lisa; "a Toulouse-Lautrec figure" who had allowed herself to be "awakened from her dream of Acapulco [by Bill] with a cigar flavored kiss from the ashcan painting period of her childhood"; a deliriously mad actress who calls herself Nina Gitana de la Primavera and is in love with an imaginary man named Manfred; Nobuko, who every day selects her kimono to be in harmony with the season, its sunlight and flowers; Varda, the creator of exquisite airy collages of women concocted from "all the legendary textiles of the world," but whose daughter stubbornly "wore Varda's torn shirts and discarded sweaters and went out with boys more sullen and mute than herself"; there is the betrayed wife of a French Consul, who invents for herself a new love, a long-dead hero of Islam, Shumla, whose "valor made the modern world seem tame and fearful." [14] Each of these brave and touching figures comes imbued with an aura of place and time; each weaves about himself a self-sustaining world of fantasy.

The themes of the nineteen vignettes are varied. Yet, upon analysis, each is revealed as a variation upon the idea of the rich creative powers of imagination. Several of the vignettes seem to say that love between man and woman is essential for each and every person regardless of age and that those who do not possess such a love in real life can just as easily summon forth from imagination the excitement and pleasure of companionship and passion. All point subtly to the vital role of creativity in every life, whether it is the charm and power of make-believe, the force of the fantasy in inventing new personalities and lives for oneself, or specific artistic creativity such as that represented by Renate, Leontine, Varda, and Judith Sands. Another recurrent theme is the absolute necessity of freedom from restrictions of emotion, feeling, and imaginative creation. Superficially, the elements of the collage seem far apart ("romantic," in Roger Shattuck's distinction), but their homogeneity of theme must make this conclusion a mixed one. Here, the elements of juxtaposition are in some ways homogeneous and in others, heterogeneous.

The varied elements of the composition are glued into place by the consistent presence of the book's one consistent character, Renate. At first, *Collages* does seem to promise a story about an energetically loving young woman who wants to unlock a secretive, moody, self-centered young man named Bruce. However, the handling of this relationship ceases, without explanation, at about page thirty shortly after Bruce has unwittingly dramatized his own uncontrollable egotism; when a forest fire threatens to destroy Renate's house in the wooded hills of southern California, Bruce rescues nothing but a huge portrait of himself. After this incident, Bruce is mentioned only once, desultorily, and the intuitive reader assumes that the more vivid Renate has moved on to more promising relationships. From this point on, *Collages* consists, not of Renate's life, but of brilliant, sharply cut, jewellike presentations of the amazing people she meets through her job as a hostess at the Paradise Inn. It is, in fact, because of her stability and her completeness that Renate's contribution to the composition is understated and almost hidden. She alone among the characters is not a fragment. The artist Varda says he cannot use her for a subject because she is *"femme toute faite."* He explains that he needs "unformed women, unfinished, undesigned women [whom he] can mold to [his] own pattern." [15]

Like other works that have been constructed according to the principle of juxtaposition, *Collages* demands an alert and dexterous reader. The message that is insisted upon by the book's slowly revolving motion is the increasingly familiar view that art and life are indistinguishably entwined. As in all of her earlier works, in *Collages* Miss Nin refuses to categorize her characters as "imaginary" or as "real," emphasizing the falseness of such a distinction. A coordinate reading of her *Diary* with her novels shows how the same persons and situations appear in both; they are just described with greater intensity and with a higher luster in the novels. Furthermore, Miss Nin's choice of materials and themes emphasizes over and over again the manifold ways in which dream and imagination can enrich daily life through compensation, through revelation, and through prophecies conveyed in images. Finally, in *Collages* Miss Nin dramatizes the interlocking creative powers of art and life, at the same time finalizing the circular shape by ending the book with the same passage with which it opens:

> Vienna was the city of statues. They were as numerous as the people who walked the streets. They stood on the tip of the highest towers, lay down on stone tombs, sat on horseback, kneeled, prayed, fought animals and wars, danced, drank wine and read books made of stone. . . .[16]

There is this important difference between the opening and closing passage; identical except for the difference of the vowels in "tip" and "top," the one was composed by Miss Nin, the other ostensibly by a writer named Judith Sands, who appears to represent Djuna Barnes. The reader must take his clue from Jorge Luis Borges' story "Pierre Menard Author of Don Quixote" and find the meaning in the juxtaposition of author and passage. Enriching the idea that the two authors may be mirror images and the suggestion that two or more writers might very well—unbeknownst to each other—compose identical paragraphs, is a second clue provided by the fact that one of the characters, a Doctor Mann, has come to seek out Judith Sands because he finds a replica of himself in a character in her famous book (obviously *Nightwood*): "Every novelist knows that at one time or another he will be confronted with the incarnation of one of his characters. Whether that character is based on a living person or not, it will draw into its circle those who resemble it. Sooner or later the portrait will attract its twin, by the magnetism of narcissism, and the author will feel this inhabitant of his novel come to life and hear his character speaking as he had imagined." [17] In just such a way, life and art come face to face with each other in Anaïs Nin's book and Judith Sands's manuscript, forming a circular configuration in which it is impossible to separate one from the other and in which neither can ever achieve independence or ultimate completion without the other. One of the wisest personages in *Collages* is the wife of the French Consul, a woman who, when her husband seeks youth and hope in relationships with young girls, finds a beautiful solace in the adoration of an heroic man who has been dead for some time. What the Consul's wife knows is that "Nothing is ever finished." [18]

Numerous writers besides Miss Nin have responded to the challenge of creating mobile structures, and some have produced books that suggest various ingenious and intriguing methods of overcoming the linear thrust that is imposed upon the novel by the physical nature of the book. Most novelists who experiment with structure discard the established concept that the book must be read from beginning to end, continuously, in a sequence that proceeds from page to page. These writers employ discontinuity, not merely as a means of eliminating transitions between prose passages that are contiguous, but more importantly, as a means of realigning the spatial and temporal expressive capacities of the book. Discontinuity provides a mode of attack on the traditional concept of the book as a medium whose physical properties impose upon its contents a certain type of order, and of demonstration, by example, of an alternative concept of the book. This desire literally to take the book apart and to reorganize its spatial dynamics is the extreme example to date of the spatialization of time. The destruction of the sequential progress of the book from one numbered page to the next represents the abandonment of conventional chronology. The new order, if, indeed, another is substituted for the one that has been cast aside, is based upon the combination of various perspectives on the subject, arranged spatially.

The "spatialization" consists in replacing the traditional temporal orientation of substance to book with a spatial orientation that takes into account such potential organizing elements as the nature of the page, of the binding, of typography, and of the relationships among the pages when they are blank. That these features of the book may be exploited in the creation of mobile constructs has been demonstrated by several writers who are both inventive and bold. Among the novels that constitute attempts to capture motion in a mobile structure are three that merit close structural analysis. Each embodies a different sort of approach to the problem of overcoming the apparent linear nature of the book *qua* book. They are Julio Cortázar's *Hopscotch* (*Rayuela*), Marc Saporta's *Composition No. 1*, and Michel Butor's *Mobile: Study for a Representation of the United States* (*Mobile: étude pour une représentation des États-Unis*).

Cortázar's 635-page book is preceded by a "Table of Instructions" ("Tablero de Dirección") which includes a statement that *Hopscotch* is many books, but two books above all. The reader is then advised to read in normal order the first fifty-six chapters. He will then have completed the first "book" and may, if he wishes, "ignore with a clean conscience what follows." However, if he chooses to go on to the second "book," he must begin with chapter 73, omitting 57 through 72, and complete the book by proceeding, when he has finished one chapter, to the next one that is indicated at the close of each completed chapter. If he does this, he will discover that 73 leads back to 1, 1 to 2, 2 to 116, 116 back to 3, 3 to 84, and so on. Chapters 57 through 155 are called "Capítulos prescindibles" ("expendable chapters"). And if the reader decides to follow the author through this maze and at some point loses his way, he may easily regain his track by consulting the table in the front of the book which lists the prescribed order of reading from chapters 73 to 131.

As Cortázar has promised, the first fifty-six chapters do comprise a conventional novel whose subject is the self-exile in Paris of an Argentinian intellectual, Horacio Oliveira. This "book," however, has two parts: the first thirty-six chapters presented "From This Side" ("Del Lado de Allá") and the remaining twenty "From the Other Side" ("Del Lado de Acá"). The former depict Oliveira's last months in Paris beginning with his gradual breakup with his mistress, la Maga, and ending in a sordid debauch with a *clocharde*, arrest, and jail. These chapters form a coherent unit, an excellently written and frequently moving account in the traditional narrative manner of life in Paris among bewildered pseudointellectuals and would-be artists; and they could easily pass for a novel complete in themselves. These chapters are autonomous, as are the individual stories that constitute *The Innocent* (*Die Schuldlosen*) and the novellas that make up *Cities of the Interior*.

A contrasting spatial dimension is provided by the second part of the first "book." Chapters 37 to 56 are set in Buenos Aires. Along with Oliveira, who has returned to his native city, the featured characters are a happily married couple named Traveler and Talita. The new setting, the new characters, and their happy and zany life evoke a strong contrast to the former Parisian sections. Indeed, as Michel Butor pointed out in "L'Espace du roman," each *lieu* illuminates another by contrast. Paris comes into much sharper focus when it is viewed in Buenos Aires, just as Buenos Aires has defined itself clearly for the Argentines who had abandoned it for Paris. In Buenos Aires, Oliveira adds more and more bizarre psychic experiences to his stockpile until eventually he succumbs to a persistent fantasy that Talita is la Maga and that Traveler, his *Doppelgänger,* is some aspect of himself that he must trap and destroy. He becomes mad, but ambiguously so, for he is perhaps both wise and happy, and he is surely transfigured. One might conclude that since Oliveira's has been the major perspective from which the reader has had to view the events of the first fifty-six chapters, his madness calls for a new perspective or a combination of perspectives. The book, after all, does continue, though Oliveira has found his personal salvation in lunacy.

As has been indicated in Chapter 6, the "expendable chapters" of *Hopscotch* comprise a collection of perspectives from which the materials of the "unexpendable" chapters are reviewed a second time around. Most of these "chapters" consist of literary quotations documented with their sources. The longest cover a few pages; the shortest consist of a single sentence. A rough analysis of these perspectives provides the following breakdown into three categories: the "Morelliana," a collection of excerpts from the ostensible diary of an aging novelist that constitute an extensive aesthetic of the antinovel; the occasional reflections of Oliveira upon some of the events and situations that are presented in the first "book"; and, third, a mass of quotations from a wide range of printed materials. Some perspectives constitute additional interpretations of relations among the characters presented in the first "book": the mystic implications of the odd trinity formed by Traveler, Talita, and Oliveira; how Oliveira's love affair with Pola was experienced by Pola herself (the earlier perspective was la Maga's); or how the South American childhoods of Oliveira and la Maga affected their personalities.

When one begins to read *Hopscotch* for the second time, that is, with the "expendable" chapters interspersed with those that more nearly contain narrative, he immediately understands that Cortázar is attempting something like the total truth by multiplying and varying the perspectives from which certain fixed characters and situations are seen by the reader. No incident, character, situation, or attitude is allowed to remain in the very incomplete exposure of Oliveira's single perspective. Each must be seen again—and in a very different light—from the new perspective that is embodied by the juxtaposition of the perspective of the "expendable" chapter with that of the original portion. Sometimes the resultant effect is mockery. This entry ("Chapter 85") is used, for example, to deflate the intellectual pretentiousness of Oliveira and his friends: "LIVES which end like literary articles in newspapers and magazines, so pompous on page one and ending up in a skinny tail, back there on page thirty-two, among advertisements for secondhand sales and tubes of toothpaste." [19] At other times, the effect of the juxtaposition may be of pathos or of irony. When the lonely and obscure, though

great, writer Morelli is taken to the hospital after he has been hit
by an automobile, Cortázar provides a perspective that bitterly
ridicules society's sense of values in selecting celebrities:

> HOSPITAL *Items*
> The York County Hospital informs us that the Dow-
> ager Duchess of Grafton, who Sunday last fractured a leg,
> had a restful day yesterday.
> *The Sunday Times,* London [20]

Sometimes the additional perspective simply presents the other
side of an argument or intellectual proposition stated in the first
reading. In this way, the piety and deep religious belief of
Meister Eckhart are contrasted to the cool and rational denials
of God in a typically Existentialist argument. Another frequent
type of contrast is found in the juxtaposition of the general and
the specific aspects of the same subject or thought. For example,
Morelli's anguished speculation, " 'there is a place in man from
where [sic] the whole of reality can be perceived' " [21] is followed
by a metaphorical explanation of why Oliveira clings so desperately to an idealized version of Talita: she seems to him a figure
holding up a candle along a dark path.

One of the most effective of *Hopscotch*'s many "coagulations"
of meaning is a sequence that embodies an implicit comment on
the universality of brutality. During an all-night party at which
the members of the Serpent Club get "high" on vodka and jazz,
Wong allows Oliveira to see his prized photos, a series of snap-
shots depicting the step-by-step knife torture of a woman in
Peking around 1920. In the second reading, this episode is followed by an "expendable" chapter consisting of an AP release
describing the execution of one Lou Vincent in the electric chair;
the tone is dry, abrupt, reportorial. Next in position are some
very acerbic remarks of Clarence Darrow condemning the violent
revenge taken by society on child criminals; this is in connection with the Leopold-Loeb case. The reader is now returned to
the muggy, boozy atmosphere of the party just in time to hear
la Maga, in a rare mood of self-pity, offer to tell the club members

how she was raped at thirteen by a drunken, red-eyed tenement dweller. Oliveira protests; he has evidently heard the story, and he does not want—now when their relationship is ending—to be obliged to feel sympathy for la Maga. She persists, encouraged by Gregorovius who is now paying her court, and has barely begun the story when Cortázar breaks it off by directing the reader's attention toward a different, if related, scene: a narrative account of how the rapist, Ireneo, as a child deliberately captured a grub for the torture of a colony of ants and sat watching in a state of high excitement as they methodically tore it apart. This sequence of comments on sadistic acts closes on a note that prohibits comforting portmanteau conclusions. Morelli, the old writer-philosopher, forbids the reader to make a mental wrapup of what he has just read: "If the volume or the tone of the work can lead one to believe that the author is attempting a sum, hasten to point out to him that he is face to face with the opposite attempt, that of an implacable *subtraction*." This thought will take the attentive reader back to a comment of Oliveira's, a retort to Gregorovius' advice to la Maga to give "a general idea" of the rape. Snaps Oliveira, " 'There's no such thing as a general idea.' " [22] Each brutal action has its own reality, its own set of motivations and repercussions, its own bestowals and reverberations of suffering. To group such actions together and to generalize about them is merely a form of dodging recognition of their discrete authenticity.

At times, Oliveira is ruthless in forcing the reader to adjust his angle of vision to the insight provided by a violently changing perspective on an event. In one of the novel's strongest scenes, la Maga's baby son, Rocamadour, dies while his mother, who has been ineffectually nursing him, is unaware even though she is in the room at the time with Gregorovius. The scene takes place right after la Maga and Oliveira's decision to part, and she is still caught between the two men, grieving for Oliveira's loss, yet vaguely attracted to the calculated warmth of Gregorovius. It is Oliveira who discovers that Rocamadour has died. True to his life pattern of choosing the surprising, the perverse, even the shocking action, he deliberately withholds the news from la Maga through the interminable course of a second all-nigh drinking party attended by the carousing members of the Serpent Club. One by one, Oliveira whispers the truth to the others. But not to la Maga. By treating the scene in this manner, Cortázar effectively makes the reader a guilty accomplice, privy to unpalatable news, a member of that nasty little circle of deluded and self-deluding bohemians who are too busy talking about "reality" to respond to the death in their midst. Only la Maga, when eventually she herself discovers Rocamadour's death, possesses sufficiently simple direct emotions to become at once hysterical with grief, remorse, and guilt, and furiously contemptuous of the bitter, unyielding Oliveira. Except in his imagination, this intensely cruel scene is the last one in which la Maga and Oliveira see each other during the long, complex course of *Hopscotch*.

Naturally, an episode such as the one just described cannot possess the same horror and power on the second reading. It is probably a good thing, for the second time around, Rocamadour's death is made to appear grotesquely funny by the appending of a newspaper story called "Riesgos del Cierre Relámpago" ("The Perils of the Zipper"):

> THE *British Medical Journal* speaks of a new type of accident that can befall boys. This accident is caused by the use of a zipper in place of buttons in trouser flies (our medical correspondent informs us).
>
> The danger lies in the prepuce's being caught in the fastener. Two cases have already been reported. In both of them circumcision had to be resorted to in order to free the child.
>
> The accident is more likely to occur when the child goes to the bathroom unaccompanied. . . .[23]

These examples provide only a sample of the richness Cortázar has achieved by his unique method of construction. His announcement that *Hopscotch* consists of "many books" is no exaggeration: there are the stories of Oliveira's psychic quest, of Traveler and Talita's love, and of la Maga's emotional daring. There is, besides, the group portrait of exiled intellectuals in Paris, the comic picture of the Buenos Aires madhouse, the aesthetic of fiction provided by Morelli, the bits and pieces of witty or lyrical statements, and the snatches of poetry that are scattered among the pages in the form of citations or insights expressed by the author himself. The highly suggestive structure of *Hopscotch* allows the author an immense freedom to combine perspectives on such a scale that he is truly constructing several books simultaneously—and doing so in such a way that the novel spills over into life much as does *The Counterfeiters*, the masterpiece of Morelli's hero, André Gide.

An imaginative reader may easily take the hint embodied in the "Tablero de Dirección" and continue making new constructs from the different arrangements of "expendable" and "unexpendable" chapters. By virtue of its peculiar structure consisting of movable parts which can be arranged in an endless variety of ways, *Hopscotch* is limited only by the total possible number of combinations that can be derived from its 155 parts. Since the book's meanings depend upon the relationships among these parts, one could go on reading *Hopscotch* forever. Presumably, this is why the anonymous reviewer for the Fort Worth *Telegram* said he would like to take it to a desert island.[24]

A book that is structurally very closely related to *Hopscotch* is Marc Saporta's *Composition No. 1*. It constitutes an ingenious attack on the novel as a narrative and is an ambitious attempt to invite the reader's participation in the making, or "putting together," of the book. *Composition No. 1* is literally a mobile work. The author has designed the parts and presented them to the reader, but he has refused to give them any sequential organization. Saporta's novel consists of 150 loose and unnumbered pages. The majority by far portray completed "actions" (thoughts, longings, descriptions, fantasies, or conversations), but a few pages can be extracted according to their contents and rearranged into sequences representing phases of a single action conveyed on four, five, or six pages. The nearly exclusive use of the present tense gives each "action" equal value and makes the reader squirm when he attempts linear organization on his own behalf. The prose style is simple, clear, predominantly descriptive, and apparently objective; that is, it is relatively free from emotional coloring or imaginative distortion. With the loose pages in his hand, the reader is invited "to shuffle these pages as though they were a pack of cards. To cut them, if he wishes, with the left hand, as if he were consulting a fortune-teller. The order in which the leaves emerge from the game will dictate the destiny of X." [25]

Taking as a clue the fact that a nonobjective painting by X's mistress is, in the novel, called "Composition No. 1," some critics have said that the final effect of *Composition No. 1* is like looking at an abstract painting. It is, instead, more like playing with one of those "do-it-yourself" sculptures that are found in most museums of modern art. One has before him a group of elements of various kinds; their nature is established and so are the broad outlines of the structure within which one is invited to arrange these elements; still, there are a great many patterns that may be worked out within this loose and general structure. In *Composition No. 1*, the possible patterns into which one may arrange the book's pages are related to a range of perspectives from the totally subjective to the totally objective. One may, if he wishes, adopt the attitude that everything in the book is the result of daydream, nightmare, or delirium. Or, one may adopt instead the opposite attitude and assume that everything actually did happen, although the reader cannot discover the exact order in which the reported events must have occurred.

When one has read about two-thirds of *Composition No. 1*, two things become obvious. The first is that one may, if he wishes, arrange the 150 pages into a conventional novel about an upper-middle-class Frenchman in his early to mid-forties who has an unsatisfactory job and a miserable marriage, who bears a highly idealized love for a German or Scandinavian girl named Dagmar, and who either has committed, or contemplates committing, two criminal acts: the rape of a housemaid who is under twenty and the theft of a very large sum of money. The same qualities that may make him capable of rape and theft enabled X during the war to be very brave in defense of a Jewish friend against right-wing terrorists, in distributing handbills at the Sorbonne for the maquis, and in carrying out various other espionage activities that are described in part but that are never fully detailed. If such a conventional composition is formed, the childhood "bits" serve to explain X's nature.

Second, the enterprising reader will realize that this traditional approach to the organization of the pages is very far from being the only alternative, or the most interesting one. For example, the reader might begin with the wartime pages, move on to the childhood, then to the automobile accident, back to the marriage, and so on, in any order that pleases his fancy. A jagged effect might be achieved by alternating, page for page, fantasy materials with supposed "actual" incidents. One might do this, that is, if he were able clearly to distinguish the difference. Eventually, Marc Saporta provides a conventional explanation for the disorder of the composition in the suggestion that X, a victim of an auto accident, is lying in a hospital room delirious, receiving impressions of his life as they pass through his receptive but passive mind. But this explanation does not serve to order the chronological relationships of the 150 pages, since nearly all of them are written in the present tense.

In *Composition No. 1*, Marc Saporta suggests that the reality of a man's life is found in clusters of incidents and feelings which are set off, one from another, not by their temporal dimension, nor even by their "reality," but by their obsessive power and emotional force. By deliberately obscuring distinctions in time and the boundary between what is merely desired and what is actually experienced, Saporta forces the reader's attention to focus upon those patterns of deep and consistent fascination that define personality and form destiny. The most ingenious reader will never be able to make the 150 pages of *Composition No. 1* form any other *type* of composition than a portrait of X. The styles may change, with the different structures that are built up from the 150 fragments, but X will remain the subject, regardless of the treatment. Saporta has retained a measure of control over his creation by limiting the perspective to but a single view of the subject. One cannot escape being there with X, looking at X's life, whether from the vistas of his dreams, his memories, or of his day-by-day experiences. Julio Cortázar, by contrast, retains for himself a structural power—since he directs the order in which the fragments of *Hopscotch* are to be read—and grants the reader a vast freedom of interpretation in searching and bestowing relationships upon the conglomerations of multiple perspectives that are brought to bear on the subjects of the book.

Both works, however, embody procedures for making the novel flexible in space, by obscuring or concealing temporal dimensions, and for endowing it with expanded powers of complex organization and with greater spatial and temporal expressive capacities. Both are mobile in the most literal sense, and they embody enormously interesting suggestions for the structural evolution of the novel.

A third experiment that abounds in structural variations that produce clear impressions of movement is Michel Butor's *Mobile*.[26] It is very nearly a totally *constructed* book; there is very little actual "writing" in it. Inadvertently providing a splendid example of "closed-field" theory at work, Michel Butor has collected certain kinds of materials and arranged them in patterns of his own design. The book contains the names of towns and cities, followed by brief phrases identifying their location; strings of one-line images; one- or two-line descriptions of automobiles and their drivers; brief statements of historical fact; descriptions of birds and flowers; the repeated greeting, "Hello, Al" (or "John" or "Harry") in which the name of the individual being greeted constantly changes; descriptions of Howard Johnson restaurants in which the flavors of advertised ice cream constantly change; statements of American Indian history; quotations from American mail-order catalogues and other types of advertisements; names of political figures; excerpts from the writings of Benjamin Franklin, Thomas Jefferson, William Penn, and from the testimonial accounts of members of the "peyote" religions of the Southwest; descriptions of the three great monuments in Washington, D.C.; brief phrases denoting the time of the day or night or of some other natural phenomenon that suggests a personal observation of the sort that might be noted in a diary. The spatial treatment and organization of these fragments results in a mobile construct that has a distinct character of its own but that is, at the same time, both flexible and movable. *Mobile* may be read from the back toward the front, or vice versa, or dipped into at any point. One may start or stop anywhere without losing either the theme or the feeling of the book, for it insinuates its being in all conceivable directions. At the same time, *Mobile* has a definite linear axis. It suggests a swift trip by automobile through the United States. It suggests, as well, a film. As he turns pages, the United States seems to unroll before the reader's eyes as on a vast cinemascope screen.

The three factors that are largely responsible for *Mobile*'s character as a mixed free and progressive structure that evokes the motion of a long, rambling automobile trip, are grammatical, typographical, and spatial. Apart from the many quotations, virtually all the "writing" consists of fragments: of phrases and isolated words. Grammatical shortcuts are frequent. As in American journalism and advertising, verbs are often omitted. Like Gertrude Stein, Butor prefers the present and the progressive present tenses for their capacity to suggest something going on at the same moment that it is described. Although one's first impression suggests that many type faces are employed in *Mobile*, there are actually only three: large capitals, normal type such as one finds in any book, and italicized type. The page is rectangular but quite close to square, and Butor scarcely ever uses more than half or two-thirds of any one page. Left- and right-hand pages must be read as a unit. Space, too, has its role to play; Hawaii, for example, is isolated in the center of an otherwise blank page. The principle of organization is simple repetition, or "insistence," as Gertrude Stein would urge.

                    pitch dark in
CORDOVA, ALASKA, the Far North, closest to the dreadful, the
          abominable, the unimaginable country where it is already
Monday when it is still Sunday here, the fascinating, sinister country
with its unexpected satellite shots, the country of bad dreams that pur-
sue you all night and insinuate, among your daylight thoughts, despite
all your efforts, so many tiny ruinous whisperings like a leak in the ceiling of an old room, the monstrous country of bears,—pitch dark in

DOUGLAS, near Glacier Bay National Monument (any natural or
          archaeological curiosity considered worthy of being preserved
from the indiscretion of settlers or tourists is called a national monument),

pitch dark in
DOUGLAS, Mountain Time, ARIZONA, the Far West,—the Navajo
Indian Reservation. (Most of the approximately five hundred
thousand Indians of the United States live on reservations scattered
throughout the country, to which they have gradually been confined
during the occupation of the land by the white invader. It would not be
kind to compare them to concentration camps. It would even be rather
unfair: some of these reservations are tourist attractions.)

*"Despite the bigness of the Southwest, little things—sights, sounds, and
smells—often create the most lasting impressions. Here are some:*
—strings of scarlet chili drying against adobe walls,
—golden aspens mantling a mountain's shoulders,
—lithe relaxation of Navajos outside a trading post,
—awkward speed of a fleeing roadrunner,
—massive thunderhead dragging its braids of rain,
—immobility of tumbleweeds banked against a fence,
—line of resigned autos waiting out a flash flood,
—single-file string of steers approaching a waterhole,
—echoes and silences in a great cliff-dwelling ruin,
—bawling of restless cattle at a roundup,
—heady aroma of campfire coffee,
—carefree boys 'in the raw' splashing in a stock tank,
—squeal of a fighting, bucking horse at a rodeo,
—wail of a coyote—and yapping of others—at night,
—drum throbs and shrill chant of an Indian dance,

—musty odor of creosote bush after rain,
—bray of a distant wild burro just after sunrise,
—harsh smell of singed flesh at a branding corral,
—sudden pelting rush of a summer thunderstorm,
—unbelievable immensity of the Grand Canyon,
—juiciness of thick steak broiled over mesquite coals,
—stars that you can reach from your sleeping bag,
—splash and tug of a mountain trout hitting your fly,
—tang of enchiladas smothered in chili sauce," (from The American
Southwest *by Dodge and Zim, "with more than 400 subjects in full color,*
—Natural Wonders,
—Indian Villages,
—Historic Sites,
—Scenic Routes,
—Guide Maps,
—Public Parks,
—Minerals,
—Animals,
—Birds,
—Trees,
—Flowers").

Petrified Forest National Monument,—pitch dark in

FLORENCE, on the Gila River, near Casa Grande National Monument,

The opening pages of *Mobile,* eight and nine, offer four modes of spatial and typographical variation. The names of the towns—Cordova, Alaska, and Douglas, Arizona—are printed in capitals, but the dry factual description accompanying each name is printed in regular type. This practice is consistent throughout the book. The opposing placement and the capitals draw the eye horizontally across the page (the descriptions of Cordova and Douglas balance each other) and suggest to the mind that these towns, despite vast differences in their locations and climates, are spiritually similar, perhaps even indistinguishable from each other. The third mode consists of the ironically employed parentheses that contain a sarcastic remark about America's treatment of the native Indians. This is to become one of *Mobile*'s most forcefully repeated themes. Total visual symmetry of the two pages is avoided. The fourth mode of variation consists of a list of sense impressions in mild commercial jargon reprinted from a book called *The American Southwest* by Dodge and Zim. This list narrows down to unadorned citations of objects that are to be found in this part of the United States: "Indian Villages," "Historic Sites," "Scenic Routes," "Guide Maps," and so on.

Near the bottom of page ten, the line broadens out again to bring into absurd conjunction the Petrified Forest and Florence, on the Gila River (evoking an ironic allusion to Florence, Italy). The repetition of "pitch dark" ought to be noticed; it refers not just to the absence of moon and stars but to another of *Mobile*'s recurrent themes, the American treatment of the Negro. The opposite page, eleven, on which the portions of type are balanced vertically, tells one that it is "not so dark" in Florence as in the Petrified Forest. Now a new element is introduced: short phrases in italic type lined up beneath one another vertically and printed uniformly close to the left margin: *"Blue night," "The mountains at night," "The alarm clock goes off."* One cannot know if these lines represent someone's thoughts or, if so, whose, but the notations seem to introduce a personal, more intimate note. It is also clear that this vertical line is intended (as in montage organization) to be read *against* the horizontal line. Another visual mode appears, if one observes that the names of the towns Florence and Georgetown are printed along a diagonal plane slanting from upper left to lower right, thus cutting up the space along a third axis. On this page, too, is introduced what will become another recurrent theme, the description of the Buick. Generally, the drivers of the cars are summed up for the reader by a swift, incisive description of a hat, dress, suit, or complexion. In terms of *Mobile*'s racial theme, it is significant that Georgetown (named after the first president) is the seat of "White County" and that it is also the location of a Zuñi reservation. "British Petroleum" links the corruption and economic exploitation of the "old" world with that of the "new." To reinforce this connection, Butor often calls Americans the "American Europeans."

This sample analysis of four pages should be adequate to convey the feel and tone of *Mobile* and to illustrate how Michel Butor's spatial and typographic treatment of his materials as described in "Le livre comme objet" results in a composition in which form and content are as indistinguishable, as inextricably functions of each other as in the finest poetry. The essence of *Mobile* is clearly stated in its title. It is a verbal approximation of the type of sculpture that is called a "mobile." It *may* remain stationary, but it may also move, for its individual parts are movable. It retains its formal integrity regardless of the angle from which it is viewed. But despite the facts that its parts may be separated from the whole and read in isolation and that these parts possess structural coherence in themselves, the work as a whole has a single unifying form. Its plasticity is its most revolutionary feature. Roland Barthes expressed this idea when he wrote of *Mobile*, "It has a decidedly plastic finality." He went on to describe the book's unique structure: "*Mobile*, that is to say, a fastidiously constructed armature (the moving part of a dynamo or motor) in which all the junctures, in being slightly movable (the factor that permits the subtlety of the game of combinations), paradoxically produce the most flowing of movements." [28]

Mobile is the extreme, but by no means the unique, example of how space as an elemental mode of organization may replace time in the mobile structure whose organization lends itself to multiplicity and to variety of arrangement with the cooperation of an imaginative reader. All the novelists whose works have been discussed in this and in the preceding chapter are striving to undermine the traditional relation of the novel to time and to the principle of cause and effect as these are embodied in the novel's traditional progressive movement from one page to another. The substitution of spatial for temporal organization is perhaps less obvious in the stable constructs treated in Chapter 8 than it is in the mobile structures that are analyzed in this chapter, but it is evident nonetheless—nowhere more clearly than in the procedure of novelistic "construction" from bits and pieces of prose arranged into architectural components.

The idea of the novel as a spatial entity consisting of prose passages that have been superimposed upon one another and juxtaposed so that they form representational or abstract patterns embodies an attempt to expand the scope of the novel in two very large areas: first, as has often been said in these pages, to bring the novel's famed capacity for realism into a closer harmony with the realities of the twentieth century; second, to extend by means of thought, investigation, and experimentation the expressive powers of the book. Technical experimentation serves the evolving needs of realism. Scarcely any writer today is more firm in his assertion of the mutual dependence of realism and experimentation than is Michel Butor. He has expressed this conviction again and again, in his novels as well as in his criticism. "Research into new forms, in revealing new subjects, reveals new relationships. After a certain amount of reflection, realism, formalism and symbolism in the novel may appear to constitute an indissoluble unity." [29]

Notes

1. Arnold Hauser, "Space and Time in the Film," *The Social History of Art*, reprinted in *Film: A Montage of Theories*, edited by Richard Dyer MacCann (New York, 1966), p. 191.
2. Waldo Frank, "The Major Issue," *The Novel of Tomorrow and the Scope of Fiction: By Twelve American Novelists* (Indianapolis, 1922), p. 51.
3. Roger Shattuck, *The Banquet Years* (New York, 1961), p. 39.

4. Henry Moore, quoted by Herbert Read, *A Concise History of Modern Sculpture* (New York, 1966), p. 163.
5. Shattuck, p. 348.
6. Michel Leiris, *Aurora* (Paris, 1946), p. 57: "de découvrer dans ses sillons de vallées et de fleurs la linge majeure de leur destin."
7. Leiris, p. 189: "orienté vers une vie souterraine."
8. Maurice Fourré, *Tête-de-Nègre* (Paris, 1960), p. 138.
9. Fourré, p. 240: "M. Maurice, notre Créateur décédé, a laissé tomber le cordonnet sanglant des Marionnettes."
10. Gertrude Stein, "Portraits and Repetitions," *Lectures in America* (New York, 1967), p. 195.
11. Getrude Stein, *The Making of Americans* (New York, 1934), p. 37.
12. For her explanation, see "The Gradual Making of the Making of Americans," *Lectures in America*, p. 153.
13. Shattuck, p. 348.
14. Anaïs Nin, *Collages* (Chicago, 1964), pp. 55, 106, 111, 59, 62, 95.
15. Nin, pp. 70, 71.
16. Nin, p. 122.
17. Nin, pp. 113–14.
18. Nin, p. 92.
19. Julio Cortázar, *Hopscotch* (New York, 1966), p. 336. *Rayuela* (Buenos Aires, 1963), p. 465: "Las vidas que terminan como los artículos literarios de periódicos y revistas, tan fastuosos en la primera plana y rematando en una cola desvaída, allá por la página treinta y dos, entre avisos de remate y tubos de dentífrico."
20. Cortázar, p. 437. Spanish version, p. 619:
"*Inválidos.*
Del Hospital del Condado de York informan que la Duquesa viuda de Grafton, que se rompió una pierna el domingo último, pasó ayer un día bastante bueno.
The Sunday Times, Londres"
21. Cortázar, p. 336. Spanish version, p. 466: " 'Quizá haya un lugar en el hombre desde donde pueda percibirse le realidad entera.' "
22. Cortázar, p. 422, 57. Spanish version, p. 595, 78:
"*Morelliana.*
Si el volumen o el tono de la obra pueden llevar a creer que el autor intentó una suma, apresurarse a señalarle que está ante la tentativa contraria, la de una *resta* implacable."
" 'No hay ideas generales,' " dijo Oliveira."
23. Cortázar, p. 408. Spanish version, p. 574:
"El British Medical Journal informa sobre una nueva clase de accidente que pueden sufrif los niños. Dicho accidente es causado por el empleo de cierre relámpago en lugar de botones en la bragueta de los pantalones (escribe nuestro corresponsal de medicina).
El peligro está en que el prepucio quede atrapado por el cierre. Ya se han registrado dos casos. En ambos hubo que practicar la circuncisión para liberar al niño.
El accidente tiene más probabilidades de ocurrir cuando el niño va solo al retrete. . . ."

24. Reprinted on the cover of the New American Library's Signet paperback edition.
25. Marc Saporta, *Composition No. 1* (Paris, 1962): "de battre ces pages comme un jeu de cartes. De couper, s'il le désire, de la main gauche, comme chez une cartomancienne. L'ordre dans lequel les feuillets sortiront du jeu orientera le destin de X."
26. The analysis of *Mobile* presented in Chapter 9 is based, understandably, on the original French edition of the book.
27. Michel Butor, *Mobile: Study for a Representation of the United States* (New York, 1963), pp. 8–11. *Mobile: étude pour une représentation des États-Unis* (Paris, 1962), pp. 8–11. These four pages follow.

> nuit noire à
> CORDOUE, ALASKA, l'extrême Nord, l'extrême proximité de l'ef-
> froyable, l'abominable, l'inimaginable pays où il est
> déjà lundi tandis qu'ici il est encore dimanche, fascinant pays sin-
> istre avec ses envols de satellites inattendus, le pays des cauchemars
> qui vous poursuivent toute la nuit, et insinuent entre vos pensées
> du jour, malgré tous vos efforts, tant de minuscules susurrements
> dévastateurs comme une infiltration d'eau dans le plafond d'une
> chambre ancienne, le monstrueux pays des ours,—nuit noire à
>
> DOUGLAS, près du monument national de la baie des Glaciers (on
> appelle monument national une curiosité naturelle ou
> archéologique que l'on a jugée digne d'être préservée de l'indiscré-
> tion des amateurs ou des colons),

nuit noire à
DOUGLAS, temps des montagnes, ARIZONA, far-west,—la réserve
des Indiens Navajos (les Indiens des États-Unis, au
nombre d'environ cinq cent mille, vivent pour la plupart dans des
réserves dispersées sur tout le territoire, où ils ont été parqués peu
à peu lors de l'occupation progressive du pays par l'envahisseur blanc.
Il ne serait pas gentil de les comparer à des camps de concentration.
Ce serait même un peu injuste : certaines de ces réserves sont
touristiques).

« *En dépit de l'immensité du Sud-Ouest, ce sont souvent de petites
choses vues, entendues, senties, qui créent les impressions les plus
durables. En voici quelques exemples :*
—*des lacets de chili écarlate, séchant contre des murs de terre,*
—*un manteau de trembles dorés couvrant les flancs d'une montagne,*
—*souple relaxation de Navajos aux portes d'une épicerie,*
—*l'allure inquiétante de l'oiseau-coureur en fuite,*
—*une massive tête d'orage traînant après soi ses tresses de pluie,*
—*une file d'autos résignées attendant la fin d'une brusque
inondation,*
—*une file de bœufs attendant au point d'eau,*
—*les échos et silences dans une grande ruine pueblo,*
—*le beuglement du bétail qu'on rassemble,*
—*l'arôme entêtant du café sur un feu de bois,*
—*de jeunes garnements à poil s'éclaboussant dans un réservoir,*
—*le cri perçant d'un cheval rebelle à un rodéo,*
—*le gémissement d'un coyote et le jappement des autres en réponse
la nuit,*
—*la palpitation d'un tambour, et le chant strident d'une danse
indienne,*

—*l'odeur moisie de la brousse après une averse,*
—*le braiment lointain d'un âne sauvage au lever du jour,*
—*l'âcre odeur de chair brûlée dans un corral où l'on marque les bêtes,*
—*soudain l'orage d'été attaque sa lapidation,*
—*l'inimaginable immensité du grand Canyon,*
—*le jus d'un épais steak grillé sur des braises,*
—*l'éclaboussement et la secousse d'une truite happant votre mouche,*
—*la saveur des enchiladas enrobées dans leur sauce au piment* »
  (*extrait du* « *Sud-Ouest américain, par Dodge et Zim, avec plus de quatre cents illustrations en couleurs,*
—*merveilles de la nature,*
—*villages indiens,*
—*sites historiques,*
—*routes pittoresques,*
—*itinéraires,*
—*parcs publics,*
—*minéraux,*
—*animaux,*
—*oiseaux,*
—*arbres,*
—*fleurs* »).

Le monument national de la Forêt Pétrifiée,—nuit noire à

FLORENCE, sur la rivière Gila, près du monument national de la Casa Grande,

nuit déjà moins noire à
FLORENCE, temps central.

Bleu nuit.

Les monts Ozarks,—passée la frontière du Sud-Ouest,

FLORENCE.

GEORGETOWN, comté de White ou comté Blanc.

Les monts la nuit.

Sur la route une Buick (vitesse limitée à 60 miles).

GEORGETOWN, chef-lieu de Williamson,—en continuant vers l'ouest,

GEORGETOWN, NEW MEXICO,—la réserve des Indiens Zunis.
LA GRANGE, comté de Lee, ARKANSAS.

Le réveil sonne.

B. P.

28. Roland Barthes, "Littérature et discontinu," *Critique* (October, 1962), pp. 825, 826: "Il a bien une finalité plastique."
   "*Mobile,* c'est-à-dire armature minutieusement articulée, dont toutes les brisures, en se déplaçant de très peu (de que permet la finesse du jeu combinatoire) produisent paradoxalement le plus lié des mouvements."
29. Michel Butor, "Le roman comme recherche," *Répertoire,* II (Paris, 1963), p. 11: "La recherche de formes nouvelles, révélant de nouveaux sujets, révèle des relations nouvelles. A partir d'un certain degré de réflexion, réalisme, formalisme et symbolisme dans le roman apparaissent comme constituant une indissociable unité."

Conclusion

There can be no genuine conclusion to a description of a process. The process continues, scarcely ever in the neat ways that can be predicted even by the most conscientious observer. In *Space, Time and Structure in the Modern Novel* one has presented a careful account of certain important related trends in the modern novel, and, in doing so, has stressed an aspect of the novel that has been very nearly neglected in studies of the genre written in English: its structure. In order to bring a balance to the existing criticism of the novel, one has sought to concentrate not only on structure, but also to use as examples of architectonic structure books whose excellence has often been recognized in passing by critics who have been, at the same time, unwilling to discuss them in detail. One thinks of such works as *Impressions d'Afrique, Nightwood, Aurora, The Cannibal, Hopscotch, Composition No. 1,* and *Mobile.*

Bold and difficult works of art must depend, at least while they are newly evolving, on the intelligence and good will of critics who will commit themselves to the actions of understanding and of explaining to others the ways in which the formidable book can be approached. Except for very few critics, in the United States the modernist novel—in English and in translation alike—has generally been rebuffed by the established literary critics and journalists, most of whose sensibilities, tastes, and values reflect the social and political ambience of the 1930s, and by a self-indulgent reading public, whose imaginations have gone flaccid through lack of use and whose capacity for active participation in art has been undermined by more easily available cliché-ridden entertainments. The result is that the serious experimental novel in the tradition of Turgenev, Flaubert, James, Richardson, Joyce, and Woolf, has barely managed to survive. At that, one can never know what astonishing and enthralling novels lie hidden in the filing cabinets of publishers or agents or in the dusty drawers of discouraged novelists.

The author has a hope for this book, a modest hope that it will reach those who teach literature in high schools, colleges, and universities and those who write about it in the quarterlies and little magaines and that, reaching these people, it will help to unroll paths of understanding—perspectives, in short—on great numbers of books that have been avoided and neglected. Not just the vigor of the novel as an aesthetic act but its very survival depends upon the capacity for response of a perhaps small, but an adventurous, curious, quick group of readers who are willing to approach certain novels as they approach poetry, bringing to it wide-open expectations, an eagerness to be surprised, and the confidence in the novelist to assume that his difficult book is a serious and meaningful action, worthy of that sort of deep concentration that includes among its considerable powers both the playful and the mysterious.

Bibliography

Novels

Barnes, Djuna. *Nightwood*. New York, 1961.
Beckett, Samuel. *Malone muert*. Paris, 1951. Translated by the author as *Malone Dies*. New York, 1956.
———. *Molloy*. Paris, 1951. Translated by Patrick Bowles in collaboration with the author as *Molloy*. New York, 1955.
———. *Murphy*. New York, 1957.
———. *Watt*. Paris, 1953.
Borges, Jorge Luis. *Ficciones*. Buenos Aires, 1956. Translated by Emecé Editores, Buenos Aires, as *Ficciones*. New York, 1962.
Broch, Hermann. *Die Schlafwandler: 1818 Pasenow, oder die Romantik; 1903 Esch, oder die Anarchie; 1918 Huguenau, oder die Sachlichkeit*, 3 vols. Munich, 1931–32. Translated by Willa and Edwin Muir as *The Sleepwalkers: A Trilogy: Part One: The Romantic (1888); Part Two: The Anarchist (1903); Part Three: The Realist (1918)*. New York, 1964.
———. *Die Schuldlosen: Roman in elf Erzählungen*. Munich, 1950.
———. *Der Tod des Vergil*. New York, 1945. Translated by Jean Starr Untermeyer as *The Death of Virgil*. New York, 1965.
Butor, Michel. *Degrés*. Paris, 1960. Translated by Richard Howard as *Degrees*. New York, 1961.
———. *L'Emploi du temps*. Paris, 1957. Translated by Jean Stewart as *Passing Time*. New York, 1960.

————. *Mobile: étude pour une représentation des États-Unis.* Paris, 1962. Translated by Richard Howard as *Mobile: Study for a Representation of the United States.* New York, 1963.

————. *Passage de Milan.* Paris, 1954.

Cortázar, Julio. *Rayuela.* Buenos Aires, 1963. Translated by Gregory Rabassa as *Hopscotch.* New York, 1966.

Desnos, Robert. *La Liberté ou l'amour!* Paris, 1962.

Döblin, Alfred. *Berlin Alexanderplatz: die Geschichte von Franz Biberkopf.* Berlin, 1929. Translated by Eugene Jolas as *Alexanderplatz Berlin: The Story of Franz Biberkopf.* New York, 1931.

Dos Passos, John. *Manhattan Tranfer.* New York, 1959.

————. *U.S.A.: The 42nd Parallel; Nineteen Nineteen; The Big Money.* New York, 1930.

Fourré, Maurice. *Tête-de-Nègre.* Paris, 1960.

Fuentes, Carlos. *Cambio de piel.* Guaymas, Mexico, 1967. Translated by Sam Hileman as *Change of Skin.* New York, 1967.

Gide, André. *Les Faux-Monnayeurs.* Paris, 1925. Translated by Dorothy Bussy as *The Counterfeiters.* New York, 1927.

Gracq, Julien. *Un beau ténébreux.* Paris, 1945. Translated by W. J. Strachan as *A Dark Stranger.* New York, 1950.

————. *Au Château d'Argol.* Paris, 1945. Translated by Louise Varèse as *The Castle of Argol.* Norfolk, Connecticut, 1951.

Hawkes, John. *The Beetle Leg.* New York, 1951.

————. *The Cannibal.* New York, 1962.

————. *The Lime Twig.* New York, 1961.

————. *Second Skin.* New York, 1963.

————. *Two Novels: "The Goose on the Grave" and "The Owl."* New York, 1954.

Leiris, Michel. *Aurora.* Paris, 1946.

Lowry, Malcolm. *Under the Volcano.* New York, 1947.

Musil, Robert. *Der Mann Ohne Eigenschaften.* Berlin, 1952. Translated by Eithne Wilkins and Ernst Kaiser as *The Man Without Qualities.* New York, 1965.

Nabokov, Vladimir. *Pale Fire.* New York, 1963.

Nin, Anaïs. *Cities of the Interior: Ladders to Fire; Children of the Albatross; The Four-Chambered Heart; A Spy in the House of Love.* Denver, 1959.

————. *Collages.* Chicago, 1964.

————. *House of Incest.* Denver, 1958.

————. *Seduction of the Minotaur.* Denver, 1961.

————. *Under a Glass Bell*. Denver, 1948.

Robbe-Grillet, Alain. *Dans le labyrinthe*. Paris, 1959. Translated by Richard Howard as *In the Labyrinth* in *Two Novels by Robbe-Grillet*. New York, 1965.

————. *Les Gommes*. Paris, 1953. Translated by Richard Howard as *The Erasers*. New York, 1964.

————. *La Jalousie*. Paris, 1957. Translated by Richard Howard as *Jealousy* in *Two Novels by Robbe-Grillet*. New York, 1965.

————. *La Maison de rendez-vous*. Paris, 1965. Translated by Richard Howard as *La Maison de Rendez-vous*. New York, 1966.

————. *Le Voyeur*. Paris, 1955. Translated by Richard Howard as *The Voyeur*. New York, 1958.

Roussel, Raymond. *Impressions d'Afrique*. Paris, 1963. Translated by Lindy Foord and Rayner Heppenstall as *Impressions of Africa*. London, 1966.

Sanguineti, Edoardo. *Capriccio italiano*. Milan, 1963.

Saporta, Marc. *Composition No. 1*. Paris, 1962.

Sarraute, Nathalie. *Les Fruits d'or*. Paris, 1963. Translated by Maria Jolas as *The Golden Fruits*. New York, 1964.

————. *Martereau*. Paris, 1953. Translated by Maria Jolas as *Martereau*. New York, 1959.

————. *Le Planétarium*. Paris, 1959. Translated by Maria Jolas as *The Planetarium*. New York, 1960.

————. *Portrait d'un inconnu*. Paris, 1948. Translated by Maria Jolas as *Portrait of a Man Unknown*. New York, 1958.

————. *Tropismes*. Paris, 1957. Translated by Maria Jolas as *Tropisms*. London, 1963.

Stein, Gertrude. *The Making of Americans*. New York, 1934.

————. "Tender Buttons: Objects, Food, Rooms," *Selected Writings*. Edited by Carl Van Vechten. New York, 1946.

————. *Three Lives*. New York, 1933.

Unamuno, Miguel de. *Amor y pedagogía*. Barcelona, 1902.

————. *Niebla*. Madrid, 1914. Translated by Warren Fite as *Mist*. New York, 1928.

Woolf, Virginia. *To the Lighthouse*. New York, 1927.

————. *Mrs. Dalloway*. New York, 1925.

————. *The Waves*. New York, 1931.

Works of Nonfiction by Novelists Involved in This Study

Broch, Hermann. *James Joyce und die Gegenwart, Rede zu Joyces 50 Geburstag.* Vienna, 1936.
Butor, Michel. *Le Génie du lieu.* Paris, 1958.
———. *Répertoire: études et conférences, 1960–64.* 2 vols. Paris, 1948–63.
Gide, André. *Journal des "Faux-Monnayeurs."* Paris, 1927. Translated by Justin O'Brien as *Journal of "The Counterfeiters."* New York, 1927.
Hawkes, John. "Interview," *Wisconsin Studies in Contemporary Literature,* VI (Summer, 1965), 141–55.
Leiris, Michel. "De la Littérature considérée comme une tauromachie," *Les Temps Modernes* (May, 1946), 1456–68.
———. Introduction to Raymond Roussel's "Comment j'ai écrit certains de mes livres," *La Nouvelle Revue Française,* XLIV (1935).
Nin, Anaïs. *The Novel of the Future.* New York, 1968.
———. *Realism and Reality.* Yonkers, New York, 1946.
Robbe-Grillet, Alain. *Pour un nouveau roman.* Paris, 1963. Translated by Richard Howard as *For a New Novel.* New York, 1965.
Roussel, Raymond. "Comment j'ai écrit certains de mes livres," *La Nouvelle Revue Française,* XLIV (1935), 575–82.
Sarraute, Nathalie. *L'Ere du Soupçon: essais sur le roman.* Paris, 1956. Translated by Maria Jolas as *The Age of Suspicion: Essays on the Novel.* New York, 1963.
Stein, Gertrude. *Composition as Explanation.* London, 1926.
———. *How to Write.* Paris, 1931.
———. *Lectures in America.* New York, 1967.
———. *Picasso.* London, 1939.
Woolf, Virginia. *The Common Reader: First Series.* New York, 1929.
———. *Mr. Bennett and Mrs. Brown.* London, 1928.

General Critical and Aesthetic Works

Apollinaire, Guillaume. "L'Esprit nouveau et les poëtes," *Mercure de France* (December 1, 1918), 1–29. Translated by

Roger Shattuck as "The New Spirit and the Poets," *Selected Writings of Apollinaire*. New York, 1948, 227–37.

——. *Les Peintres cubistes, méditations esthétiques*. Paris, 1912. Translated by Lionel Abel as *The Cubist Painters, Aesthetic Meditations*. New York, 1962.

Astre, Georges-Albert. "Les deux langages," *La Revue des Lettres Modernes*, V (1958), 135–49.

Bahr, Hermann. *Expressionismus*. Munich, 1919.

Balakian, Anna E. *The Literary Origins of Surrealism: A New Mysticism in French Poetry*. New York, 1947.

——. *Surrealism: The Road to the Absolute*. New York, 1959.

Barthes, Roland. "L'Activité structuraliste," *Lettres Nouvelles* (February, 1963), 71–80.

——. "Littérature et discontinu," *Critique* (October, 1962), 817–29.

Beach, Joseph Warren. *The Twentieth Century Novel: Studies in Technique*. New York, 1932.

Bergonzi, Bernard. "The New Novel and the Old Book," *The Listener* (March 23, 1967), 391–92.

Bithell, Jethro. *Modern German Literature: 1880–1950*. London, 1959.

Blanchot, Maurice. *L'Espace littéraire*. Paris, 1955.

——. *Le Livre à venir*. Paris, 1959.

——. "Le Roman, oeuvre de mauvaise foi," *Les Temps Modernes* (April, 1947), 1304–17.

Bloch-Michel, Jean. "Nouveau roman et culture des masses," *Preuves* (March, 1961), 17–28.

Bluestone, George. *Novels into Film*. Berkeley, California, 1961.

Booth, Wayne C. *The Rhetoric of Fiction*. Chicago, 1961.

Bouchareine, R. "Film, roman et entourage concret, lumières sur l'univers quotidien," *La Revue des Lettres Modernes*, V (1958), 166–81.

Bourin, André. "Techniciens du roman," *Les Nouvelles Littéraires* (January 22, 1959), 1–4.

Breton, André. *Les Manifestes du surréalisme*. Paris, 1955.

Bryan, C. D. B. "Cortázar's Masterpiece," *The New Republic* (April 23, 1966), 19–23.

Cocteau, Jean. "Note, en toute hâte," *La Nouvelle Revue Française*, XLI (1933), 464.

Deutsch, Babette. *Poetry Handbook: A Dictionary of Terms*. New York, 1957.

Dort, Bernard. "Sur l'espace," *Esprit* (July 8, 1958).

Duvignaud, Jean. "Dialogue ininterrompu," *La Revue des Lettres Modernes*, V (1958), 150–54.

Edel, Leon. *The Modern Psychological Novel*. New York, 1959.

Eisenstein, Sergei. *Film Form*. Translated by Jay Leyda. New York, 1957.

Forster, E. M. *Aspects of the Novel*. London, 1927.

Fowlie, Wallace. *Age of Surrealism*. Bloomington, Indiana, 1950.

Frank, Joseph. "Spatial Form in the Modern Novel," *Critiques and Essays in Modern Fiction: 1920–1951*. Edited by John W. Aldridge. New York, 1952.

Frank, Waldo. "The Major Issue," *The Novel of Tomorrow and the Scope of Fiction: By Twelve American Novelists*. Indianapolis, 1922.

————. "The Novel as Poem," *The New Republic* (August 20, 1945), 226–28.

Freedman, Ralph. *The Lyrical Novel: Studies in Hermann Hesse, André Gide and Virginia Woolf*. Princeton, 1963.

Frohock, W. M. "Introduction to Butor," *Yale French Studies*, No. 24 (Summer, 1959), 54–61.

Fuentes, Carlos. "A Demanding Novel: *Hopscotch*," *Commentary* (October, 1966), 142–43.

Giedion, Sigfried. *Space, Time and Architecture: The Growth of a New Tradition*. Cambridge, Massachusetts, 1941.

Gillet, Joseph E. "The Autonomous Character in Spanish and European Literature," *Hispanic Review*, XXIV (July, 1956), 179–90.

Gordon, Carolyn and Allen Tate. *The House of Fiction*. New York, 1950.

Grabo, Carl H. *The Technique of the Novel*. New York, 1928.

Harss, Luis and Barbara Dohmann. *Into the Mainstream: Conversations with Latin American Writers*. New York, 1967.

Hauser, Arnold. *The Social History of Art and Literature, II*. London, 1951.

Herd, Erich W. "Hermann Broch and the Legitimacy of the Novel," *German Life and Letters*, XIII (1960), 262–77.

Holthusen, Hans Egon. "Crossing the Zero Point: German Literature Since World War II," *French and German Letters Today*. Washington, D.C., Reference Department, The Library of Congress, 1960, 39–53.

Hoog, Armand. "The Surrealist Novel," *Yale French Studies*, No. 8 (1951).

Howe, Irving, ed. *Literary Modernism.* New York, 1967.

Howlett, Jacques. "Notes sur l'objet dans le roman," *Esprit* (July 8, 1958), 67–72.

———. "Thèmes et tendances d'avant-garde dans le roman aujourd'hui," *Les Lettres Nouvelles* (February, 1963), 139–48.

Hulme, T. E. "Bergson's Theory of Art," *Speculations.* London, 1936. 143–69.

Humphrey, Robert. *Stream-of-Consciousness and the Modern Novel.* Berkeley, California, 1959.

James, Henry. *The Future of the Novel.* Edited by Leon Edel. New York, 1956.

Jens, Walter. *Deutsche Literatur der Gegenwart.* Munich, 1961.

Kandinsky, Wassily. *Uber das Geistige in der Kunst.* Munich, 1912. Translated as *Concerning the Spiritual in Art.* New York, 1947.

Kanters, Robert. "Situation présente du 'nouveau roman,'" *Le Figaro Littéraire* (March 26, 1959).

Kenner, Hugh. "Art in a Closed Field," *Virginia Quarterly Review*, 30 (Autumn, 1962), 597–613.

———.*Flaubert, Joyce and Beckett: The Stoic Comedians.* Boston, 1962.

Kermode, Frank. *The Sense of an Ending: Studies in the Theory of Fiction.* New York, 1967.

Kumar, Shiv K. *Bergson and the Stream of Consciousness Novel.* New York, 1963.

Lawrence, D. H. "Why the Novel Matters," *Phoenix: the Posthumous Papers of D. H. Lawrence.* Edited by Edward D. McDonald. New York, 1936. 533–38.

LeSage, Laurent. *The French New Novel.* University Park, Pennsylvania, 1962.

Littlejohn, David. "The Anti-Realists," *Daedalus* (Spring, 1963), 250–64.

Loy, J. Robert. "'Things' in Recent French Literature," *PMLA*, 71 (March, 1956), 27–41.

Lubbock, Percy. *The Craft of Fiction.* New York, 1957.

de Magny, Olivier. "Écriture de l'impossible," *Les Lettres Nouvelles* (February, 1963), 125–38.

Matthews, J. H. *Surrealism and the Novel.* Ann Arbor, Michigan, 1966.

McCarthy, Mary. "Characters in Fiction," *The Humanist in the Bathtub*. New York, 1964. 195–216.

Mendilow, Adam Abraham. *Time and the Novel*. London, 1952.

Meyer, Leonard B. *Music, the Arts, and Ideas: Patterns and Predictions in Twentieth-Century Culture*. Chicago, 1967.

Meyerhoff, Hans. *Time in Literature*. Berkeley, California, 1955.

Morrissette, Bruce. "The New Novel in France," *Chicago Review*, 15 (Winter–Spring, 1962), 1–19.

Mourlet, Michel. "Cinéma contre roman," *La Revue des Lettres Modernes*, V (1958), 155–65.

Mudrick, Marvin. "Character and Event in Fiction," *Yale Review* (Winter, 1961), 202–18.

Muir, Edwin. *The Structure of the Novel*. London, 1928.

Nadeau, Maurice. *Histoire du surréalisme*. Paris, 1946. Translated by Richard Howard as *The History of Surrealism*. New York, 1965.

Nathan, Monique. " 'Visualisation' et vision chez Virginia Woolf," *La Revue des Lettres Modernes*, V (1958), 270–74.

Ortega y Gasset, José. *Obras completas*, III. Madrid, 1947. Relevant to this study are "La Deshumanización del Arte," translated by an unnamed person for Doubleday and Company, as *The Dehumanization of Art*. New York, 1956; and two essays, "La Doctrina del Punto de Vista" and "Del Sentido Histórico de la Teoría de Einstein" (both collected in "El Tema de Nuestro Tiempo"). These essays have been translated by James Cleugh as "The Doctrine of the Point of View" and "The Historical Significance of the Theory of Einstein" and printed in *The Modern Theme*. New York, 1961.

Peyre, Henri. *French Novelists of Today*. New York, 1967.

Picasso, Pablo. "Conversations with Picasso" by Christian Zervos, *The Creative Process*. Edited by Brewster Ghiselin. Berkeley, California, 1954.

Picon, Gaëtan. "Du roman expérimental," *Mercure de France* (June, 1957), 300–304.

Pingaud, Bernard. "Je, vous, il," *Esprit* (July, 1958), 91–99.

———. "Y a-t-il quelqu'un?" *Esprit* (July, 1958), 83–86.

Read, Herbert. *A Concise History of Modern Painting*. New York, 1966.

———. *A Concise History of Modern Sculpture*. New York, 1966.

———. *The Philosophy of Modern Art*. New York, 1953.

Reid, Benjamin L. *Art by Subtraction: A Dissenting Opinion of Gertrude Stein.* Norman, Oklahoma, 1958.

Roudiez, Leon S. *Michel Butor: Columbia Essays on Modern Writers.* New York, 1965.

San Lazzaro, G. di. *Klee, A Study of His Life and Work.* Translated from the Italian by Stuart Hood. London, 1957.

Sanouillet Michel. *Dada à Paris.* Paris, 1968.

Sartre, Jean-Paul. Preface to *Portrait d'un inconnu* by Nathalie Sarraute. Paris, 1948. 7–16.

———. *Situations I.* Paris, 1947. Translated by Benita Eisler as *Situations.* New York, 1965.

Scholes, Robert. "For Nonrealistic Fiction," *The New York Times Book Review* (October 22, 1967), 2.

Shattuck, Roger. *The Banquet Years: The Origins of the Avant-Garde in France: 1885 to World War I.* New York, 1961.

Sokel, Walter Herbert. *The Writer in Extremis: Expressionism in Twentieth-Century German Literature.* New York, 1964.

Spender, Stephen. *The Struggle of the Modern.* London, 1963.

Stoltzfus, Benjamin. *Alain Robbe-Grillet and the New French Novel.* Carbondale, Illinois, 1964.

Strelka, Josef. *Kafka, Musil, Broch und die Entwicklung des modernen Romans.* Vienna, 1959.

Sutherland, Donald. *Getrude Stein: A Biography of Her Work.* New Haven, 1951.

Sypher, Wylie. *Rococo to Cubism in Art and Literature.* New York, 1960.

Webster's New Collegiate Dictionary. Springfield, Massachusetts, 1949.

Weightman, J. C. *The Novelist as Philosopher.* New York, 1962.

———. "Robbe-Grillet," *Encounter,* XVIII (March, 1962).

"What's New in the Novel?" *Yale French Studies,* No. 8 (1951).

Williams, Raymond. "Realism and the Novel," *Partisan Review* (Spring, 1959), 200–213.

Wilson, Edmund. *Axel's Castle: A Study in the Imaginative Literature of 1870–1930.* New York, 1931.

Wöfflin, Heinrich. *Kunstgeschichtliche Grundbegriffe: das Problem der Stilentwicklung in der neueren Kunst.* Munich, 1923. Translated by M. D. Hottinger as *Principles of Art History: The Problem of the Development of Style in Later Art.* New York.

Worringer, Wilhelm. *Abstraktion und Einfühlung: ein Beitrag zur Stilpsychologie.* Munich, 1908. Translated by Michael Bullock as *Abstraction and Empathy.* London, 1953.

———. *Formprobleme der Gotik.* Munich, 1912. Translated as *Form Problems of the Gothic.* New York, 1918.

Ziolkowski, Theodore. *Hermann Broch: Columbia Essays on Modern Writers.* New York, 1964.

Index